262143 055

*Measuring Inequality
of Opportunities in
Latin America and the Caribbean*

Measuring Inequality of Opportunities in Latin America and the Caribbean

Ricardo Paes de Barros,
Francisco H. G. Ferreira,
José R. Molinas Vega, and
Jaime Saavedra Chanduvi

with

Mirela de Carvalho, Samuel Franco,
Samuel Freije-Rodríguez, and
Jérémie Gignoux

A COPUBLICATION OF PALGRAVE MACMILLAN
AND THE WORLD BANK

© 2009 The International Bank for Reconstruction and Development / The World Bank
1818 H Street NW
Washington DC 20433
Telephone: 202-473-1000
Internet: www.worldbank.org
E-mail: feedback@worldbank.org

1 2 3 4 12 11 10 09

A copublication of The World Bank and Palgrave Macmillan.

Palgrave Macmillan
Houndmills, Basingstoke, Hampshire RG21 6XS and
175 Fifth Avenue, New York, N. Y. 10010
Companies and representatives throughout the world

Palgrave Macmillan is the global academic imprint of the Palgrave Macmillan division of St. Martin's Press, LLC and of Palgrave Macmillan Ltd. Macmillan® is a registered trademark in the United States, United Kingdom and other countries. Palgrave® is a registered trademark in the European Union and other countries.

The authors have asserted their rights to be identified as the authors of this work in accordance with the Copyright, Designs and Patents Act 1988.

This volume is a product of the staff of the International Bank for Reconstruction and Development / The World Bank. The findings, interpretations, and conclusions expressed in this volume do not necessarily reflect the views of the Executive Directors of The World Bank or the governments they represent.

The World Bank does not guarantee the accuracy of the data included in this work. The boundaries, colors, denominations, and other information shown on any map in this work do not imply any judgement on the part of The World Bank concerning the legal status of any territory or the endorsement or acceptance of such boundaries.

ISBN: 978-0-8213-7745-1 (Paperback)   ISBN: 978-0-8213-7747-5 (Hardcover)
eISBN: 978-0-8213-7746-8   DOI: 10.1596/978-0-8213-7745-1

Library of Congress Cataloging-in-Publication Data

Measuring inequality of opportunities in Latin America and the Caribbean.
    p. cm.
  Prepared by Ricardo Paes de Barros and others.
  ISBN 978-0-8213-7745-1 -- ISBN 978-0-8213-7746-8 (electronic)
  1. Latin America—Economic conditions—1982– 2. Caribbean Area—Economic conditions—1945– 3. Latin America—Social conditions—1982– 4. Caribbean Area—Social conditions—1945– 5. Equality—Latin America. 6. Equality—Caribbean Area. 7. Children—Government policy—Latin America. 8. Children—Government policy—Caribbean Area. I. Barros, Ricardo Paes de, 1954– II. World Bank.
  HC125.M38 2008
  330.98—dc22
                                                                    2008037311

Cover design: ULTRAdesigns

Latin American Development Forum Series

This series was created in 2003 to promote debate, disseminate information and analysis, and convey the excitement and complexity of the most topical issues in economic and social development in Latin America and the Caribbean. It is sponsored by the Inter-American Development Bank, the United Nations Economic Commission for Latin America and the Caribbean, and the World Bank. The manuscripts chosen for publication represent the highest quality in each institution's research and activity output and have been selected for their relevance to the academic community, policy makers, researchers, and interested readers.

Advisory Committee Members

Alicia Bárcena Ibarra, Executive Secretary, Economic Commission for Latin America and the Caribbean, United Nations

Inés Bustillo, Director, Washington Office, Economic Commission for Latin America and the Caribbean, United Nations

José Luis Guasch, Senior Adviser, Latin America and the Caribbean Region, World Bank; and Professor of Economics, University of California, San Diego

Santiago Levy, Vice President for Sectors and Knowledge, Inter-American Development Bank

Eduardo Lora, Principal Adviser, Research Department, Inter-American Development Bank

Luis Servén, Research Manager, Development Economics Vice Presidency, World Bank

Augusto de la Torre, Chief Economist, Latin America and the Caribbean Region, World Bank

Other Titles in the Latin American Development Forum Series

China's and India's Challenge to Latin America: Opportunity or Threat? (2009) by Daniel Lederman, Marcelo Olarreaga, and Guillermo E. Perry, editors

Does the Investment Climate Matter? Microeconomic Foundations of Growth in Latin America (2008) by Pablo Fajnzylber, José Luis Guasch, and J. Humberto López, editors

The Impact of Private Sector Participation in Infrastructure: Lights, Shadows, and the Road Ahead (2008) by Luis Andres, José Luis Guasch, Thomas Haven, and Vivien Foster

Innovative Experiences in Access to Finance: Market-Friendly Roles for the Visible Hand? (2009) by Augusto de la Torre, Juan Carlos Gozzi, and Sergio L. Schmukler

Job Creation in Latin America and the Caribbean: Trends and Policy Challenges (2009) by Carmen Pagés, Gaëlle Pierre, and Stefano Scarpetta

Remittances and Development: Lessons from Latin America (2008) by Pablo Fajnzylber and J. Humberto López, editors

Fiscal Policy, Stabilization, and Growth: Prudence or Abstinence? (2007) by Guillermo Perry, Luis Servén, and Rodrigo Suescún, editors

Investor Protection and Corporate Governance: Firm-Level Evidence across Latin America (2007) by Alberto Chong and Florencio López-de-Silanes, editors

Natural Resources: Neither Curse nor Destiny (2007) by Daniel Lederman and William F. Maloney, editors

Raising Student Learning in Latin America: Challenges for the 21st Century (2007) by Emiliana Vegas and Jenny Petrow

Beyond Survival: Protecting Households from Health Shocks in Latin America (2006) by Cristian C. Baeza and Truman G. Packard

Emerging Capital Markets and Globalization: The Latin American Experience (2006) by Augusto de la Torre and Sergio L. Schmukler

The State of State Reform in Latin America (2006) by Eduardo Lora, editor

Beyond Reforms: Structural Dynamics and Macroeconomic Vulnerability (2005) by José Antonio Ocampo, editor

Privatization in Latin America: Myths and Reality (2005) by Alberto Chong and Florencio López-de-Silanes, editors

Keeping the Promise of Social Security in Latin America (2004) by Indermit S. Gill, Truman G. Packard, and Juan Yermo

Lessons from NAFTA: For Latin America and the Caribbean (2004) by Daniel Lederman, William F. Maloney, and Luis Servén

Globalization and Development: A Latin American and Caribbean Perspective (2003) by José Antonio Ocampo and Juan Martin, editors

Is Geography Destiny? Lessons from Latin America (2003) by John Luke Gallup, Alejandro Gaviria, and Eduardo Lora

The Limits of Stabilization: Infrastructure, Public Deficits, and Growth in Latin America (2003) by William Easterly and Luis Servén, editors

About the Authors

Ricardo Paes de Barros holds a PhD in Economics from the University of Chicago and a Post PhD from the International Growth Center at Yale University. Since 1979, he has been a researcher at the *Instituto de Pesquisa Econômica Aplicada* (IPEA) where he has been conducting research on inequality, education, poverty, and labor markets in Brazil and Latin America. He has been a visiting professor at Yale University and a Director of Social Studies of IPEA. He has been awarded the Haralambos Simedionis and Mario Henrique Simonsen prizes, and admitted by the President of Brazil, Luiz Inácio Lula da Silva into the *Ordem Nacional do Mérito Científico*.

Francisco H. G. Ferreira is a Lead Economist with the Development Research Group at the World Bank and has published widely on both theoretical and empirical issues related to inequality. Chico (as he is known) is a coeditor of the *Journal of Economic Inequality* and a former editor of *Economía* (the journal of the Latin American and Caribbean Economic Association—LACEA). He was a codirector of the team that wrote the *World Development Report 2006*, on equity and development. He holds a BSc (Economics), MSc, and PhD from the London School of Economics, and was a professor of economics in Rio de Janeiro between 1999 and 2002.

José R. Molinas Vega is a Senior Economist with the Poverty Reduction and Economic Management Unit in the Latin America and the Caribbean Region at the World Bank. His research interests include social capital, rural development, the political economy of social service delivery, economics of education, poverty analysis, and applied macroeconomics. He has been Academic Director of the Master's Program in Economics and professor of development economics and macroeconomics at the Catholic University of Asunción (Paraguay). Before joining the World Bank, he was Director of Instituto Desarrollo in Asunción. José holds a PhD in economics from the University of Massachusetts, Amherst. He has been a Visiting Fellow at the Kellogg Institute of the University of Notre Dame.

Jaime Saavedra Chanduvi is Manager for the Poverty and Gender Group, Poverty Reduction and Economic Management Unit, in the Latin America and the Caribbean Region of the World Bank. His major areas of interest include poverty reduction, labor markets, and social policies. He was Executive Director and Principal Researcher at Grupo de Análisis para el Desarollo (GRADE) in Lima, and a Principal Advisor to the Ministry of Labor and Social Promotion in Peru. He has been President of the Executive Committee of the Network on Inequity and Poverty of the IDB-World Bank-LACEA. He has been a board member at LACEA, the Nutrition Research Institute, and the National Council of Labor in Peru. He has held a teaching position at Pontificia Universidad Católica del Peru and Universidad del Pacífico in Peru, and has been a visiting researcher at the University of Toronto. Dr. Saavedra holds a PhD in economics from Columbia University.

Mirela de Carvalho is with the Instituto de Pesquisa Econômica Aplicada (IPEA).

Samuel Franco is with the Instituto de Estudos do Trabalho e Sociedade (IETS).

Samuel Freije-Rodríguez is with the World Bank.

Jérémie Gignoux is with the World Bank.

Contents

Foreword

Over the past decade, faster growth and smarter social policy have reversed the trend in Latin America's poverty. Too slowly and insufficiently, but undeniably, the percentage of Latinos who are poor has at long last begun to fall. This has shifted the political and policy debates from poverty toward inequality, something to be expected in a region that exhibits the world's most regressive distribution of development outcomes—outcomes such as income, land ownership, and educational achievement.

The inequality debate is a loud and acrimonious one. It has polarized Latin America's politics and blurred its development vision. It has called into question the very role of the state: should it try to redistribute wealth or protect property rights? Encourage social equality or enforce private contracts? And yet, for all its ideological and emotional intensity, this has been the wrong debate. Much more important than inequality of outcomes among adults is inequality of opportunity among children. The debate should not be about equality (equal rewards for all) but about equity (equal chances for all), because the idea of giving people equal opportunity early in life, whatever their socioeconomic background, is embraced across the political spectrum—as a matter of fairness for the left and as a matter of personal effort for the right.

The problem is that we have never been able to systematically measure inequality of opportunity, in Latin America or anywhere else. The development community simply lacked the methodological tools to monitor equity, making it all but impossible to design, implement, and evaluate public policies that target human opportunity. While the citizens of the region feel the uneven playing field under their feet—that personal sense that one's destiny is predetermined by circumstances over which one has no control or responsibility, such as skin color, gender, birthplace, or family wealth—their leaders have proved unable to do much about it.

This book is a breakthrough in the measurement of human opportunity. Written by a team of researchers from the World Bank, Brazil's Instituto de Pesquisa Economica Aplicada, and Argentina's Universidad de la Plata, it builds sophisticated formulas to answer a rather simple question: how much influence do personal circumstances have on the access that children get to the basic services that are necessary for a productive life? For example, is the probability of a girl's access to clean water (a nutritional must), or piped sewerage (a health shield), or electricity (a necessity for reading), or completion of the sixth grade (a predictor of higher education) in any way affected by her race, her mother's literacy, or her father's salary? As the answers are aggregated across services, children, and circumstances, a picture arises of how equitable (or not) a society is. In fact, with data representing some 200 million children and spanning roughly the last decade, a Human Opportunity Index is constructed for each of the 19 largest Latin American countries. And a different light is shed over old development paradigms and new development insights. Four are mentioned here to illustrate the analytical and policy possibilities that the new methodology opens.

First, between a quarter (Colombia) and half (Guatemala) of the income inequality that we observe among adults in Latin America is due to the circumstances they faced when they started out in life—at the very outset, through no fault of their own. And while their race, sex, and location all played a role, no circumstances were more powerful than their mothers' education and their fathers' incomes. In other words, Latinos are right to feel that they are condemned by a playing field that is not level—it is not.

Second, looking across Latin American countries at a single point in time, we see no obvious correlation between inequality of outcomes among adults and inequality of opportunity among children. This gives rise to "inequality traps" in countries where, without additional policy action, children will have little chance to even out the inequality lived by their parents (as in Colombia or Panama). It also gives rise to "intergenerational transitions" (as in Brazil or Chile) where adults suffer high levels of inequality but children face even higher odds of prospering. Put differently, societies can, with their actions, alter their equity profiles.

Third, a more complete diagnosis of a country's development stage can be drawn. While the United Nations Development Programme's Human Development Index—a composite of average literacy, life expectancy, and income—provides a good, ex post reading of how well adults have fared, the Human Opportunity Index developed in this book gives an ex ante evaluation of how likely it is that children are to fare well. Like the World Bank's Doing Business rankings (a proxy for the quality of the business environment), which provide a thorough reading of the obstacles firms need to overcome to succeed, the Human Opportunity Index shows the obstacles children need to overcome to succeed. In both cases, a more holistic, and more useful, picture emerges.

Finally, what does it all mean for policy making? A lot. Many existing social policies and programs are already opportunity enhancing. But new points of emphasis are revealed. Early life interventions, from pregnancy monitoring and institutional births to toddlers' nutrition and neurological development, get a new sense of priority. So do preschool access (such as pre-kindergarten social interaction) and primary school achievement (such as reading and thinking ability). The physical security, reproductive education, mentoring, and talent screening of adolescents, all areas that are often overlooked, gain new relevance. A battery of legal and institutional preconditions gain new meaning, from birth certificates, voter registration, and property titles to the enforcement of antidiscrimination, antitrust, and access-to-information laws. And blanket subsidies that, at the margin, are consumed by those who do not need them (free college for the rich, to name one), turn into opportunity-wasting aberrations.

Needless to say, producing a methodology to measure human opportunity, and applying it across countries in one region, is just a first step. On the one hand, technical discussions and scientific vetting will continue, and refinements will surely follow. On the other, applying the new tool to a single country will allow for adjustments that make the findings much more useful to its policy realities (for example, work is already under way for Brazil and Chile, countries where the threshold to define what a "basic" service is may be higher than the Latin American average). And fascinating comparative lessons could be learned by measuring human opportunity in developed countries—across, say, the states of the United States or the nations of Europe. But the main message this book delivers remains a powerful one: it is possible to make equity a central purpose, if not the very definition, of development. That is, perhaps, its most important contribution.

Marcelo M. Giugale
Director, Poverty Reduction and Economic Management
Latin America and the Caribbean Region
The World Bank

Acknowledgments

This report was prepared jointly by a team of researchers from the World Bank; IPEA and IETS from Brazil; and Universidad de la Plata, Argentina. Leonardo Gasparini and Leopoldo Tornarolli at CEDLAS-Universidad de la Plata coordinated a team in charge of processing household surveys. Maria Caridad Araujo (World Bank) provided support during early stages of the project. Able research assistance was provided by Ezequiel Molina (World Bank), Marcos Silva (IETS), and Pablo Guzman and Gabriela Farfan (CEDLAS-Universidad de la Plata). Comments were received from participants of seminars and workshops held by Comision Nacional de Evaluacion-CONEVAL (Mexico), Ministry of Planning and Budgeting (Brazil), Ministry of Long Term Planning (Brazil), IPEA (Brazil), MIDE-PLAN (Chile), Oficina de Planeamiento y Presupuesto (Uruguay), and Fedesarrollo (Colombia), as well as the XI Meeting of the Network on Poverty and Inequality held in Santo Domingo. The team received advice and comments at different stages of the process from Marcelo Giugale, Tito Cordella, Aline Coudouel, Emmanuel Skoufias, Gabriel Demombynes, Estanislao Gacitua, Luis Andres, Gladys Lopez-Acevedo, Augusto de la Torre, John Newman, Julio Loayza, Fernando Blanco, Christian Gonzalez, Facundo Cuevas, Waleska Garcia-Corzo, Rossana Polastri, Lars Moller, Ana Lucía Armijos, Emily Sinnott, Seynabou Sakho, Florencia T. Castro-Leal, and Jasmin Chakeri (World Bank); Guillermo Perry (formerly at the World Bank and currently at Fedesarrollo, Colombia); Pranab Bardhan (University of California, Berkeley); and John Roemer (Yale University). Other peer reviewers were Jesko Hentschel and Peter Lanjouw (World Bank) and Luis Felipe Lopez Calva (UNDP). Chris Humphrey, Emmy Yokoyama, and Indu John Abraham contributed in editing the document. Jonna Lundwall, Ane Perez Orsi de Castro, and Anne Pillay provided logistical support throughout the process. The following people provided invaluable comments in the preparation of the report: Wilson Jimenez (ARU Foundation, Bolivia); Marcelo Neri (Fundação

Getúlio Vargas, Brazil); Dante Contreras (Universidad de Chile); Iris Salinas (MIDEPLAN, Chile); Mauricio Santamaria (Fedesarrollo, Colombia); Pablo Sauma (University of Costa Rica); Rolando Guzman (the Dominican Republic); Carlos Larrea (Andean University Simón Bolívar, Ecuador); Alberto Leyton (World Bank, El Salvador); Sigfrido Lee (CIEN, Guatemala); Clara Ana Coutinho (World Bank, Jamaica); Rodrigo Garcia Verdu (Mexico); Ardito Barletta (Asesores Estratégicos, Panama); Javier Escobal (GRADE, Peru); and Cecilia Llambi (CINVE, Uruguay). The National Statistical Offices in the region provided general feedback on the document and validated the comparability among surveys used to create the Human Opportunity Index and the questions used from the surveys in each country and how they were harmonized to generate the variables. We would especially like to express our gratitude to the National Statistical Offices of Bolivia, Brazil, Colombia, Costa Rica, the Dominican Republic, Ecuador, El Salvador, Honduras, Mexico, Panama, Paraguay, Peru, and Uruguay. José Molinas Vega and Jaime Saavedra Chanduvi are the Task Team Leaders of this project.

Abbreviations

CCC	Chile Crece Contigo
CEDLAS	Centro de Estudios Distributivos, Laborales y Sociales (Universidad Nacional de La Plata, Argentina)
CONEVAL	Comisión Nacional de Evaluación (Mexico)
D-index	dissimilarity index
ECV	Encuesta de Calidad de Vida (Colombia, Ecuador)
ENAHO	Encuesta Nacional de Hogares (Peru)
ENCOVI	Encuesta Nacional sobre Condiciones de Vida (Guatemala)
ENV	Encuesta de Niveles de Vida (Panama)
GDP	gross domestic product
HOI	Human Opportunity Index
IDB	Inter-American Development Bank
IETS	Instituto de Estudos do Trabalho e Sociedade (Brazil)
IPEA	Instituto de Pesquisa Econômica Aplicada (Brazil)
IRT	item response theory
LAC	Latin America and the Caribbean
MxFLS	Encuesta Nacional sobre Niveles de Vida de los Hogares (Mexico)
OECD	Organisation for Economic Co-operation and Development
PISA	Program for International Student Assessment
PNAD	Pesquisa Nacional por Amostra de Domicílios (Brazil)
PPP	purchasing power parity
RGES	Regime of Explicit Health Guarantees (Chile)
UNDP	United Nations Development Programme
WDR	*World Development Report*

Overview

Imagine Maria, a six-year-old girl living in rural Guatemala. She has four brothers and sisters, and her mother is an illiterate widow who earns about $180 per month as a subsistence farmer. What are Maria's chances of becoming a prominent lawyer or a university professor? Not very high, and certainly a lot lower than those of a six-year-old boy growing up in Guatemala City with two parents in his home, both with a secondary education and a good income, and only one sibling. Many people in Latin America, like Maria, face difficult odds of achieving economic and social success because of circumstances beyond their control: gender, race, location of birth, or their family background. Equality of opportunity is about giving Maria and all other children in the world the same chance to be successful in life.

Reducing inequality is one of the main development challenges in Latin America. Inequality is pervasive, resilient, and judged to be fundamentally unfair by many. Despite this reality, the political and policy debates about if, how, and by how much inequality should be reduced are often polarizing. Left and right do not easily agree on what redistributive policies should be implemented, if any. Attitudes toward inequality and toward redistribution vary sharply. One reason is that people usually tolerate (and maybe agree with) income inequality arising from differences in choices made, effort extended, and talents put to use by individuals, while they view as fundamentally unfair inequality arising from differences in opportunities.

As mentioned by the Commission on Growth and Development (2008), inequality of opportunity, which creates unfair differences in starting points, can be toxic—in particular if opportunities are systematically denied to specific groups of the population. Equality of opportunity seeks to level the playing field so that circumstances such as gender, ethnicity, birthplace, or family background, which are beyond the control of an individual, do not influence a person's life chances. Success in life should depend on people's choices, effort, and talents, not on their circumstances at birth.

Until now, no systematic measures—comparable to the Gini or other measures of economic inequality—have existed to summarize the level of inequality of opportunity observed in Latin America. This book aims to fill this gap, using two different techniques. The first technique, discussed in chapters 2 and 3, develops a Human Opportunity Index to measure differences in opportunity among children. The basis for the first technique is the recognition that as long as some children in a country do not have access to specific basic services that are critical for future advancement in life, such as primary education or running water, and as long as that access is influenced by circumstances, like gender or ethnicity, inequality of opportunity will prevail. The Human Opportunity Index can be used to track a country's progress toward the goal of providing all children equal access to these basic opportunities, simultaneously tracking both the overall coverage and the equity of their distribution. The index, described in detail in chapters 2 and 3, can serve as a tool to help guide public policies aimed at equalizing opportunity. If the inequality of outcomes today reflects past inequality in basic opportunities, it is all the more important now for policy makers to be able to track the allocation of basic opportunities among children so they can design policies to break intergenerational cycles of inequality and improve future outcomes.

The second technique, discussed in chapters 4 and 5, builds on measures of income inequality, consumption inequality, and inequality in educational achievement, and estimates the share of current outcome inequality that can be explained by circumstances that are beyond the control of the individual. This is interpreted as the share of inequality that can be related to inequality in opportunity. In a sample of countries of the region, conservative estimates show that between one-half and one-quarter of current inequality of consumption reflects inequality of opportunity, a very sizable share. Using this same measuring technique, it is also possible to generate opportunity profiles describing the characteristics of the most-disadvantaged groups.

This overview chapter briefly outlines the main findings of the study. It begins with an explanation of the Human Opportunity Index described in chapters 2 and 3, including the estimates for 19 Latin American countries and possible policy applications of the index. Next, the overview briefly outlines the analysis in chapters 4 and 5, which estimates the share of existing unequal outcomes in income, consumption, and education associated with unequal opportunity. The overview concludes with final remarks.

The Human Opportunity Index

The Human Opportunity Index is a synthetic measure of inequality of opportunity in basic services for children. The index is inspired by the social welfare function proposed by Sen (1976), and posits that a development process in which society attempts to equitably supply basic opportunities requires ensuring that as many children as possible have access to those basic opportunities, with a target of universalism; it requires distributing available basic opportunities increasingly toward the more disadvantaged groups. The Human Opportunity Index summarizes in a composite indicator two elements: (i) how many opportunities are available, that is, the coverage rate of a basic service; and (ii) how equitably those opportunities are distributed, that is, whether the distribution of that coverage is related to exogenous circumstances. Hence, an increase in coverage of a basic service at the national level will always improve the index. However, if that increase in coverage is biased toward a disadvantaged group (for example, children in a poor region), it will further reduce inequality of opportunity, increasing the index more than proportionally.

This study defines *basic opportunities* as a subset of goods and services for children, such as access to education, to safe water, or to vaccinations, that are critical in determining opportunity for economic advancement in life. These are either affordable by society at large already, or could be in the near future, given the available technology. Universal provision of basic opportunities is a valid and realistic social goal. In the case of children, most societies agree on the importance of a set of basic opportunities, at least at the level of intentions; even if different societies might have different standards about the right set of basic opportunities, there is some global consensus on a few of them, just as there is consensus regarding the Millennium Development Goals. Here we include as basic opportunities variables related to education (completion of sixth grade on time, and school attendance at ages 10–14) and housing conditions (access to clean water, sanitation, and electricity). Other basic opportunities can be added, but these were available from reasonably comparable available household surveys.

The Human Opportunity Index focuses on coverage and inequality of opportunities among children for three main reasons:

- First, from an empirical standpoint, the principle of equality of opportunity as "leveling the playing field" can be readily operationalized by measuring children's access to basic goods and services that are critical for the full development of a child. For children, access defines "opportunity," because children (unlike adults) cannot be expected to make the efforts needed to access these basic goods by themselves.

- Second, from a policy standpoint, evidence indicates that interventions to equalize opportunity early in the lifecycle of an individual are significantly more cost effective and successful than interventions later in life.

- Third, focusing on children helps put inequality of opportunity at the center of the policy debate. As pointed out by the *World Development Report 2006* (World Bank 2006), on the day of their birth, children cannot be held responsible for their family circumstances, despite the fact that these circumstances—such as race, gender, parents' income and education, and urban or rural location—will make major differences in the lives they lead.

   To get a sense of the importance of the inequitable distribution of opportunity, consider the case of having access to electricity. Despite the high average access to electricity in most countries in the region, there is not much equity across groups, as can be seen when comparing the average probability for access to electricity for two different children (figure 1). One child has four siblings in a rural single-parent household, with an illiterate parent and a household per capita income of US$1 a day. The other has one sibling in an urban two-parent household, and both parents have completed secondary education and earn a household per capita income of

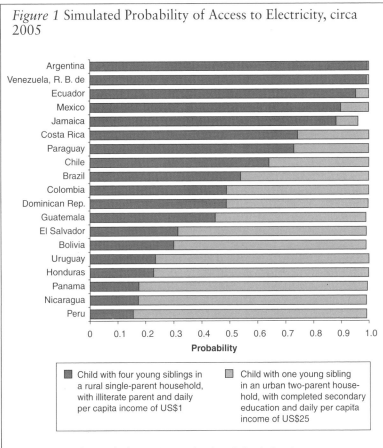

Figure 1 Simulated Probability of Access to Electricity, circa 2005

Child with four young siblings in a rural single-parent household, with illiterate parent and daily per capita income of US$1

Child with one young sibling in an urban two-parent household, with completed secondary education and daily per capita income of US$25

Source: Authors' calculations (regression-based simulations).

US$25 a day. The differences in access to electricity are considerable, and vary tremendously across Latin America. In Chile, a relatively rich child's opportunity is almost double that of a child from a poorer background, while in Peru and Nicaragua the difference is more than sixfold. Similar pronounced differences are documented in services such as access to water, sanitation, and electricity as well as education.

Methodology for Building the Human Opportunity Index

As noted, the Human Opportunity Index synthesizes into a single indicator measurements of both the level of basic opportunities in a society and how equitably those opportunities are distributed. The first component of the index—the average coverage rate for a given basic opportunity—can be readily determined using household survey data. The second component—the equity of opportunity distribution—requires a more involved calculation.

Our measure of inequality of opportunity is a version of the dissimilarity index (D), widely used in sociology and applied to dichotomous outcomes. The D-index measures the dissimilarity of access rates for a given service for groups defined by circumstance characteristics (for example, gender, location, parental education, and so forth) compared with the average access rate for the same service for the population as a whole. If the equal opportunity principle is consistently applied, an exact correspondence between population and opportunity distributions should be observed. That is, if half the population is in circumstance group A, 35 percent in group B, and 15 percent in group C, opportunities should be distributed in the same proportions. The D-index ranges from 0 to 1 (0 to 100 in percentage terms), and in a situation of perfect equality of opportunity, D will be zero.

Access probability gaps are at the heart of the D-index (figure 2 illustrates this with an example). The horizontal line represents the average probability in the entire population that a child will have access to clean water. The bars represent the access of probability of specific groups. The D-index is a weighted average of the absolute differences of group-specific access rates (p_i) from the overall average access rate, $\bar{p}$.

The D-index in figure 2 will be higher than zero, and will capture the fact that children of illiterate parents living in rural areas have a much lower probability of having access to safe water than their counterparts in urban areas with literate parents. There can be as many probability gaps as there are possible combinations of group-defining circumstances. For example, 20 income groups, 7 family-size groups, and whether one is in a rural or urban setting already generates 280 probability gaps. If augmented with parental education and the gender of the child, the total number of probability gaps would be very large. The exact procedure to calculate the p_i's involves an econometric specification.

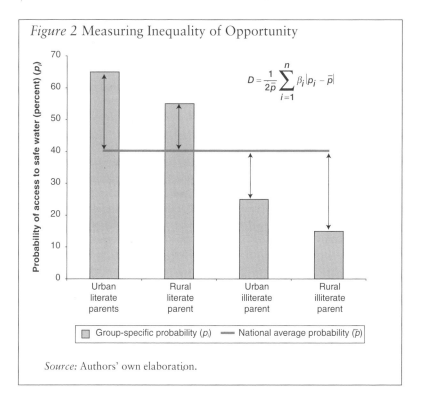

Figure 2 Measuring Inequality of Opportunity

$$D = \frac{1}{2\bar{p}} \sum_{i=1}^{n} \beta_i |p_i - \bar{p}|$$

Group-specific probability (p_i) ▬ National average probability ($\bar{p}$)

Source: Authors' own elaboration.

The D-index can be interpreted as showing the fraction of all available opportunities that needs to be reassigned from better-off groups to worse-off groups to achieve equal opportunity for all. In one of the education indicators, finishing sixth grade on time, for example, Guatemala's D-index score is 27 percent, indicating that 27 percent of total opportunities for finishing sixth grade on time have to be reallocated to ensure equal chances for all. By contrast, in Chile less than 3 percent of these opportunities need to be reallocated to ensure equal chances for all children. The average for this indicator in Latin America and the Caribbean as a whole is 11 percent. The regional average for school attendance at ages 10 to 14 is 3 percent, for water is 12 percent, for sanitation 26 percent, and for electricity 10 percent.

The Human Opportunity Index (O) incorporates into a single composite indicator both overall access rates and the D-index measure of opportunity distribution. Analogous to Sen's welfare function that combines income per capita with income distribution indicators, this index combines average access to opportunities ($\bar{p}$) with how equitably those opportunities are distributed (D). The proposed index is given by

$$O = \bar{p}(1-D).$$

On an intuitive level, the Human Opportunity Index takes access to a basic opportunity, the coverage rate, and "discounts" it if those opportunities are allocated inequitably. Two forces drive the index: for a given level of D, an increase in the prevalence of opportunities (that is, a higher $\bar{p}$) increases the index, while an improvement in the way existing opportunities are allocated (a reduction in D) will also improve the index. Hence, the index is Pareto-consistent, in that it will improve if the overall average access to a given opportunity increases, no matter how access is distributed—at least someone is better off, and no one is worse off. However, the D-index gives much greater weight to those opportunities allocated to a disadvantaged sector of the population than to those allocated to an advantaged group, and is therefore a distribution-sensitive measure.

Human Opportunity Index Results for 19 Countries in Latin America and the Caribbean

The study calculated Human Opportunity Indexes using data from nationally representative household surveys for 19 Latin American and Caribbean countries over a period of approximately a decade (1995–2005). The criterion was to choose two comparable surveys as close as possible to 1995 and to 2005. Together, the surveys are representative of nearly 200 million children ages 0–16 from 19 Latin America and Caribbean countries. The five basic opportunity variables considered were completing sixth grade on time, school attendance at ages 10–14, and access to water, sanitation, and electricity (figure 3).

The Human Opportunity Index for completion of sixth grade on time shows that in Jamaica, Mexico, Argentina, Chile, Ecuador, and Uruguay more than 75 percent of all opportunities needed to ensure universal access are available *and* have been allocated according to an equality of opportunity principle. In contrast, in Honduras, El Salvador, Brazil, Nicaragua, and Guatemala this indicator is below 50 percent. Scores across the 19 countries range from 24 percent in Guatemala to 86 percent in Jamaica. The Human Opportunity Index for school attendance for children ages 10 to 14 illustrates that all countries score very high levels: above 75 percent. Scores across the 19 countries range from 77 percent in Guatemala to 98 percent in Chile. This is a much narrower gap (22 percentage points) than in the case of completion of sixth grade on time. For these two educational variables, the regional average is 62 percent and 90 percent, respectively. In these educational opportunities, as well as in those related to housing conditions, described below, the value of the Human Opportunity Index is in all cases below the coverage rate. This is because in all cases the D-index, which exclusively measures how available opportunities are allocated, has a positive value.

For access to water, variance within the region is larger, with Jamaica, Nicaragua, Peru, El Salvador, and Paraguay lagging below the 50 percent mark, while Costa Rica, Chile, Brazil, and Argentina are above 90 percent.

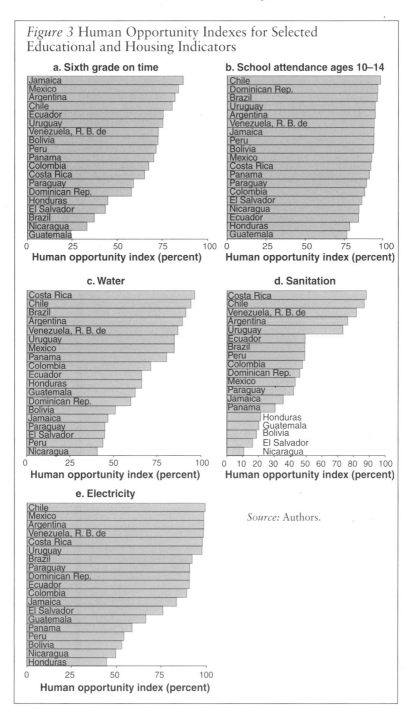

Figure 3 Human Opportunity Indexes for Selected Educational and Housing Indicators

a. Sixth grade on time

Jamaica
Mexico
Argentina
Chile
Ecuador
Uruguay
Venezuela, R. B. de
Bolivia
Peru
Panama
Colombia
Costa Rica
Paraguay
Dominican Rep.
Honduras
El Salvador
Brazil
Nicaragua
Guatemala

0   25   50   75   100
Human opportunity index (percent)

b. School attendance ages 10–14

Chile
Dominican Rep.
Brazil
Uruguay
Argentina
Venezuela, R. B. de
Jamaica
Peru
Bolivia
Mexico
Costa Rica
Panama
Paraguay
Colombia
El Salvador
Nicaragua
Ecuador
Honduras
Guatemala

0   25   50   75   100
Human opportunity index (percent)

c. Water

Costa Rica
Chile
Brazil
Argentina
Venezuela, R. B. de
Uruguay
Mexico
Panama
Colombia
Ecuador
Honduras
Guatemala
Dominican Rep.
Bolivia
Jamaica
Paraguay
El Salvador
Peru
Nicaragua

0   25   50   75   100
Human opportunity index (percent)

d. Sanitation

Costa Rica
Chile
Venezuela, R. B. de
Argentina
Uruguay
Ecuador
Brazil
Peru
Colombia
Dominican Rep.
Mexico
Paraguay
Jamaica
Panama
Honduras
Guatemala
Bolivia
El Salvador
Nicaragua

0 10 20 30 40 50 60 70 80 90 100
Human opportunity index (percent)

e. Electricity

Chile
Mexico
Argentina
Venezuela, R. B. de
Costa Rica
Uruguay
Brazil
Paraguay
Dominican Rep.
Ecuador
Colombia
Jamaica
El Salvador
Guatemala
Panama
Peru
Bolivia
Nicaragua
Honduras

0   25   50   75   100
Human opportunity index (percent)

Source: Authors.

The Latin American situation as a whole is much worse for sanitation than for water services, with a regional average of 67 percent in the case of water and 43 percent in the case of sanitation; four Central American countries plus Bolivia show scores below 30 percent. Regarding electricity, several countries have practically reached universal access, while others, such as Peru, Bolivia, Honduras, and Nicaragua, show Human Opportunity Index scores of around 50 percent.

Some countries—El Salvador, Guatemala, and Nicaragua—have low levels for all the different opportunities considered, while Chile is close to universal access in most cases. The performance of a few countries diverges widely when measuring different opportunities. For instance, Jamaica is close to providing access to all in education, but is very far from universality for water and sanitation. Brazil is close to universal access in electricity, at midway in sanitation, and has much room for improvement in education.

To construct a single summary indicator that can facilitate the measurement of opportunity in each country, all five different indicators of children's opportunities—completing sixth grade on time, school enrollment at ages 10–14, and access to water, sanitation, and electricity—were incorporated into an overall Human Opportunity Index (table 1). We first average the indexes for water, sanitation, and electricity into a single index of housing conditions. This is then averaged with the education index, encompassing completion of sixth grade on time and school enrollment for children ages 10–14. The results show that across the different opportunities considered, Argentina, Chile, Costa Rica, Uruguay, and República Bolivariana de Venezuela are closest to universality. Guatemala, Honduras, and Nicaragua are farther from that target, both because of low coverage and because the existing coverage is not equitably distributed.

Analyzing Changes in the Human Opportunity Index

Progress in the Human Opportunity Index varies substantially across countries and across the specific opportunities. In educational opportunities, Brazil and four Andean countries have made above-average improvements over the 1995–2005 period. Countries with below average growth are mainly those with relatively high levels of opportunities already reached (for example, Chile and República Bolivariana de Venezuela). In contrast, Guatemala is a country with initial low levels and below average change in educational opportunities (figure 4). The case of housing conditions is different. Countries still needing substantial progress in housing conditions, for example, Panama and Nicaragua, have only small improvements. Conversely, Chile and Costa Rica, with relatively high initial positions, have improved enough in this area over the 10-year period to reach almost

Table 1 Summary Human Opportunity Index (HOI), circa 2005

Country	HOI for education	HOI for housing conditions	Human Opportunity Index
Argentina	89	88	88
Bolivia	83	41	62
Brazil	67	77	72
Chile	90	93	91
Colombia	78	69	74
Costa Rica	79	94	86
Dominican Republic	77	65	71
Ecuador	80	69	74
El Salvador	65	46	55
Guatemala	51	50	50
Honduras	62	44	53
Jamaica	90	55	73
Mexico	88	75	82
Nicaragua	59	34	46
Panama	81	57	69
Paraguay	74	59	67
Peru	83	49	66
Uruguay	85	85	85
Venezuela, R. B. de	84	89	86
Average	76	64	70

Source: Authors.

universal access. Countries such as Peru, Mexico, Brazil, and Paraguay have also recorded large improvements in their opportunities for housing conditions, although substantial additional efforts are needed to equalize opportunities among all children.

By definition, progress in the Human Opportunity Index can occur by (i) increases in average access $(\bar{p})$, and (ii) increases in equality of opportunity $(1-D)$ of the existing opportunities. The empirical analysis shows that two-thirds of the improvements in the Human Opportunity Index are driven by an increase in the total supply of available opportunities, and a third by a reduction of inequities in the distribution of the available opportunities. This tendency varies across countries and basic opportunities, however. For instance, with regard to water, some countries, like El Salvador, have increased average total access and the equality of opportunity in a relatively balanced fashion. Others, like Nicaragua and Guatemala, have expanded opportunity only by increasing average access. If those new opportunities had been allocated in a more equitable fashion, favoring proportionally more children in rural areas or those whose parents are less educated, the overall Human Opportunity Index score for those countries

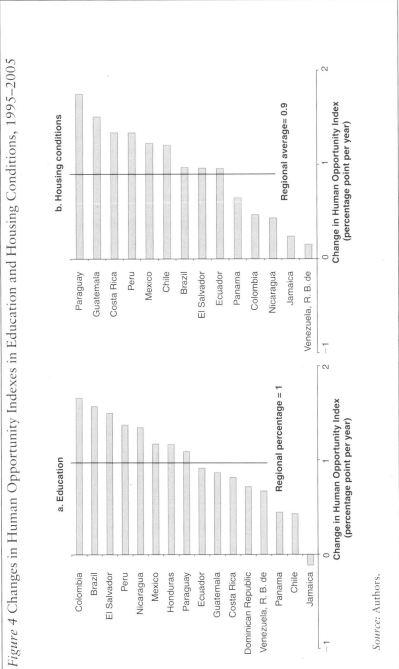

Figure 4 Changes in Human Opportunity Indexes in Education and Housing Conditions, 1995–2005

a. Education

b. Housing conditions

Source: Authors.

would have risen further. This happened, for instance, in countries like Paraguay and Mexico, in the case of water, Peru and Chile in the case of sanitation, and El Salvador and Brazil in the case of electricity. That is, in several instances, increases in opportunities have been implemented paying particular attention to disadvantaged groups, improving equality of opportunities more than proportionally. But progress is not homogeneous, either across countries or across basic opportunities.

To implement policies that reduce inequality of opportunities, a clear understanding of which key exogenous circumstances are unfairly influencing access of children to basic services is needed. The results indicate that parental education is an important divide in educational opportunity in Latin America and the Caribbean. In 17 out of 19 countries, it is the most important explanation of inequality of sixth grade completion on time. Inequality in enrollment between girls and boys is significant, together with parental education, as a determinant behind inequities in access to school for children between 10 and 14. In contrast, location is the most important circumstance in explaining inequality of opportunity in housing conditions for children. Without a doubt the urban-rural divide is the most important circumstance in explaining inequality of opportunity in basic housing infrastructure. Parental education and income have a smaller but still important role in explaining why many children do not have access to basic infrastructure services.

Expanding Policy Uses of the Human Opportunity Index

The basic opportunities considered in the Human Opportunity Index here —completing sixth grade on time, school enrollment at ages 10–14, electricity access, and water and sanitation services—are generally agreed-on aspirations for universal coverage in Latin America and the Caribbean, and indeed the world. However, the Human Opportunity Index can be readily used to examine other opportunities that might be of interest to a particular government. For example, an exercise for Chile considered access to computers and the Internet as basic opportunities for children. The results indicate that while Chile has had considerable success in expanding coverage and equity for many basic opportunities, it still has considerable challenges ahead regarding computer and Internet access (figure 5).

Another use of the Human Opportunity Index is to analyze inequality of opportunity within a country. An analysis made at the subnational level for Brazil showed that the Human Opportunity Index varied significantly across states, and that progress over time across regions has been uneven. Looking at completion of sixth grade on time, richer Brazilian states have values that are well below the average for Chile, the best performer in the region (figure 6). At the other end of the scale, the poor states of the northeast are doing worse than Guatemala and Nicaragua, the worst-performing countries in the region. In Brazil, the wealthy states of Santa Catarina and São Paulo perform four times better on the Human Opportunity Index than the poor states of Alagoas and Piauí.

The Relationship between Inequality of Opportunity and Inequality in Outcomes

The exact nature of the dynamic relationship between current inequality of outcomes and past inequality of basic opportunities for children is complex and not easily disentangled. One specific purpose of the Human Opportunity Index is helping countries focus not simply on unequal outcomes, which are not easy to redress, but also on inequality of basic opportunities, which most people agree is unfair and should be reduced as much as possible.

When looking at Latin American countries today, income inequality and inequality of opportunity reveal interrelated but distinct stories. Some countries, such as Costa Rica and Uruguay, show relative income equality and low inequality of opportunity for children (table 2). Other countries with high income inequality today, for example, Brazil and Chile, might have less inequality in the future because equitable access to basic opportunities is improving as a result of long-standing pro-active government policies (although the current levels in these countries are very different). Other countries, for example, Guatemala and Honduras, might still be trapped in a situation of high income inequality and very unequal opportunities for children, suggesting that stronger equity-oriented policies are needed. These are just examples—all countries face unique challenges.

As long as large differences like those found in Latin America exist in basic opportunities, children will have systematically different chances of success in life. As a whole, societies with greater inequality of basic opportunities among children are more likely to show inequalities later in the lifecycle, despite individuals who beat the odds through their effort, talent, and luck.

But inequality in basic opportunities determined by circumstances outside the control of the person will interact with other differences in opportunities that arise throughout life, such as opportunities to access tertiary education or obtain a high quality job, among others. Hence, the book also uses another approach, complementary to the Human Opportunity Index, that measures the share of current outcomes that can be attributed to inequality of opportunity. That measure is applied to income, earnings, and consumption for adults and to educational achievement for young people. The approach is described in the next section.

Figure 5 Human Opportunity Index and Coverage Rate: Chile, 2006

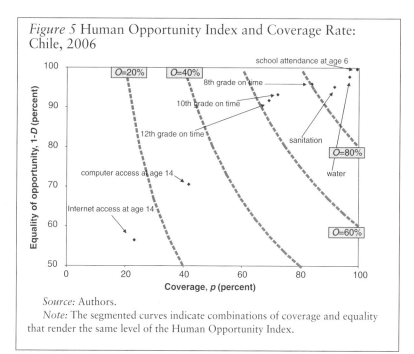

Source: Authors.

Note: The segmented curves indicate combinations of coverage and equality that render the same level of the Human Opportunity Index.

Figure 6 Human Opportunity Index: Completion of Sixth Grade on Time in Brazil by State, 2005

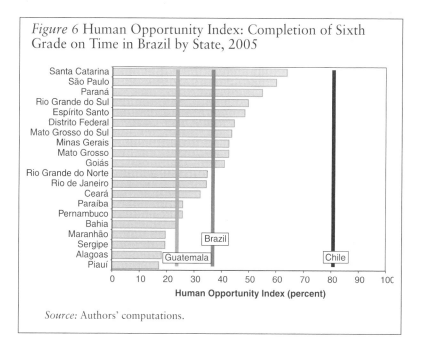

Source: Authors' computations.

Table 2 Income and Opportunities

	Level of income inequality	
Level of opportunity	*Relatively low income inequality*	*Relatively high income inequality*
Lower basic opportunities for children	*Puzzling:* El Salvador	*Inequality trap:* Bolivia Honduras
Higher basic opportunities for children	*Relative equality:* Argentina Costa Rica Uruguay Venezuela, R. B. de	*In transition:* Brazil Chile Colombia

Source: Authors' compilation based on World Bank and Universidad Nacional de la Plata: Socio-Economic Database for Latin America and the Caribbean (SEDLAC).

Estimating the Share of Unequal Opportunity in Unequal Outcomes

Outcomes such as earnings, income, occupational advancement, health status, or educational achievement in Latin America show marked inequalities that stem, at least partially, from inequality of opportunity. When some of the inequality observed in the outcome of interest can be attributed to exogenous circumstances, such as a person's gender or family background, it reflects inequality of opportunity in a society. In an ideal world, inequality in outcomes should reflect only differences in effort and choices individuals make, as well as luck.

Based upon this idea, inequality of opportunity can be estimated by decomposing outcome inequality into a portion resulting from circumstances that lie beyond the individual's control, and a residual component that rewards choices made, effort put forth, luck, and talent. Individuals cannot be held accountable for the component resulting from circumstances such as birthplace, gender, ethnicity, or parental background because they are exogenous and beyond their control. Moreover, there is a social consensus that these exogenous circumstances should not have an effect on individual outcomes. That component is a measure of inequality of opportunity—a reflection of the influence of those circumstances on overall inequality. This is a "consequential" approach in which inequality of opportunity is reflected by the importance of circumstances in explaining inequality of outcomes. It complements the Human Opportunity Index by measuring the "results" caused, in part, by the inequality of basic opportunities among children, but adding other mechanisms through which these exogenous circumstances may have an effect on outcome inequality.

In conceptual terms, the approach for estimating inequality of opportunity as a share of total outcome inequality is simple. First, six variables related to circumstances exogenous to the individual were identified from the most comprehensive data sets available: gender, race or ethnicity, birthplace, the educational attainment of the mother, the educational attainment of the father, and the main occupation of the father. In each country, the sample data were partitioned into groups or "cells," such that all individuals in any given cell have exactly the same combination of the six circumstances. The difference in outcomes *between* cells can be attributed to inequality of opportunity, while the differences *within* cells can be considered the result of effort or luck.

A comparative assessment of inequality of economic and educational opportunities was undertaken using this methodology for seven Latin American countries (Brazil, Colombia, Ecuador, Guatemala, Mexico, Panama, and Peru), based on data from nationally representative household surveys and international education assessments.

Inequality of Economic Opportunity

Inequality of economic opportunity was assessed first for labor earnings, household income, and household consumption. It was conservatively estimated to account for between one-fifth and one-third of overall earnings inequality in the seven Latin American countries reviewed (table 3). Brazil had the highest (most unequal) estimate at 34 percent, and Colombia the lowest at 20 percent. When analyzing household income instead of individual earnings, inequality of opportunity accounted for a slightly larger portion of overall inequality, with conservative estimates ranging from 20 percent in Mexico to 37 percent in Guatemala. When household consumption per capita was used, the share of total inequality was even higher, ranging from one-quarter in Colombia and Mexico to one-half of overall inequality in Guatemala.

It is interesting to note that high outcome inequality does not always imply high shares of inequality of opportunity. The most unequal countries are not necessarily those in which the importance of opportunity in explaining inequality is high. Inequality of opportunity, measured in this way, picks up something quite different from outcome inequality. There may be a positive correlation between inequality of outcomes and of opportunity shares, and, indeed, the mechanisms of intertemporal reproduction of inequality would lead one to expect this. But they are different concepts.

Table 3 Share of Inequality of Economic Opportunity
(percent)

Indicator	Brazil	Colom-bia	Ecuador	Guate-mala	Mexico	Pana-ma	Peru
Labor Earnings							
Overall inequality	61	60	63	78	75	57	67
Share of inequality							
of opportunity	34	20	25	29	23	25	21
Per capita income							
Overall inequality	69	55	41	61	71	63	55
Share of inequality							
of opportunity	32	25	29	37	20	35	29
Per capita consumption							
Overall inequality	—	44	35	40	63	38	35
Share of inequality							
of opportunity	—	26	34	52	26	42	34

Source: Authors' calculations based on household surveys.

Note: — = Not available. Overall inequality measured by the mean log deviation. Inequality of opportunity shares are nonparametric estimates.

Specific circumstances may have different roles in generating inequality of opportunity. Across all indicators of economic welfare analyzed here, the circumstances with the greatest impact on generating inequality of economic opportunity were family background variables: education levels of both parents (with the mother's having a stronger effect) and occupation of the father. Ethnicity and birthplace had smaller effects, but they were still sizable, particularly in Guatemala and Panama. Indeed, the importance of an indigenous background in Guatemala and Panama helps account for the overall higher levels of inequality of opportunity in those countries.

Another way to consider the inequality of economic opportunity is to determine the characteristics of the most-disadvantaged groups. Using the same circumstance variables as above, *opportunity profiles* identify the most-disadvantaged "types"—groups of the population characterized by exogenous circumstances—in each country for whom inequality of opportunity relegated them to the bottom of the socioeconomic ladder. For example, it is found that the poorest 10 percent of the population in Brazil comprises groups that are black or mixed race, born in the north or northeast, with parents who worked in agriculture and had low education. In all countries except Colombia, ethnic minorities constitute more than two-thirds of the portion of the poorest 10 percent (table 4). This would show that ethnicity is one key circumstance, exogenous to the

Table 4 What Circumstances Characterize the Most Economically Disadvantaged Groups?
(Percentage of individuals in circumstance groups that are in the bottom 10 percent of the distribution of consumption)

	Brazil	*Colom-bia*	*Ecuador*	*Guate-mala*	*Mexico*	*Pana-ma*	*Peru*
Member of ethnic minority	100	33	61	100	65	75	100
Father without education	89	77	87	99	72	58	100
Mother without education	91	96	98	99	94	93	99
Father's occupation in agriculture	88	—	93	100	94	84	—

Source: Authors' calculations based on samples of individuals ages 30 to 49 from the following household surveys: Brazilian PNAD 1996, Colombian ECV 2003, Ecuadorian ECV 2006, Guatemalan ENCOVI 2000, Mexican MxFLS 2002, Panamanian ENV 2003, and Peruvian ENAHO 2001.
Note: — = Not available. In the case of Brazil, consumption was replaced by income, because data on consumption were not available.

individual, that defines his belonging to the group with the poorest start. Family background was a second key variable to characterize individuals in the poorest decile. Specifically, in all countries, all people in the poorest decile had an uneducated mother. In countries with relevant data, more than 80 percent of the most disadvantaged individuals have their father in agriculture activities. And finally, birthplace: all individuals of the poorest decile in Brazil were born in the north or northeast; in Panama, 76 percent were born in rural areas; in Guatemala, 100 percent were born in the north and northeast; in Mexico, 65 percent were born in the south center and the south. Interestingly, when analyzing the richest 10 percent, there was no clear identification with birthplace. The circumstances most important in ranking groups at the very bottom of the opportunity scale are not necessarily the same as those accounting for the largest shares of inequality in the overall decomposition. In particular, race and ethnicity are more important determinants of severe opportunity deprivation than of opportunity shares of overall inequality. Family background variables, like parental education and occupation, are salient for both.

Inequality of Opportunity in Educational Achievement

Inequality of opportunity can also be reflected in educational outcomes. The book presents the results of a comparative assessment of inequality of opportunity in educational achievement in five Latin American countries, as well as in nine North American and European countries. Education outcome data come from the internationally comparable exams administered by the Program for International Student Assessment (PISA). Total inequality in educational achievement was decomposed into a component resulting from a set of circumstances and a second component encompassing individual efforts, talent, and luck, using the same technique as for economic inequality. The predetermined circumstances used in all countries were gender, mother's and father's education, father's occupation, and school location. Information on race or ethnicity was not available for all countries in the education sample, and hence was not included.

Inequality of opportunity was estimated to account for between 14 percent and 28 percent of overall inequality in reading achievement in Latin America, and for between 15 percent and 29 percent in mathematics achievement, as a conservative estimate. As with economic outcomes, the circumstances that had the largest impact on opportunity shares were family background variables, notably mother's education and father's occupation. School location was particularly important in Mexico, revealing large geographic inequalities in educational achievement in that country. The impact of gender on opportunity shares of educational achievement inequality was found to be limited.

Compared with Organisation for Economic Co-operation and Development countries, the median Latin American country seems to be more opportunity unequal with regard to educational achievement, with about 20 percent of total inequality accounted for by circumstances. Meanwhile, in the typical industrial country, 15 percent of inequality is associated with the same circumstances. Because total outcome inequalities were also higher in Latin America, this pattern is even more pronounced in levels, with Argentina and Peru recording the highest estimates of inequality of educational opportunity.

Opportunity profiles of the circumstance types with the least and most advantages in educational opportunity reveal that for all countries, the most-disadvantaged groups tended to include a disproportionate share of children of agricultural workers and parents with little or no schooling (table 5). In Chile and Mexico, most disadvantaged individuals are studying in rural areas, whereas in Argentina and Brazil, a significant proportion are found in urban areas. Boys are a majority of those in the most-disadvantaged groups for reading. It is interesting to note that girls dominate among the most advantaged in both reading and mathematics achievement, as well as among the most disadvantaged for mathematics.

The influence of parental background variables in educational achievement as well as in economic outcomes reveals marked problems of intergenerational transmission of poverty—less parental education not only shapes opportunities and explains an important fraction of income inequality, but also characterizes groups at the bottom of the educational and economic ladders.

Table 5 What Characterizes Students in the Bottom 10 Percent of
Reading Performance Distribution?
*(Percentage of individuals in circumstance groups that are in the
bottom 10 percent of the distribution of reading scores)*

Circumstance	Argentina	Brazil	Chile	Mexico	Peru
Male	85	90	68	96	67
Father without education	62	66	61	86	93
Mother without education	75	80	76	87	96
Father agricultural or fishery worker	77	74	60	71	95
School located in a village or small town	42	28	61	94	–

Source: Authors' compilation using data from the PISA 2000 and 2001 surveys.
Note: Groups according to exogenous circumstances (gender, family background, school location) are defined and ordered according to mean scores; groups that account for the bottom decile of performance are kept; percentages indicate characteristics of those individuals.

Final Remarks

Equality of opportunity is about leveling the playing field for everyone from the beginning of their lives. In a region characterized by pervasive and untamed inequality of income, and where groups of the population remain excluded from socioeconomic progress, a shift in the debate toward equality of opportunities promises to be a useful guide for public policy. It is a shift in the debate and in the attention of policy makers, who recognize that much more progress can be made if countries confer a sense of urgency to the need to give the same chances to all. To do that, measuring inequality of opportunity—better, deeper, and more systematically— is critical. This book proposes tools to advance this agenda. With the Human Opportunity Index, the level and distribution of basic opportunities among children can be better measured and tracked over time. Similarly, progress in opportunity profiles of the most-disadvantaged groups can be assessed and followed in each country, as well as the importance of inequality of opportunities' share in total inequality. Inequality of opportunity appears at different moments in life, but here, the intent has been to provide a measure for estimating basic opportunities for children, and for gauging the importance of inequality of opportunities to educational outcomes among youth and economic outcomes among adults. For equality of opportunity to prevail, we posit that there is a social consensus that exogenous circumstances should not have a role. However, birthplace matters in Latin America; it determines a child's access to clean water, sanitation, and electricity. Parental education matters; it explains access to early secondary schooling and access to water and sanitation, and is strongly related to economic and educational achievement. Parental socioeconomic status is much more strongly linked to that of children than what many would perceive as just. Ethnicity matters, and seems to be a key factor in economic and educational outcomes, particularly as it characterizes the most-disadvantaged groups. These strong, undesired associations result in a complex, challenging, and urgent agenda.

This book reports progress, although heterogeneous across countries and across opportunities. The Human Opportunity Index for children has increased since 1995 for all basic opportunities (education, water, electricity, sanitation), mostly because of increases in average access, but also because, in several instances, increases in opportunities were implemented paying particular attention to disadvantaged groups, further reducing inequality of opportunity. But universality of these basic opportunities should be a target for the near future, so the policy challenge is big. And for inequality of opportunity in general, as long as birthplace, ethnicity, and family background strongly influence opportunities and individual outcomes, the Latin American population will still strongly believe that the playing field is, in fact, not level.

References

Commission of Growth and Development. 2008. *The Growth Report: Strategies for Sustained Growth and Inclusive Development.* Washington, DC: Commission on Growth and Development.

Sen, A. 1976. "Real National Income." *Review of Economic Studies* 43 (1): 19–39.

World Bank. 2006. *World Development Report 2006: Equity and Development.* Washington, DC: World Bank.

1

Inequality of Opportunity: What It Is, How It Can Be Measured, and Why It Matters

Even though poverty and inequality are related concepts, the goals of reducing them have received different levels of support. Reducing poverty is a universally accepted aim and a priority for development work, and is included as the first Millennium Development Goal. By contrast, while inequality has received a lot of attention—particularly in Latin America and the Caribbean, the region with the highest inequality in the world—consensus on promoting policies to reduce inequality has been much harder to achieve.

Inequality is traditionally measured using consumption, income, or wealth indicators. However, inequality is a characteristic of a host of other outcomes, production factors, and services that influence social and economic advancement. For example, access to education varies dramatically within most countries in the region. Take the probability of completing sixth grade on time for a 13-year-old living with one sibling in an urban, two-parent household with a daily per capita income of US$25 (in purchasing power parity terms), and compare it with a 13-year-old with four young siblings in a rural, single-parent household, where the parent is illiterate and the daily per capita household income is US$1. In a relatively rich country like Chile, the probability of a child from a richer background completing sixth grade is almost double that of a child from a poorer background. But in less rich Brazil and poorer Guatemala the probability is 15 times larger (figure 1.1).

Another example is the pronounced difference in access to basic services such as electricity. Take two children with the same characteristics

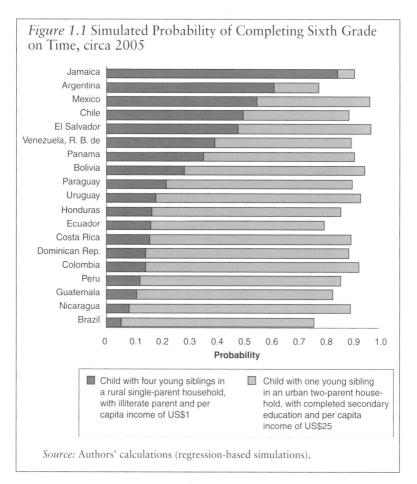

Figure 1.1 Simulated Probability of Completing Sixth Grade on Time, circa 2005

Source: Authors' calculations (regression-based simulations).

as above, but now analyze the likelihood that they live in houses where there is access to electricity from any source. Relatively rich children will all have access to electricity in almost all countries, but in countries such as Panama, Peru, and Nicaragua, less than 20 percent of poor children will have it (figure 1.2). Turning to health outcomes, the infant mortality rate among children in El Salvador with educated mothers is 25 per 1,000 live births, compared with 100 per 1,000 live births among children whose mothers have no formal education. In Haiti, the proportion of children with no access to basic immunization services is approximately 10 times larger among the poorest 20 percent than among the richest 20 percent of the population.[1]

Similar disparities are found in access to a number of other public services. These examples of inequality are all the more stark because they

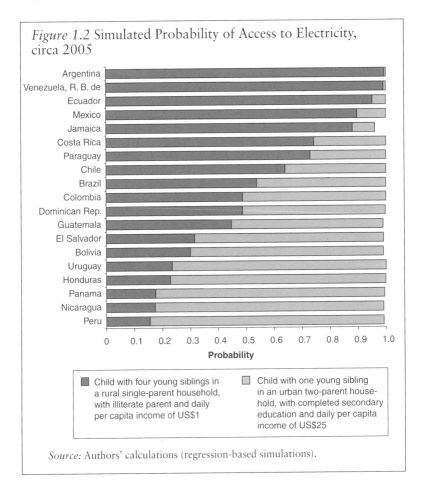

Figure 1.2 Simulated Probability of Access to Electricity, circa 2005

Probability

Child with four young siblings in a rural single-parent household, with illiterate parent and daily per capita income of US$1

Child with one young sibling in an urban two-parent household, with completed secondary education and daily per capita income of US$25

Source: Authors' calculations (regression-based simulations).

relate to children, who can hardly be considered responsible for making the choices that led to these inequalities.

Which Kind of Inequality Matters?

Should policy makers worry about inequality? Is all inequality objectionable? Worldwide, there is less agreement on this issue than might be expected. Consider, for instance, the heterogeneous responses to a question included in the World Values Survey, which asked representative samples of people in 69 countries about their views on the importance of income redistribution versus individual effort (figure 1.3). The median response was six, roughly in the middle of the spectrum. More striking was the fact

that the two most popular replies were at the two extremes: some 20 percent of the global sample felt very strongly that incomes should be made
more equal, while approximately the same number felt equally strongly
that larger inequalities were needed, as an incentive to individual effort.
These differences of views may arise simply from differences in social preferences about inequality. But there is an alternative explanation: that the
sources of inequality matter. It can be argued, for instance, that economic
inequality is neither all bad, nor all good. Whether we judge inequality to
be unfair may well depend on why some people are richer than others.

People in the Latin America and the Caribbean region face highly
unequal opportunities in life and different chances of economic success—
and, not surprisingly, very unequal outcomes. The debate about public
policy and inequality reduction must recognize that inequality is made
of heterogeneous components, some much more unfair, undesirable, and
unnecessary than others. Most people would probably view income gaps
that arise from different choices as less objectionable than those related
to ethnicity, location of birth, gender, or family background, which are all
factors beyond the individual's responsibility and thus might be deemed

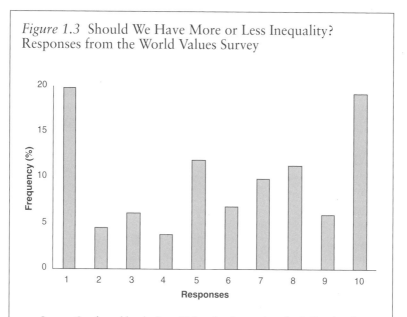

Figure 1.3 Should We Have More or Less Inequality?
Responses from the World Values Survey

Source: Conducted by the Inter-University Consortium for Political and
Social Research, based at the University of Michigan, 1999–2000, as cited in
Inglehart and others, 2004.
Note: "1" is equivalent to "incomes should be made more equal"; "10" is
equivalent to "we need larger income differences as incentives for individual
effort."

unfair. Consensus could easily be reached about the need for policies devoted to reducing or eliminating the unfair influence of some of these components. However, other potential sources of inequality may be necessary to give people proper incentives to provide the effort to acquire education and translate it into earnings. In that regard, some inequality may be tolerated, like inequality caused by differences in effort and talent, particularly when attempts to reduce it could interfere with other ethical objectives, such as privacy and individual freedom. Equality of opportunities is desirable, equality of outcomes (earnings, income, wealth) not necessarily.

Gaviria (2006) has analyzed Latin American people's views regarding equality of opportunities. Using a large sample of people from 17 countries from the region collected by Latinobarometro, he analyzed if people believed everybody had the same opportunities to move out of poverty and if poverty could be attributed to lack of opportunities or to lack of effort or talent. Seventy-four percent believed that opportunities are not fairly distributed, and 64 percent that poverty is due to factors different to effort or talent. Overall, people were pessimistic about the importance of effort for socioeconomic advancement.

Development economists view equity—in opportunities—as an important factor not only from a moral standpoint, but also as part of the development process itself. The *World Development Report 2006: Equity and Development* suggested two main sets of reasons why equity should matter for policy makers in developing (and developed) countries: (i) unequal opportunity is widely seen as intrinsically unfair, and unfairness bothers people and can lead to social conflict; and (ii) inequality in some particular circumstances (notably but not exclusively inherited wealth) can be economically inefficient. However, people do not view, and policy makers may not want to treat, all unequal outcomes the same.

In many societies, unequal opportunities caused by circumstances at birth, such as ethnicity, gender, place of origin, and family background, which are beyond the control of the individual, condition the outcomes that individuals are able to achieve in life. The inequality caused by unequal opportunities is viewed by most people as fundamentally unfair. Thus, shifting the debate from inequality of income or earnings to inequality of opportunity, and to the policies needed to tackle that inequality, might facilitate a political and policy consensus. When the focus of the debate is on inequality of income or any other outcome, the views about how much to redistribute—if any at all—and through which mechanisms would vary from left to right across the political spectrum. However, when the focus shifts to the equalization of opportunity, political consensus about the need to reduce inequity is easier to achieve, and the direction this principle gives to policy is clearer. Deliberating equality of opportunity helps policy makers differentiate between those inequalities caused by factors considered "fair" and those considered "unfair."

The number of different opportunities affecting later outcomes can be infinite, from access to basic education and nutrition when very young, to opportunities for tertiary education, to access to a decent job as an adult. This book treats some goods and services as *basic opportunities*, to focus attention on those opportunities most critical to future life outcomes, particularly for children. Most societies care deeply about providing a set of basic opportunities to children, such as access to safe water, minimum caloric intake, and basic education. These goods and services are not under the control of the child and are directly measurable indicators that can also be used to denote inequality of opportunity. In addition, these opportunities are affordable with existing technology and resources, making universal access a realistically achievable aim.

The remainder of this chapter is divided into four sections. The first examines in more detail the concepts behind inequality of opportunity and proposes a framework for the analysis of opportunity that may be useful for policy design. The second discusses the alternative approaches to measuring inequality of opportunity used in the remainder of the book. The third section summarizes the main reasons policy makers should be concerned about inequality of opportunity, while the last considers the implications for policy.

The Concept of Inequality of Opportunity

Understanding the exact meaning of the concept of inequality of opportunity and its implications requires some analytical, methodological, and even philosophical consideration. Before moving on to the detailed quantitative work of later chapters, this section seeks to carefully define inequality of opportunity and related concepts, and then construct a framework for measuring it.

Conceptual Underpinnings

The critical distinction between outcome differences that are attributable to individual responsibility and those that are not has played a central role in political philosophy in the last 40 or so years. Before John Rawls' *A Theory of Justice* (1971), most people sought to assess the fairness or equity of a social allocation solely on the basis of the distribution of outcomes. In the 1970s, spurred on by the work of both Rawls and Robert Nozick (1974), political scientists and philosophers began to consider the fairness of processes, and how final outcomes are determined both by the opportunities a person enjoys and by what he or she makes of those opportunities.

John Rawls (1971) emphasized liberty. His first basic principle of justice demanded "the most extensive liberty for each, consistent with similar liberty for others." His second principle postulated that "primary goods," which provide basic opportunities—a concept that will be returned to later—should be available to all members of society. Under his "Difference Principle," Rawls proposed that the optimal allocation of primary goods would maximize the share of the least privileged group.

Following Rawls, Ronald Dworkin (1981) equated fairness with *equality of resources*, rather than outcomes. Richard Arneson (1989) spoke of *equality of opportunity for welfare*, rather than of welfare itself. Although details and nuances differ across these various authors, the common thread was a redefinition of what Gerry Cohen (1989) calls the "currency of egalitarian justice": it seemed to most writers that fairness required the equality of *something*, but given the role of individual responsibility, it was clear that it was not simply the equality of outcomes.

Economists were not far behind. In his 1979 Tanner Lectures at Cambridge University, Amartya Sen famously asked "Equality of What?" (Sen and Hawthorne 1985). He took it as a given that most recent theories of justice associated fairness with the equal distribution of something. But it was not obvious what this something ought to be. Because "final outcomes," such as utility, or even intermediated outcomes, such as income, wealth, or education, depended in large part on choices made by individuals themselves, it seemed fair to hold individuals accountable for some of the final differences in achievement, so long as those differences followed from those choices.[2] Sen defined a person's "capabilities" as the set of possible "functionings" that he or she might enjoy, and argued that attention should focus on the distribution of those capabilities.

This book, similarly to the *World Development Report 2006: Equity and Development*, adopts a notion of fairness that is based on *equality of opportunity*. This phrase has been used equally by commentators on both the political right and left. A definition of the concept useful for this discussion is that of Roemer (1998). Roemer spoke of the outcome of interest as an "advantage" and divided the determinants of advantage into two groups: "efforts," which are subject to individual choice, and "circumstances," which are factors that lie outside the individual's control. Equality of opportunity would prevail in a situation in which the distribution of an outcome of interest is independent of circumstances. Equal opportunity levels the playing field, and everybody has, in principle, the potential to achieve the outcomes of their choosing.

Developing a Conceptual Framework

The debate about the role of public policy in reducing inequality requires a better understanding of the sources of inequality. Figure 1.4 diagrams the basic ideas behind the concept of inequality of opportunity, which will help orient the discussion. Overall outcome inequality, in the uppermost box, represents the inequality observed in outcomes such as labor earnings, household consumption per capita, educational achievement, health prevalence, or any other social outcome of interest. Outcome inequality arises from two basic sources. The first is inequality associated with differences in circumstances that the individual cannot be held accountable for and that lead people to face different opportunity sets: race, gender, the family and socioeconomic group into which they were born, the place where they were born, as well as any mental or physical characteristics they inherit at birth. As long as these predetermined circumstances affect the outcome of interest—and there is a social agreement that they should not—through any mechanism, the differences generated will be attributable to inequality of opportunity, represented in the right-hand box.

Although many would argue that this source of inequality is intrinsically unjust, not everyone would unconditionally agree that public policy must be used to reduce it. Inequality of opportunity, as well as overall inequality, is made up of heterogeneous components that must be disentangled before a consensus can be reached on the extent to which public policy should be used to reduce it.

The remainder of outcome inequality reflects differences in variables that are, to some extent, under the control of the individual. These include where individuals choose to work and live, with whom they choose to marry or cohabit, how many children they decide to have, and so forth.[3] These factors could have been different if the person had chosen a different path; individuals with identical choice sets reach different outcomes as a result of their own choices, and it is sensible to hold them accountable for those choices. That component of inequality is in the left-hand box. It is sometimes described as inequality resulting from effort and choice, but because it also includes differences resulting from postnatal random shocks (luck), it is preferably called "residual inequality."[4]

Two views of inequality of opportunity can be encompassed within this framework. The first, called "meritocratic," requires that people with identical levels of effort and choice enjoy identical outcomes. Any inequality in outcomes would map perfectly to differences in effort and choice. In this situation, circumstances might still condition the final outcome as they affect the choice set available to the individual (arrows 1 and 3, shutting down arrow 2 in figure 1.4). A second view, called "egalitarian," is from Roemer (1998). This definition requires that the distribution of outcomes be stochastically independent of any circumstances.[5] It therefore shuts down not only the direct effect of circumstances on outcomes through arrow 2, but also the indirect effect of circumstances on the set of choices facing the individual that operates through efforts and choice (arrow 3).

An example clarifies the distinction. Imagine a country in which there is no discrimination against indigenous people in the labor market, but where language barriers, cultural differences, differences in the types of schools attended, or differentiated treatment within schools result in indigenous students consistently attaining lower educational achievements. Given

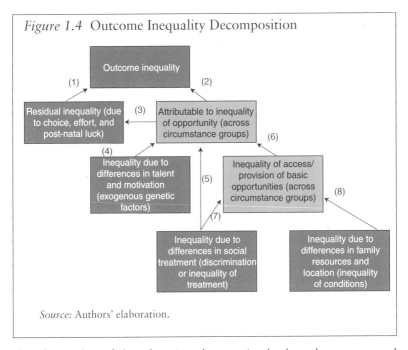

Figure 1.4 Outcome Inequality Decomposition

Source: Authors' elaboration.

that the quality of the education they receive leads to lower expected returns in the labor market, they rationally choose to invest less time in education. The labor market rewards education, and indigenous workers earn less than nonindigenous workers; for the sake of argument assume that the lower earnings are entirely due to educational differences resulting from a choice made by the individual. According to the meritocratic definition, this society would not have inequality of opportunity in its labor market, because education is part of the choice set of the individual, and people would be rewarded precisely in accordance with their educational achievements.

The egalitarian view, however, would view this society as opportunity-unequal, because outcomes are not independent of ethnicity. Circumstances (being indigenous) may not affect outcomes through the labor market, but they affect them through the educational choices ("efforts" in Roemer's terminology) of the individual, which implies that the distribution of choices finally made is different across the two groups. In this case, even if arrow 2 is shut down, circumstances are affecting outcomes through arrows 1 and 3.

As Roemer (1998) noted, the egalitarian view would mandate some form of intervention to increase the incomes of the disadvantaged group, until each percentile of the effort distribution among the advantaged group earned the same as the corresponding percentile among the disadvantaged. To compensate, indigenous workers must, theoretically, be paid more than nonindigenous workers for each unit of education (year of schooling, for example), because the level of education itself was unfairly influenced by circumstances. In the discussion of meritocracy, the egalitarian view questions where the merit comes from. If it is attributable to circumstances, it is not "true" merit (box 1.1).

Box 1.1 Meritocracy and Equality of Opportunity

Meritocracy is a notion often associated with equality of opportunity. Meritocracy awards positions of responsibility according to skill and effort. To some extent, this notion parallels Roemer's distinction made between effort and circumstances in defining equality of opportunity. But Roemer proposes an important distinction between meritocracy and equality of opportunity. His proposition is that equality of opportunity implies leveling the playing field before any competition takes place. Meritocracy is equivalent to a nondiscriminatory approach at the competition stage, where selection is based only on traits and skills that are relevant to the position in question. A "leveled playing field" conception of inequality of opportunity is equivalent to equalizing opportunities at the period of formation so that all have the chance to acquire the needed skills.

Take the example of admission to a university. The meritocracy principle will admit those most likely to do well. The equality of opportunity principle will admit the high-effort individuals across groups of individuals defined by circumstances, even if those from disadvantaged groups may not do as well in university as those from advantaged groups. According to equality of opportunity, this policy is not a waste of university resources; according to meritocracy, it is.

Equal opportunity focuses on *fairness* in regard to competition for social resources. Meritocracy focuses on *produced social outcomes*. But society must balance fairness toward those competing for resources with general social welfare. Equality of opportunity cannot imply devoting an infinite amount of resources so that any individual can acquire the skills needed for any position he or she chooses. To properly adjudicate this problem requires having a general social welfare function for society. Lacking that, there is a rule of thumb that most people would adhere to: when training people for careers and occupations, use the equality of opportunity principle. When choosing candidates for jobs, use meritocracy.

No one would recommend equality of opportunity for choosing surgeons for their children. In that case, people want meritocracy. Also, take the example of selection to professional basketball teams. Height is an important circumstance, exogenous to the individual. Yet no one would recommend equality of opportunity here. In none of these cases is it advisable to select people only according to their effort—because the welfare of patients and basketball spectators dominates.

Note: The authors thank John Roemer for his contribution to this box.

The meritocratic and the egalitarian definitions coincide only when effort is stochastically independent of circumstances. When there is no arrow 3 when circumstances do not affect the choice set, shutting down the direct effect through arrow 2 suffices to ensure that circumstances have no effect on outcomes. In general, however, this is not the case. Assume the final outcome is earnings. Earnings inequality will depend on the educational effort a young individual chooses to make. Is the educational effort independent of circumstances? Unlikely. The best (and most empirically well-established) example is the dependence of a person's own schooling (which reflects effort) on parental education (a circumstance from the viewpoint of the child).[6] In fact, intergenerational mobility and inequality of opportunity are related concepts, although they measure different effects. One can say that as long as parental income is a good predictor of individual income, intergenerational income mobility is low. Hence, inequality of opportunity is high and family background might have a large influence on economic achievement and welfare. However, that is true only under the restrictive assumption that parental income is statistically sufficient for all observed relevant circumstances. Still, the literature of intergenerational mobility is pertinent for this discussion because parental and family background is a key determinant of opportunity. As shown above, children from different family backgrounds do face very different access to basic services, and, through different channels, family background affects a host of outcomes throughout the lifetime. Box 1.2 delves into the different points of contact between the literatures of intergenerational mobility and inequality of opportunity.

But there are many other ways in which background affects effort and choices people make. In a recent experimental study in rural India, Hoff and Pandey (2006) found that children perform differently in simple tasks when their caste identity is made salient. Steele (1997) and Steele and Aronson (1995) found similar effects on performance from emphasizing stereotypes among African Americans and whites in the United States (see World Bank 2006 for a summary).

This book, in keeping with the *World Development Report 2006*, uses an approach consistent with Roemer's egalitarian definition of equality of opportunity: a society has equal opportunities when circumstances are not statistically associated with differences in important life outcomes, nor directly, nor through affecting the choice set people face.

For policy purposes, it is critical to further disentangle the elements behind inequality of opportunity to judge whether those elements are justifiable or whether policy can and should attempt to redress them. Inequality of opportunity arises from at least three sources: intrinsic and personal characteristics, discriminatory treatment, and access to social services.

First, inequality of opportunity can arise from traits that are exogenous but intrinsic to the person: the genetic endowment of talent and motivation (arrow 4, figure 1.4). To the extent that these circumstances lead to

Box 1.2 Intergenerational Mobility and Equality of Opportunity

Intergenerational mobility is the extent to which parents' incomes or occupational choices correlate with those of their offspring.[a] There are a number of points of coincidence between the mobility and equality of opportunity literatures. One relates to the role of inherited ability and, more broadly, of genes in determining both individual outcomes and the intergenerational transmission of such outcomes. Some of the specialized literature suggests that intelligence and personality are, in part, hereditary. Moreover, the role of genes is likely to be enhanced by assortative mating and other channels of cultural transmission, such as choices, preferences, and the environment in which children are raised (Feldman, Otto, and Christiansen 2000). A second has to do with the importance of social connections, networks, and influences as determinants of individual outcomes and their intergenerational transmission.

Reliable estimates of intergenerational mobility are scarce. A common measure is the elasticity of son's to father's income; the smaller the elasticity, the higher mobility will be, and the less dependent an individual's earnings on that individual's background. Recent evidence shows that mobility in the United States is much lower than in Canada, Finland, Sweden, or the United Kingdom (World Bank 2006). Mazumdar (2005) calculates a fairly high intergenerational elasticity in earnings (0.6) between fathers and sons in the United States. Moreover, he finds substantial immobility among the poorest. Children born to parents in the lowest decile are likely to remain in the poorest 50 percent, and half of them will stay among the poorest 30 percent. There are many potential reasons behind this. One developed by Mazumdar is that parents from poorer backgrounds face financial constraints early in the lifetime of the child such that they cannot "buy into" neighborhoods with higher-quality schools. Empirically, he finds that families with low net worth have a significantly higher intertemporal elasticity than families with high net worth. That is, low wealth generates an intergenerational poverty trap. This justifies paying attention to family background as a key source of inequality of opportunity.

Recent evidence for Brazil, Peru, and Chile suggests that low mobility might be more marked in Latin America than in industrial countries (IDB 2008). Ferreira and Veloso (2004) show that in Brazil, sons of fathers in the lowest quintile of the wage distribution have a 35 percent probability of remaining in that quintile. For fathers in the richest quintile, the probability of their sons staying in the same quintile is 43 percent. Of interest is that income persistence is much higher among Afro-descendants. For this group, the figures are 47 percent and 29 percent, respectively; that is, half of Afro-descendants' sons in the poorest quintiles will stay there. The corresponding figures for whites are 25 percent and 50 percent, showing low mobility for those in the richest quintile.

Box 1.2 Intergenerational Mobility and Equality of Opportunity *(continued)*

An important point is that equal opportunity might not lead directly to greater economic mobility. Equality of opportunity does not necessarily imply the elimination of all sources of economic likeness between parents and children. Specifically, equality of opportunity may not negate the effect of inherited ability or certain values, which seem to explain a large portion of outcomes and economic mobility (Jencks and Tach 2006).

But at the same time, there is room for policy interventions to equalize opportunities and promote mobility. Ashenfelter and Rouse (2000) suggest that in the presence of positive returns to schooling unrelated to ability, schools can offer an adequate environment to increase skills (and therefore incomes), enhancing both equality of opportunity and economic mobility. Furthermore, in addition to the skills that are taught in schools, these environments can have an effect on norms and preferences in ways that make individuals more attractive to employers, translating into further effects on earnings (Bowles and Gintis 2000).

a. Both sociologists and economists have contributed substantially to the theoretical and empirical understanding of economic mobility. A complete review of the two literatures can be found in Morgan, Grusky, and Fields (2006).

---

differences in productivity or achievement, or results in a meritocratic environment, the inequality of opportunity might be considered, if not just, at least acceptable.[7] From a policy perspective, some genetic disadvantages can be fixed (for example, eyesight problems), and that can have important implications for equalizing opportunities (Jencks and Tach 2006). Roemer (1998) proposes that traits that are to some extent genetic (such as inherited IQ) are circumstance variables in an education production function. In principle, a society may want to invest resources to level the playing field for low-IQ individuals. How much and how far it wants to go in this compensation is a social choice.

Second, equally talented and productive individuals are treated differently in different markets, which might generate different outcomes for individuals with otherwise similar characteristics (arrow 5). People with different circumstances (family background, race, or place of origin) might be discriminated against in the labor market and have access to different kinds of jobs and consequently to different incomes. Likewise, males and females may not be treated equally when under consideration for a job, and may be paid differently for performing the same task. Quite often, equally talented and productive individuals are treated differently, receiving different access to the best jobs or receiving different wages even when performing the same tasks. In this case, inequality is generated by the unequal treatment of equally deserving individuals. This unequal treatment of equals is usually referred to as discrimination. Although there is consensus that discrimination is unfair, the resources societies are willing to allocate to eliminating this source of inequality vary considerably and remain open to debate.

A third component is the unfair allocation of what we call "basic opportunities" (arrow 6). The number of dimensions in which inequality of basic opportunities may arise is large and may operate at different stages of the life cycle. Differences in access may be generated early in life, such as access to education, health, nutrition, and basic services, or later in life in access to tertiary education, to a good quality job, or to political voice. As defined in more detail below, basic opportunities are those that are critical for development at early stages in life, that will have a key impact on outcomes, and that countries may aspire to provide universally. Policies can and should be implemented to increase access to basic opportunities and to ensure that their provision is not systematically biased against any specific group or type of individual. Even if universal access is not achievable in the short run, equality of opportunity implies ensuring that progress in the provision of basic opportunities is not biased against anybody because of circumstances.

The sources of unequal access to basic opportunities related to circumstances can be grouped into differences in social treatment and differences in conditions. *Differences in social treatment* are mostly related to discrimination across circumstance groups (arrow 7). If access to an opportunity is biased against certain groups of the population, inequality in acquired characteristics (such as formal education) might be generated even among equally talented persons. This, in turn, will lead to unequal outcomes even in meritocratic societies. Discrimination can also operate during the process of acquisition of a characteristic. For example, different ethnic groups may be treated equally for admission to a school, but be discriminated against while studying. In all cases of discrimination, equality of opportunity is violated because equally talented and motivated individuals are being treated differently, leading to differential outcomes. Nondiscriminatory policies would be the appropriate and necessary measure in these situations.

Differences in conditions relate to family background and resources that might differ across circumstance groups (arrow 8). In this case, children of poor parents are not being discriminated against; rather, they do not have equal access to services to develop and fully utilize their talents, just because their families lack the necessary resources. Among children, unequal access to basic opportunities hampers the accumulation of human and physical capital, which eventually has an impact on outcomes such as income and earnings. Lack of resources may impair not just access to basic opportunities but also the ability to benefit from them. For example, children of poor parents may have both less access to schools and learning disadvantages (such as no books at home or illiterate parents). In this case, equally talented children from different social backgrounds are not going to have the same opportunities for reasons outside their control. Unequal access to basic opportunities may also occur because of differences in location—for example, in a society with urban-biased policies, key services may not be available in rural areas, or the quality of those services may be much lower.

Whenever a child's access to or ability to benefit from basic opportunities depends on family resources, the ideal of equal opportunity is violated and social immobility is generated. Equally talented children from different social backgrounds are not going to have the same opportunities and outcomes for reasons outside their control. The role of public policy in this case is unanimously recognized—equal access to and conditions to benefit from these specific sets of social services should be provided to all. The policy implications are critical. Countries can and have implemented policies to subsidize access to social services, at least for the poor and, in some cases, have even guaranteed minimum income to ensure that all have the necessary conditions for benefiting from available services.

There are many correlations and causal interactions between these elements of inequality of opportunity. Greater innate ability may be partly the result of early childhood stimulation (such as storytelling or playing with small children). Richer families may have access to neighborhoods with better public schools, so that access to "better" public services is correlated with family socioeconomic background, and so on. From the point of view of policy design, the correlation between the pattern of access to, use of, and benefit from public services and the other subcomponents of inequality of opportunity is absolutely critical.

From Concepts to Operationalizing Equality of Opportunity

The overall goal of this book is to make the concept *equality of opportunity* operational by developing measurement tools that can assess and track inequality of opportunity. The book starts by defining equality of opportunity as the situation in which all individuals, independent of exogenous circumstances, have the same opportunities in life. "Circumstances" as used here are socially determined exogenous factors, such as gender, race, or socioeconomic background, beyond an individual's control, and about which there is broad agreement that they should not have a role in outcomes. In a situation of full equality of opportunity, these circumstances neither hinder nor contribute to the individual's achievement.

If the measurement of inequality of opportunity is to have any policy relevance, outcome levels and their relation to circumstances must at least conceptually be influenced by social policy choices. Circumstances are factors beyond an individual's control (such as race) that should not but that actually do affect outcomes of interest (such as wages). Outcomes of interest are advantages (such as wages) that can be modified by social choice (such as subsidized education or minimum wages). Moreover, the relationship between outcomes and circumstances (wages and race) can, at least conceptually, be modified by social choice (for example, ensuring equal provision of quality education for everybody, or affirmative action programs). For this exercise to be relevant for policy, that social choice must conceptually be able to modify both the level of the outcome and, more important for present purposes, its dependence on circumstances.

Despite the attention given to inequality of opportunity by sociologists and philosophers, empirically it neither has a universal definition nor an established measurement indicator similar to those for inequality of income or earnings. In the sociology literature, inequality of opportunity has been measured as the association between family background and children's outcomes. (See, for instance, the classic work of Boudon 1974.) Economists have recently begun paying attention to the measurement of inequality of opportunity for continuous outcomes such as income, consumption, and educational achievement.[8]

This study proposes two types of measures of inequality of opportunity. The first is a Human Opportunity Index, which introduces a new way to measure inequality in discrete indicators of basic opportunities for children. The second measure builds upon existing research to estimate the share of economic and educational inequality resulting from inequality of opportunity among youth and adults. The conceptual frameworks for these two techniques for estimating inequality of opportunity are outlined below and described in more detail in chapters 2 and 4.

The Human Opportunity Index

Understanding all the factors that influence individual outcomes, such as welfare or utility, is complex, if not impossible. We recognize that those outcomes are partially determined by factors that are the individual's responsibility, but an important part is determined by circumstances that lie beyond the individual's control and that create differences in the opportunities available to each individual. An equitable development process should pursue the equalization of opportunity at all stages of an individual's life, seeking to level the playing field for all citizens.

As mentioned in the previous section, one component of inequality of opportunity is unequal access to basic opportunities. As long as some children in a country do not have access to education, health, nutrition, and basic services, and as long as access is determined by circumstances for which the child is not accountable, such as gender, ethnicity, or family background, inequality of opportunity will prevail in that country. The Human Opportunity Index is an indicator that can be used to track a country's progress toward the goal of providing all children equal access to basic services defined as critical opportunities for future advancement in life.

Given the complexity of the issue, and for methodological considerations, it is useful to focus on a limited number of specific opportunities that could be measured and tracked. Undertaking such a task first requires operationalizing the concept of "opportunity." For the purposes of this study, opportunities are defined as those variables that

- exert influence on outcomes (such as income, labor earnings, educational achievement, and the like);
- are critical for the development of an individual;
- are exogenous and not under the control of the individual but are endogenous to society and can be modified by social choice and public policy; and
- might be unfairly influenced by circumstances.

For adults, endogeneity makes classifying opportunities as the result of either effort or circumstance more difficult. What role do individual effort and choice have in, for example, the opportunity to attend tertiary education? Attendance is influenced by the choices of an individual, but also by whether adequate tertiary education institutions exist or whether family resources might preclude attendance.[9] The same could be said of an adult's access to clean water—it might depend, at least partially, on an individual's choices, but it might also depend on the supply where the individual lives. Some may argue that the location of residence for an adult is under his or her control, so the condition of an adult with or without access to water is an interplay between an opportunity and a choice the adult made.

But for a six-year-old girl, access to safe drinking water or to a primary school is clearly an exogenous opportunity. Access is controlled not by her, but by her family or society. Hence, the set of goods and services that are critical for children is defined as *basic opportunities*. Examples include access to education, basic infrastructure, immunizations, minimum nutritional levels, and a birth certificate or other identity document. Two other elements are critical to consider a service or good a basic opportunity. First, basic opportunities are critical for human development. Second, they are affordable, given the available technology; and if not affordable today for a specific country, they might be in the near future with effective policies, such that universal provision is a valid and realistic social goal. Even if different societies have different standards regarding the set of basic opportunities, there is some consensus at the global level, as exemplified by the Millennium Development Goals. In the particular case of children, most societies agree on a set of basic opportunities, at least at the level of intentions.

A development process in which society attempts to equitably supply basic opportunities requires undertaking two complementary objectives:

- Ensuring that as many people as possible have access to basic opportunities.
- If the supply of basic opportunities is limited because of resource constraints, allocating newly created opportunities first to those who, given their circumstances, are at a disadvantage, to promote equality of opportunity.

The Human Opportunity Index presented in subsequent chapters gauges progress in these two complementary objectives using a measure of inequality of opportunity that can be applied to discrete outcomes. Indicators used to approximate opportunities among children are empirically more tractable: all observed inequality related to circumstance can safely be assumed to be inequality of opportunity because children cannot be held responsible for their own access to them. The empirical analysis does not have to disentangle inequality derived from circumstance from that related to individuals' choices. Hence, because opportunities are easier to directly observe among children, and because opportunities early in life are a precondition for equality of opportunity throughout the lifetime, this study focuses on basic opportunities for children to construct a Human Opportunity Index.

This approach gauges how circumstances related to differentiated social treatment (for example, based on gender or race), family resources, or location impact inequality in basic opportunities for children. Again following figure 1.4, this is represented by arrows 7 and 8. This method proceeds in two steps. First, it measures whether *existing* opportunities are allocated equitably, by using a dissimilarity index, or "D-index," that compares different circumstance groups' probabilities for accessing a given opportunity. The D-index has an appealingly concrete interpretation: it is the share of opportunities that would have to be "reallocated" across children from different circumstance groups in a country to restore equal opportunities for all children. Second, the D-index is combined with the absolute level of basic opportunities in a society into a synthetic measure, a Human Opportunity Index. This index assesses the importance of both improving overall access to basic opportunities and ensuring that existing opportunities are allocated equitably.

Through the Human Opportunity Index, this book investigates the extent to which circumstances affect access to a set of basic opportunities related to education (completing sixth grade on time and attending school at ages 10–14) and housing (water, sanitation, and electricity). Given that data on access to these types of public services are collected in household surveys, the Human Opportunity Index can be applied to a large number of countries. Other key basic opportunities have not been included owing to data limitations. More detail on the construction of the index is provided in chapter 2.

Measuring Inequality of Opportunity

Outcomes such as income, earnings, occupational advancement, health status, and educational achievement show inequalities that stem at least partially from circumstances. When a share of unequal outcomes can be attributed to circumstance, it reflects inequality of opportunity in a society. In an ideal world, inequality in outcomes should reflect only differences in effort and choices individuals make, as well as luck and talent. Based on this idea, one way to measure inequality of opportunity is to decompose unequal outcomes into a portion resulting from circumstances that lie beyond the individual's control, and a residual component that contains reward to effort and choices (as well as luck and talent). The individual cannot be held accountable for the component resulting from circumstances, because he or she is not responsible for them. That component reflects inequality of opportunity. This approach is used in chapters 4 and 5 to assess inequality of economic opportunity and educational achievement. Referring to figure 1.4, the first component includes both the direct effect of circumstances on outcomes (arrow 2) and any indirect effect of circumstances through effort or choice (arrow 3). Thus, it captures the multiple channels through which circumstances have an impact on outcomes. The residual component includes the effects of effort, choices, luck, and talent that are not associated with differences in circumstances, if all relevant circumstances are adequately measured. Because this approach breaks down the overall observed inequality in outcomes, it is called in this book the "top-down" approach.

A method frequently used for testing the equality of opportunity in a given society consists of investigating whether the outcome distributions conditional on circumstances are different.[10] If the wage distributions among indigenous and nonindigenous people in a country were identical, one would claim that there was no inequality of opportunity in that society related to the circumstance of being indigenous. If, instead, they differed in systematic ways (for instance, such that one circumstance was always preferable to another), the hypothesis of equal opportunity would be rejected, and some of the unobserved inequality would be due to opportunity disparities between indigenous and nonindigenous people. (See Lefranc, Pistolesi, and Trannoy 2006.)

To move beyond *testing* for inequality of opportunity and toward *measuring the extent* of that inequality, the literature has relied primarily on decompositions of overall outcome inequality into the two components described above. This top-down approach is closest to the spirit of the existing literature on measuring inequality of opportunity. (See, for example, Checchi and Peragine 2005, and Bourguignon, Ferreira, and Menéndez 2007.) It uses the formalization provided by John Roemer (1998), who describes equality of opportunity as the situation where outcomes (or "advantages") are distributed independently of circumstances. Essentially, individuals in a sample are allocated to groups defined by the vector of circumstance variables that are judged to be important potential determinants of outcomes of interest—such as race, gender, ethnicity, birthplace, and family background. This procedure partitions the population into many cells, such that all persons in any given cell have identical circumstances. Once this is achieved, all the inequality *between* the cells is due to differences in circumstances, while the inequality *within* a cell is due to the residual component.[11] The share of between-group inequality is then used as a measure of inequality of opportunity.

There are two ways of applying the top-down approach: either directly estimate between-group inequality or estimate within-group inequality and subtract that from the total. These two alternative paths do not generally yield the same responses. The technical reason for this path-dependence is that when the differences within groups are eliminated first, the weights used to aggregate within-group inequality across all groups are not changed. For most inequality measures, however, when the differences between groups are eliminated first (by rescaling group means, or "standardizing the distribution"), the weights change.

Fortunately, there is one standard decomposable measure of inequality—a member of the generalized entropy class of indexes—that is path-independent in this sense. It gives the same share for inequality of opportunity whether differences between groups are estimated directly, or whether the within-group differences are estimated first and then subtracted from the total. This measure is the mean logarithmic deviation, also known as the Theil-1 index. In this book, this index is relied on mostly when using the top-down approach.[12] The decomposition described in this section can be implemented in practice both parametrically and nonparametrically.

Finally, the partition of the population into groups, which was implemented for the decompositions mentioned above, can also be used to individually identify the groups that are the most disadvantaged in the distribution of opportunity in each society. Instead of ranking individuals or households by their income levels, ranks are produced only to identify which are the broad groups, defined by circumstances, that are, on average, not sharing in social prosperity. The methodology allows identification of the characteristics of the most-disadvantaged groups, from the perspective of equality of opportunity. For example, circumstances such as ethnicity and low parental education characterize the groups that account for the bottom 10 percent of the population.

Chapters 4 and 5 present results and describe in more detail the methods touched on in this section, while the formal treatment is reserved for papers by Ferreira and Gignoux (2008a, 2008b).

The Complementarity of the Empirical Approaches

The two approaches described above are complementary. Looking from a life-cycle perspective, the more bottom-up approach of the Human Opportunity Index seeks to understand the nature of inequality in access to basic opportunities related to education and housing among children. In this sense, it looks "inside the production function" of inequality of opportunity by focusing on arrows 7 and 8 of figure 1.4. Inequality in access to basic opportunities related to circumstances will, later in life, be reflected as part of the overall effect of circumstance on outcomes.

In turn, the top-down approach focuses on outcomes among youth and adults, and estimates to what extent a specific set of circumstances affects those outcomes. The measure reflects the operation of a multiplicity of opportunities, including basic opportunities during life that have been affected by circumstances. This allows the full extent of inequality of opportunity, at least that part linked to observed circumstances, to be measured. This relates to arrows 1 through 3 in figure 1.4.

This book does not dwell directly on all situations in which opportunities are needed to improve life chances. For example, the empirical sections of the book do not directly address unequal opportunity stemming from discrimination in the labor market. The analysis of the role of circumstances on outcomes such as income or labor earnings is captured through the final net impact of circumstances on outcomes, which are mediated through specific inequalities in opportunity, including discrimination, without trying to isolate each specific effect. Other studies approaching the theme of inequality of opportunity in the Latin America and the Caribbean region from different perspectives have become available (see box 1.3).

Box 1.3 Latin American Contributions to the Equality Opportunities Literature

The work presented in this book builds upon a vast literature driven by dedicated researchers in the region who have directly and indirectly investigated issues related to basic opportunities. Researchers investigating individual country experiences in the region have contributed significantly to the growing literature using opportunities as an analytical framework. The fact that a variety of stakeholders in Latin America and the Caribbean are showing active interest in using an opportunities framework to analyze issues related to poverty reaffirms the value of efforts that aim to widen the methodological debate and bring opportunities to the top of the policy agenda.

Scott (2007) investigated inequality in income and basic education and health indicators in Mexico since the revolution (1910–20), reviewing the historical persistence and multidimensional nature of inequality. Scott concentrated on analyzing a wide range of instruments employed by the government over time, such as land reform, Progresa (Oportunidades), and social spending on universal programs in education, health,

(Box continues on the following page.)

Box 1.3 Latin American Contributions to the Opportunities Literature *(continued)*

and social security, in view of assessing the redistributive impacts of these initiatives. Núñez, Ramirez, and Taboada (2006) investigated income inequality in Colombia from the perspective of opportunities and effort, focusing on social mobility. A key finding was that if people at birth had the same opportunities, income distribution in Colombia could improve between 12 and 28 percent, depending on the inequality index used (Gini or Theil) and the unit of analysis (individuals or households).

The Economic Commission for Latin America and the Caribbean and Fundación Empresarial para el Desarrollo Educativo in 2000 collaborated to investigate equity in the coverage, quality, and intergenerational transmission of educational opportunities in El Salvador (Carrasco Guzmán 2000). Similarly, the Pan American Health Organization has played a key role in investigating issues related to access to health. In 2004, it published a study using data from six countries—the Dominican Republic, Ecuador, Guatemala, Honduras, Paraguay, and Peru—with the objective of characterizing and measuring exclusion in health (PAHO 2004).

Another strand of the literature studies intergenerational mobility through educational transmission. Schooling inequality may be partially explained by parental characteristics, which can be attributed to inequality of opportunity. This approach was used by Barros and Lam (1993) for Brazil. Behrman, Gaviria, and Szekely (2001), in a study for Brazil, Colombia, Mexico, and Peru, examined the impact of parental background in schooling and occupational status, and found that intergenerational mobility is much larger in the United States than in Latin American countries. Gaviria (2006) studied the relation between parents' and sons' years of schooling and found a stronger and larger statistical relationship in Latin America than in the United States and Europe. He found large differences in education for offspring of less-educated parents and very small differences for those with educated parents.

An important contribution to the Latin American literature is the IDB's 2008 Report on Economic and Social Progress, which focused on social exclusion. The report, *Outsiders? Changing Patterns of Exclusion in Latin America and the Caribbean*, delves into questions about the multidimensional and interrelated nature of social exclusion. The report views social exclusion as an inefficient and dysfunctional dynamic social, political, and economic process whereby individuals and groups are denied access to the opportunities and quality services necessary to live productive lives and move out of poverty.

Research into opportunities has not been confined to the academic world. In 2005, the Ministry of Finance of Chile included an analysis of inequality of opportunity in Chile, and highlighted it as a challenge for the future in its annual public report on the state of the treasury. Though relatively short, the analysis is impressive. Topics included philosophical considerations, historical foundations of inequality of opportunity from colonialism, and up-to-date data on a diverse set of important variables, such as access to education and intergenerational mobility. The ministry also produced a number of short notes on its Web site tailored toward a wider readership in an effort to gain public attention for the issue.

Why Should We Be Concerned with Inequality of Opportunity?

Inequality of opportunity, as well as its importance to the more common inequality of outcome concept, is—and if not, should be—a matter of academic and policy interest for several reasons. It is at the heart of the concern about the ability of society to increase opportunity for the most disadvantaged and provide a level playing field to all individuals. It is critical to an understanding of attitudes toward inequality and, hence, attitudes toward redistribution, which will influence the political economy framework under which public policy is defined. And it is critical to a better understanding of the relationship between inequality and growth (Ferreira 2008).

The World Bank's *World Development Report 2006: Equity and Development* (WDR) defined equity as the combination of equality of opportunity with avoidance of extreme deprivation in outcomes. This definition is consistent with a view of the development process in which the ultimate social objective is maximum sustainable expansion of opportunities for the least advantaged group, subject to a no-poverty constraint.[13] The shift of focus from inequality of outcomes to inequality of opportunity puts the need to eliminate unfair differences stemming from circumstances for which the individual is not responsible at the center of the debate.

The focus on inequality of opportunity touches on disparities that recent evidence shows are perceived as unfair. As noted in the introduction to this chapter, the WDR suggested that one of the reasons equity should matter for policy makers in developing (and developed) countries is that unequal opportunities are widely seen as intrinsically unfair, and unfairness bothers people. Intrinsic unfairness simply reflects the fact that people object to inequality of opportunity, and prefer to live in a "more just" society (see box 1.4). The 2006 WDR listed a number of manifestations of this concern, from religious teaching to the importance of equity in legal institutions, as well as a growing psychology and economics literature on the foundations of social preferences for fairness. Incontrovertible experimental evidence now exists, for instance, that individuals across a

---

Box 1.4 Social Preference and the "Ultimatum Game"

A classic example of the preference for fairness is the international results from the ultimatum game, which are inconsistent with the predictions from game theory under the maintained assumption of self-regarding preferences (also known as the rational self-interest hypothesis). In a simple ultimatum game, players A and B are matched anonymously (across computer screens that do not reveal one's identity to another), and told that they will never interact again. Player A is given some amount of money (say, $100) and is told that he must offer some share of the $100 to player B. Player B must then accept or reject the offer. If the offer is accepted, it is implemented in fact, and both players keep their allotted shares. If B rejects the offer, both players get zero. B also knows the rules.

Under the rational self-interest hypothesis, the Nash equilibrium from this game is that A should offer $1 to B, and keep $99. Since $1 > $0, B should accept this offer. In reality, relatively few offers come in at less than $30, and a nontrivial share of those offers is actually rejected. The modal offer ranges between 31 and 60 percent of the $100, depending on the context. Note that the behavior of the first player is possibly consistent with rational self-interest. If the person has any reason to believe that player B will reject the offer, it may well be perfectly selfish and rational to offer, say, $40. But the behavior of those who reject the offer is simply not consistent with rational self-interest. The dominant interpretation in the literature is that it reveals a remarkably widespread "taste for fairness." (See Falk, Fehr, and Fischbacher 2003 and Hoffman, McCabe, and Smith 1996.)

---

wide range of cultures and geographic settings are prepared to forgo real income gains in exchange for the opportunity to directly reward others who have behaved fairly and punish those seen as behaving unfairly.

Whether such social preference is learned or socially acquired (as a norm), or whether it is in fact innate, remains a matter of debate. Whatever the reason, there is now widespread agreement that fairness matters to people; and if it matters to people, it should also matter to policy makers.

These social preferences, intertwined with the perceptions about the sources of the observed inequality, have an effect on the attitudes of people toward redistributive policies. Alesina and La Ferrara (2005) showed that those who believe that the mobility process is "fair" and that society offers equal opportunity to its members so that effort and ability determine socioeconomic success, do not look favorably on government redistribution. But those who believe that social advancement is not a fair game, either because social connections are critical or because not everyone has the same opportunity to get an education, are more supportive of redistributive policies. The sources of income differences that affect individual opinions regarding redistribution are estimated by Fong (2001) using Gallup Poll data for the United States in 1998. Gaviria (2006), using Latinobarometro data, showed that in Latin America, redistributive policies are supported by those who believe that connections are critical for economic advancement, that opportunities are not the same for everybody, and that working hard is not enough to be economically successful.

Turning to another reason for unequal opportunity to be of concern, the WDR mentioned that inequality in some particular circumstances (notably but not exclusively inherited wealth) may lead to an inadequate ex post allocation of resources. As an example, it is unlikely that the ablest children are matched to the best educational opportunities. Instead, relative wealth is likely to constrain their schooling possibilities, with children from wealthier backgrounds gaining disproportionate access to the best schools. This is not only unfair, but is also likely to lead to a lower aggregate level of human capital than alternative allocations. In a similar vein, if poorer entrepreneurs have no access to credit, or access only at higher interest rates regardless of expected returns, financial capital will be allocated to some projects with lower (risk-adjusted) rates of return, while potentially better projects remain unfunded.

Finally, notions of inequality and opportunity are open to many different interpretations, and discussion of their precise meaning and policy and legal implications can become heated and controversial. For some, the basic opportunities expounded here will be considered fundamental rights. Indeed, countries such as Mexico have embedded in their constitution the right to education and other services. Several other countries incorporate access to specific services as individual constitutional rights, although specific policies on how those rights are to be translated into effective provision are generally vague. A further discussion on the perspective of right can be found in box 1.5.

What Does Measuring Inequality of Opportunity Mean for Policy?

The quantitative tools described in this book are intended to help measure inequality of opportunity in different countries and across time. Adequate measurement is the first step to being able to use the concept for public policy, allowing policy makers to track an individual country's progress over time in providing equity of certain opportunities related to certain circumstances, and also to compare policy experiences across countries, to gain perspective and seek lessons that can be applied elsewhere. We do not explore here the specific policies that countries should undertake to

Box 1.5 Beyond Measurement: The Perspective of Rights

Rights themselves are a challenging concept—scholars have debated the nature of rights for centuries. Many choose to introduce a dichotomy into rights: "I have a right to X means that either someone else has an obligation to provide me with X or that no one should stop me from having X." The former is a positive right and the latter is a negative right. This simple dichotomy underlies much of the ongoing political and social debate about what should be considered a right and in what sense. A negative view would contend that a child cannot be denied access to education by anyone, while a positive view would argue that someone (usually the state) carries the responsibility to provide that child with access to education.

A further consideration is what good is a right if there are no available forms of redress. In the context of widespread corruption among judges, prohibitive costs of legal counsel for the poor, and a lack of basic knowledge of rights, some have questioned what rights mean to people in the world. Legal rights, which are included in national legislative frameworks and backed by governmental power, are but one category of rights in public discourse. The concept of human rights, for example, as articulated in the Universal Declaration of Human Rights and adopted by the United Nations General Assembly in 1948, has been used primarily to promote a set of social conditions seen as fundamental to human well-being and dignity. However, they are not always enforceable; their "power" lies in persuasion and shaming, not in the courts or through police. So if a child has a right to education, the question that follows is, what kind of right? And what does conferring rights status on this basic opportunity really mean on a daily basis in any particular country?

Recent efforts to develop innovative approaches to integrating a rights-based perspective into social policy through "social guarantees" in Chile reaffirm the ongoing dedication of societies to defining a socially acceptable framework for reducing poverty and improving well-being. Chile's Regime of Explicit Health Guarantees (RGES), introduced between 2003 and 2005, guarantees the universal provision of health services for a selection of prioritized health problems, while also defining maximum waiting periods and total yearly amounts a family can spend on those services. The RGES uses a range of tools to ensure social guarantees: a solid legal framework, mechanisms of redress and enforcement (maximum waiting periods for resolution of claims also exist), extensive publicity campaigns, and monitoring systems that ensure the continual improvement of services. Public debate played a pivotal role in establishing societal consensus around the initiative. Following from this, another concept strongly linked with both opportunities and rights is justice. A country's legal system and the rights that it protects originate in society's sense of what is socially just. Notions of justice range from the relatively abstract to clear principles communicated through religious institutions.

Note: This box was written by Estanislao Gacitua-Mario.

improve opportunity for all citizens, but rather focus on contributing to better measurement of inequality of opportunity.

To the extent that unequal access to social services and unequal opportunity to benefit from them are systematically related to exogenous factors (such as gender, ethnicity, place of origin, or family background), they are clearly a constituent part of the inequality of opportunity. This is particularly true for children because family resources, family characteristics, where they were born, and their own traits are certainly exogenous. Few would question the unfairness of children's unequal access to and opportunity to fully benefit from social services resulting from any of these factors. The Human Opportunity Index can track a country's progress toward providing basic opportunities to all children, and whether existing opportunites are being allocated according to a principle of equality of opportunity. As such, the index sheds light on which specific basic opportunities require more attention, either because of inequitable distribution or low absolute levels. It also helps to identify the more disadvantaged segments of the population and to determine where policies should place more emphasis, given financial, managerial, and technological constraints.

To both widen the coverage and promote the equality of basic opportunities for children, public policy should be oriented toward directing marginal investments so as to increase basic opportunities for the most disadvantaged groups, helping equalize access to education, sanitation, water, and electricity. This, in turn, implies shifting the pattern of resources spent by society such that disadvantaged groups receive proportionately more. Considering existing technologies and resources, most countries in Latin America are currently realistically able to make universal access to basic opportunities, at least the ones considered here, a policy goal for the near future. In Latin America, social expenditures have increased sharply; according to data from the Economic Commission for Latin America and the Caribbean, between 1990 and 2003, social expenditures rose from 9.6 percent to 12.8 percent of GDP, consistent with an increase of 45 percent in expenditures per capita. Overall expenditures, however, are not large compared with international standards, nor are overall tax revenues. But changing the pattern of distribution of public expenditures is a pending challenge. The policy challenges countries face are complex when the goal of increasing opportunity for those that are more disadvantaged has to face up against the higher marginal costs of providing opportunities to those subgroups of the population.[14] For example, education expenditure patterns in Latin America usually reveal that public resources per student are higher in richer areas, reinforcing the unequal pattern that comes from family out-of-pocket expenditures. Breaking the cycle of intergenerational persistence of inequality requires modifying expenditure patterns, and modifying institutional barriers to doing so.

A development process that equalizes opportunity implies devoting more resources to providing opportunities to disadvantaged groups. There is a leap, however, from the theoretical construct to the practical policy application. Shifting expenditure and investment patterns is an economic and political process and also presents implementation challenges. For example, it might be less costly to increase equality of opportunity when a population is geographically concentrated rather than dispersed. In that case, community-level targeting might have a different impact on equalizing opportunities than targeting at the individual level, but costs might also be different. The only fair process would be one in which new opportunities are randomly distributed to individuals from disadvantaged populations, but that process might not be technologically feasible. The principles and the measurement tools presented here can still guide policy choices among the different technologically, economically, and administratively feasible expansion paths to allow a country to provide the most opportunities in the fairest manner.

The second part of the book, which uses a top-down approach to decompose observed adult income into a component resulting from circumstances exogenous to the individual and a residual component resulting from effort, choice, and luck, generates two different kinds of output that may be useful to policy makers. The first, of course, is simply a lower-bound measure of the degree of inequality of economic opportunity in a society. It is not a perfect measure because it provides an assessment of the inequality associated with only six observed circumstances. But it is informative and can be presented either as an indicator of the *level of inequality of opportunity* or as a measure of the *opportunity share of overall inequality*. Both numbers are discussed for the seven countries for which the appropriate data were available. If estimated repeatedly over time, these indicators can provide governments and other social actors with a useful diagnostic of how the distribution of opportunities is evolving in their countries.

The shift of focus from inequality of incomes or earnings to inequality of opportunity is critical for policy makers and development practitioners in Latin America. A better understanding of the importance of inequality of opportunity in the determination inequality of outcomes may change attitudes toward redistribution. People dislike and consider unfair inequality associated with differences in circumstances, which many argue should be compensated for by society. By highlighting that component of inequality attributable to circumstances, this type of analysis can help build a social and political consensus on both the necessity of and the best means for addressing inequality of opportunity. As such, the focus on inequality of opportunity may have a greater impact on improving economic performance than might a focus on inequality of income.

Measuring the inequality of opportunity allows policy instruments to focus more exactly on the component of unequal outcomes caused by factors outside individual control, while not affecting differences resulting from individual choice and the application of effort, which are usually viewed as fair. The tools presented in the following chapters can help promote a consensus on the need to focus the policy debate urgently on how to increase equity, identify the specific populations most in need, and provide guidance on the kinds of policies needed to effectively provide the same chances to all.

Notes

1. See chapter 2 in World Bank (2006).

2. Sen was also particularly concerned with interpersonal comparability of utility, and with the fact that different people may have different maps from the commodity to the utility space. Though important in their own right, those issues are tangential to the discussion at hand.

3. Note that many of the choices an individual makes will then be predetermined circumstances for the next generation.

4. The role of luck (or pure randomness) in the analysis of inequality of opportunity is neither a simple matter nor completely settled. It is generally agreed that one's "initial position" (the luck of birth) should be seen as a circumstance. But luck during one's lifetime may be treated differently depending on whether participation in the lottery is voluntary (as in actual gambling, but also in choosing to fight a war) or not. See Lefranc, Pistolesi, and Trannoy (2006) for a good summary. This book groups postnatal luck with effort and choice, and refers to it as a residual component.

5. Formally, $F(y \mid c) = F(y)$, where y denotes the (univariate) outcome of interest, and c denotes the full vector of circumstances.

6. Among many good surveys, see Solon (1999) and Bowles and Gintis (2002).

7. Even in a meritocratic environment, some might dislike a society where only one type of talent has a large economic value and only a small fraction of the population has that talent.

8. See, for instance, Betts and Roemer (1999), Bourguignon, Ferreira, and Menéndez (2007), Checchi and Peragine (2005), Waltenberg and Vandenberghe (2007), Schuetz, Ursprung, and Woessmann (2005), and Lefranc, Pistolesi, and Trannoy (2006).

9. Providing educational subsidies for talented individuals will equalize opportunity and reduce the influence of parental income on access to tertiary education.

10. Because if $F(y \mid c) \neq F(y), \exists c$, the egalitarian definition of equal opportunities is violated.

11. The "identifying assumption" that underpins the claim that between-group inequality is "due" to circumstances is essentially that all material circumstance variables are observed and used in the partition of the population. The robustness of this assumption can be assessed by means of a Monte Carlo simulation exercise. See Bourguignon, Ferreira, and Menéndez (2007).

12. This goes back to a result attributed to Foster and Shneyerov (2000), and the implications for the measurement of inequality of opportunity are discussed in Ferreira and Gignoux (2008a).

13. See Bourguignon, Ferreira, and Walton (2007) and Roemer (2006) for a discussion.

14. It is likely that the actual dynamics of the interrelation between coverage and equality of opportunity is determined by the relative price of providing access to different population groups.

References

Alesina, A., and E. La Ferrara. 2005. "Preferences for Redistribution in the Land of Opportunities." *Journal of Public Economics* 89 (5-6): 897–931.

Arneson, R. 1989. "Equality and Equality of Opportunity for Welfare." *Philosophical Studies* 56: 77–93.

Ashenfelter, O., and C. Rouse. 2000. "Schooling, Intelligence, and Income in America." In *Meritocracy and Economic Inequality*, ed. K. Arrow, S. Bowles, and S. Durlauf. Princeton, NJ: Princeton University Press.

Barros, R. P., and D. Lam. 1993. "Desigualdade de renda, desigualdade em educação e escolaridade das crianças no Brasil." *Pesquisa e Planeamiento Econômico* 23 (2): 191–218.

Behrman, J., A. Gaviria, and M. Szekely. 2001. "Intergenerational Mobility in Latin America." Working Paper No. 002914, FEDESARROLLA.

Betts, Julian R., and John E. Roemer. 1999. "Equalizing Educational Opportunity through Educational Finance Reform." Department of Economics Paper No. 99-8, Department of Economics, University of California at Davis.

Boudon, R. 1974. *Education, Opportunity, and Social Inequality*. New York: Wiley.

Bourguignon, F., F. H. G. Ferreira, and M. Menéndez. 2007. "Inequality of Opportunity in Brazil." *Review of Income and Wealth* 53 (4): 585–618.

Bourguignon, F., F. Ferreira, and M. Walton. 2007. "Equity, Efficiency and Inequality Traps: A Research Agenda." *Journal of Economic Inequality* 5 (2) : 235–56.

Bowles, S., and H. Gintis. 2000. "Does Schooling Raise Earnings by Making People Smarter?" In *Meritocracy and Economic Inequality*, ed. K. Arrow, S. Bowles, and S. Durlauf. Princeton, NJ: Princeton University Press.

———. 2002. "The Inheritance of Inequality." *Journal of Economic Perspectives* 16 (3): 3–30.

Carrasco Guzmán, Alvaro. 2000. "Equity in Education in El Salvador." *CEPAL Review* 70: 165–79.

Checchi, D., and V. Peragine. 2005. "Regional Disparities and Inequality of Opportunity: The Case of Italy." IZA Discussion Paper No. 1874, Institute for the Study of Labor, Bonn, Germany.

Cohen, G. A. 1989. "On the Currency of Egalitarian Justice." *Ethics* 99: 906–44.

Dworkin, R. 1981. "What Is Equality? Part 1: Equality of Welfare." *Philosophy & Public Affairs* 10: 185–246.

Falk, Armin, Ernst Fehr, and Urs Fischbacher. 2003. "On the Nature of Fair Behavior." *Economic Inquiry* 41 (1): 20–6.

Feldman, M., S. Otto, and F. Christiansen. 2000. "Genes, Culture, and Inequality." In *Meritocracy and Economic Inequality*, ed. K. Arrow, S. Bowles, and S. Durlauf. Princeton, NJ: Princeton University Press.

Ferreira, F., and J. Gignoux. 2008a. "Inequality of Economic Opportunities in Latin America." www.worldbank.org/lacopportunity. Washington, DC: World Bank.

———. 2008b. "Towards an Understanding of Socially Inherited Inequalities in Educational Achievement: Evidence from Latin America and the OECD." www.worldbank.org/lacopportunity. Washington, DC: World Bank.

Ferreira, Sergio G., and Fernando A. Veloso. 2004. "Intergenerational Mobility of Wages in Brazil." Unpublished.

Fong, C. 2001. "Social Preferences, Self-Interest and the Demand for Redistribution." *Journal of Public Economics* 82 (2): 225–46.

Foster, J., and A. Shneyerov. 2000. "Path Independent Inequality Measures." *Journal of Economic Theory* 91: 199–222.

Gaviria, A. 2006. *Movilidad social y preferencias por redistribución en América Latina*. DOCUMENTOS CEDE 2006-03. Universidad de los Andes, Bogota.

Hoff, Karla, and Priyanka Pandey. 2006. "Discrimination, Social Identity, and Durable Inequalities." *American Economic Review* 96 (2): 206–11.

Hoffman, Elizabeth, Kevin McCabe, and Vernon L. Smith. 1996. "On Expectations and the Monetary Stakes in Ultimatum Games." *International Journal of Game Theory* 25 (3): 289–301.

IDB (Inter-American Development Bank). 2008. *Outsiders? The Changing Patterns of Exclusion in Latin America and the Caribbean*. Washington, DC: Inter-American Development Bank.

Inglehart, Ronald, Miguel Basanez, Jaime Diez-Medrano, Loek Halman, and Ruud Luijkx, eds. 2004. *Human Beliefs and Values: A Cross-Cultural Sourcebook Based on the 1999–2002 Values Surveys*. Mexico, Distrito Federal: Siglo Veinteiuno.

Jencks, C., and L. Tach. 2006. "Would Equal Opportunity Mean More Mobility?" In *Mobility and Inequality*, ed. S. Morgan, D. Grusky, and G. Fields. Palo Alto, CA: Stanford University Press.

Lefranc, A., N. Pistolesi, and A. Trannoy. 2006. "Inequality of Opportunities vs. Inequality of Outcomes: Are Western Societies All Alike?" Working Paper No. 54, Society for the Study of Economic Inequality, Palma de Mallorca, Spain.

Mazumdar, Bhashkar. 2005. "The Apple Falls Even Closer to the Tree than We Thought: New and Revised Estimates of the Intergenerational Inheritance of Earnings." In *Unequal Chances: Family Background and Economic Success*, ed. Samuel Bowles, Herbert Gintis, and Melissa Osborne. Princeton, NJ: Princeton University Press.

Morgan, S., D. Grusky, and G. Fields. 2006. *Mobility and Inequality: Frontiers of Research in Sociology and Economics*. Palo Alto, CA: Stanford University Press.

Nozick, Robert. 1974. *Anarchy, State and Utopia*. New York: Basic Books.

Núñez, J., J. C. Ramírez, and B. Taboada. 2006. *Desigualdad de ingresos, esfuerzos y oportunidades - un estudio del caso colombiano*. DOCUMENTO CEDE 002296, Universidad de Los Andes, Bogota.

PAHO (Pan American Health Organization). 2004. *Exclusion in Health in Latin America and the Caribbean*. Washington, DC: PAHO

Rawls, John. 1971. *A Theory of Justice*. Cambridge, MA: Harvard University Press.

Roemer, John E. 1998. *Equality of Opportunity*. Cambridge, MA: Harvard University Press.

———. 2006. "Review Essay: *The 2006 World Development Report: Equity and Development.*" *Journal of Economic Inequality* 4 (2): 233–44.

Scott, J. 2007. *Desigualdad de oportunidades y políticas públicas en México: el fracaso del proyecto redistributivo.* SDTE 330, El Centro de Investigación y Docencia Económicas.

Schuetz, Gabriela, Heinrich Ursprung, and Ludger Woessmann. 2005. "Education Policy and Equality of Opportunity." CESifo Working Paper No. 1518, CESifo GmbH, Munich.

Sen, Amartya, and Geoffrey Hawthorne. 1985. *The Standard of Living (Tanner Lectures in Human Values).* Cambridge: Cambridge University Press.

Solon, G. 1999. "Intergenerational Mobility in the Labor Market." In *Handbook of Labor Economics,* vol. 3A. ed. O. Ashenfelter and D. Card. Amsterdam: North Holland.

Steele, C. M. 1997. "A Threat in the Air: How Stereotypes Shape Intellectual Identity and Performance." *American Psychologist* 52 (6): 613–29.

Steele, C. M., and J. Aronson. 1995. "Stereotype Threat and the Intellectual Test Performance of African Americans." *Journal of Personality and Social Psychology* 69 (5): 797–811.

Waltenberg, Fabio D., and Vincent Vandenberghe. 2007. "What Does It Take to Achieve Equality of Opportunity in Education? An Empirical Investigation Based on Brazilian Data." *Economics of Education Review* 26 (6): 709–23.

World Bank. 2006. *World Development Report 2006: Equity and Development.* Washington, DC: World Bank.

2

A Human Opportunity Index for Children

An equitable development process should pursue the equalization of opportunities at all stages of an individual's life, seeking to level the playing field for all citizens. One component of inequality of opportunity is the unequal access of children to the "basic opportunities" needed to get a fair start in life. As long as all children in a country do not have access to education, health, nutrition, and basic services and access is correlated to circumstances for which the child is not accountable, such as gender, ethnicity, or family background, inequality of opportunity will prevail in that country. A goal of social and economic policy should be to reduce that correlation as much as possible and provide a level playing field to all children. Focusing on reducing inequality of opportunity is then a useful policy guidepost, and a critical first step is to have an adequate measure of this inequality.

This chapter seeks to measure inequality of opportunity by developing a Human Opportunity Index, a composite indicator that combines two elements: (i) the level of coverage of basic opportunities necessary for human development, such as primary education, water and sanitation, and electricity; and (ii) the degree to which the distribution of those opportunities is conditional on circumstances exogenous to children, such as gender, income, or household characteristics. This new index assesses the importance of both improving overall access to basic opportunities and ensuring its equitable allocation. By doing so, it can serve as a tool to help steer public policies with the aim of equalizing opportunity.

The Human Opportunity Index is calculated for a set of opportunities related to education (completion of sixth grade on time and school attendance for children ages 10–14) and housing conditions (access to clean water, adequate sanitation, and electricity), and then summarized in a single overall index. Applied to discrete outcomes, it combines the two elements—coverage ($\bar{p}$) and inequality of opportunity (D)—in a single calculation in which coverage of a basic opportunity is adjusted by how unequally it is distributed.[1] The level of opportunity measured by this index can be interpreted as the number of existing opportunities in a given society that have been allocated based on an equal opportunity principle.

A critical step in estimating how existing basic opportunities are distributed is the development of a measure of inequality of opportunity, the D-index. It measures dissimilar access rates to a given basic opportunity for groups of children defined by circumstance characteristics (specifically, children's area of residence, gender, parents' level of education, per capita family income, number of siblings, and presence of two parents at home) compared with the average access rate to the same service for the population of children as a whole. The D-index ranges from 0 to 100, in percentage terms, and in a situation of perfect equality of opportunity, D will be zero. The D-index has an interesting interpretation as the fraction of all available opportunities that need to be reallocated from children of better-off groups to children of worse-off groups to restore equal opportunity.

The Human Opportunity Index uses data from 36 nationally representative household surveys for 19 Latin American and Caribbean countries over a period of approximately a decade (1995–2005). Together, the surveys represent nearly 200 million children ages 0–16 from the region. The results show remarkable improvement in opportunities in most countries in the region because of both improvement in coverage and more equitable allocation of opportunities. Still, countries have not improved uniformly in all basic opportunities and, in many cases, are far from providing universal access.

This chapter proceeds as follows. The next section discusses in more detail the motivation for choosing the selected basic opportunities and circumstance variables, as well as the data sources used for the estimations. The following section presents results on the first component of the Human Opportunity Index—the total coverage levels of each opportunity in the countries being studied. The methodology for the second component of the Human Opportunity Index, the distributional equality of basic opportunities for children—the D-index—and national estimates are presented in the third section. The fourth section provides the analytical framework for the Human Opportunity Index and reports empirical results for the 19 Latin American and Caribbean countries. The fifth section concludes by summarizing the findings.

Defining Basic Opportunities for Children

Basic opportunities are services that are critical for children's development. They are exogenous for the child, i.e., the child is a passive receiver, and societies see universal provision as a valid social goal. Examples include access to primary education, early childhood education, immunizations, minimum nutritional levels, sanitation, clean water, electricity, and a birth certificate or other identity document. They are exogenous from the point of view of the child, because access is controlled not by her, but by her family or society. And universal provision of these basic opportunities is a valid and realistic social goal because they are affordable, given the available technology. And if they are not affordable today for a specific country, they might be in the near future through effective policies. Even if different societies might have various standards regarding the set of basic opportunities, in the case of children, most societies agree on a set of basic opportunities, at least at the level of intentions. This chapter focuses on inequality and coverage of basic opportunities among children for three main reasons:

- First, from an empirical standpoint, opportunities can be operationalized by measuring children's access to basic goods and services critical for the full development of a child. For children, access defines opportunity, because children (unlike adults) cannot be expected to make the efforts needed to access these basic goods by themselves.
- Second, from a policy standpoint, evidence indicates that early intervention in the life cycle of an individual to equalize opportunities is significantly more cost effective and successful than attempting interventions later in life.
- Third, focusing on children clarifies the message that socially determined inequality of opportunity is unfair and helps put opportunity equalization at the center of the policy debate. As pointed out by the *World Development Report 2006* (World Bank 2006), on the day of their birth, children cannot be held responsible for their family circumstances, despite the fact that these circumstances—such as race, gender, parents' income and education, and urban or rural location—will make major differences in the lives they lead.

Basic opportunities are those essential to ensuring that today's children will have the potential, as adults, to better achieve the outcomes of their choosing. A vast array of basic opportunities are relevant to policy and critical for children's future development. This chapter focuses on basic opportunities related to education and housing conditions. Aside from its intrinsic importance, data from household surveys to allow comparison across time and across a large number of countries are available for variables in these spheres.[2]

For education, the completion of sixth grade on time is used as a proxy for a child's opportunity for basic education. Primary schools must be of sufficient quality to provide the differentiated instruction required to get all children promoted through the first six years of schooling on time, avoiding grade repetition or very low marks. If schooling quality is good, the child will learn the content needed to be promoted from grade to grade, regardless of his or her circumstances. In a world of equality of opportunity, all children, regardless of their circumstances, should have access to basic quality education. In practice, this variable is measured by computing the probability of having ended sixth grade on time for all children ages 12 to 16.[3] Some education systems, as in Jamaica, implement automatic promotion in primary education, while others do not, which may create comparability problems. This chapter also uses school attendance for those ages 10–14. This variable measures the gross attendance rate (that is, school attendance independent of grade) for children between the ages of 10 and 14. This measure thus includes children in late primary or early secondary education (depending on the country system).

A child's access to adequate housing conditions is a critical element of the opportunity for a healthy life. Three conditions have been selected for this study: access to water, to sanitation, and to electricity. Several studies have found a strong and negative relationship between children's mortality rates and improved water sources and sanitation facilities (see Abou-Ali Hala 2003; Galiani, Gertler, and Schargrodsky 2005; Fuentes, Pfütze, and Seck 2006; and Rutstein 2000; among others). Improved water, sanitation, and hygiene are the only ways to reduce the incidence of diarrhea and related serious long-term consequences, which include making children more vulnerable to malnutrition and opportunistic infections (such as pneumonia), and physical or mental stunting for the rest of their lives. The World Health Organization estimates that approximately 1.4 million children under age five die every year, mostly in developing countries, from diarrheal diseases attributed to unsafe water supply and inadequate sanitation and hygiene (WHO 2002, 1). Water and sanitation are primary drivers of public health, and should be considered basic opportunities for all children.

Access to electricity is also a basic opportunity for children. Electricity improves quality of life with respect to alternative sources of energy for lighting, cooking, and heating, such as kerosene and wood fuel. The provision of electricity to households allows for improved conditions for studying in the evenings; for avoiding deaths produced by indoor biomass cook stove pollution (particularly among young children and mothers); for accessing information and entertainment via radio, television, and the Internet; for freeing parents' time from domestic chores so they could potentially spend that time improving the process of raising their children; and for home and community safety. Studies have documented that children spend more time studying after electricity is provided (Gustavsson 2007); electricity also allows access to modern educational techniques using computing, as in rural Peru (Bajak 2007).[4] Replacing kerosene lamps with electricity has also been shown to reduce eye irritation, coughing, and nasal problems, and reduce the substantial number of children who die annually from accidental kerosene poisoning (Kaufman et al. 2000). Electricity also helps ease the domestic workload—women in rural areas can spend the equivalent of two working days per week in fuelwood collection (Budlender, Chobokoane, and Mpetsheni 2002).

For water, sanitation, and electricity, all children ages 0 to 16 are included in the sample. The indicator for each of these basic opportunities consists of the percentage of children ages 0 to 16 who live in a household with access to the utility. Each utility is considered separately and simple criteria are used for identifying from the surveys the access of a household to each opportunity. Most surveys in the region do not ask about potable (safe) water, but about the location of the water source and the system used for distribution. This variable takes the value of one if the household has access to water from the public network inside the dwelling or inside the property.[5] For recording access to sanitation, the variable is set equal to 1 when the house is connected to a public sewerage system or to a septic tank.[6] For electricity, the variable is equal to 1 if the household has access to electricity from any source.

Recorded access to a basic opportunity may hide substantial differences in the quality of the service. For instance, access to electricity does not guarantee complete 24-hour service or adequate wattage. Frequent blackouts and diminished wattage hinder the benefits a family can draw from access to electricity, with effects ranging from reliability of food conservation in refrigerators to hours of light for evening studying. Similar statements can be made with respect to completion of primary education on time and access to water and sanitation. Data access and comparability limitations make it difficult to gauge quality in basic opportunities. At this stage, for comparability purposes, the analysis is limited to indicators that measure quantity and not quality. Further analysis at the country level should incorporate the quality dimension, because quality of services is a critical area of improvement in all countries, and also because there are large inequalities in quality of services across different groups of the population.

A child's circumstances are defined by variables common to all surveys: (i) gender,[7] (ii) child's area of residence (urban or rural), (iii) the number of years of schooling of the family head, (iv) per capita family income, (v) either single-parent or two-parent household, and (vi) the number of siblings ages 0–16. These six circumstances are used for the analysis of access to education, water, sanitation, and electricity. Race and ethnicity would be extremely relevant in analyzing access to basic goods and services, as would more detailed location information (municipality, locality, or even neighborhood). However, these variables are not present in all nationally representative household surveys in the 19 LAC countries, and hence are not considered.

The estimates in this chapter use data from 35 nationally representative household surveys for 19 LAC countries over a period of approximately

Table 2.1 Countries, Surveys, and Years

Country	Survey	Survey years	
Argentina	Encuesta de Impacto Social de la Crisis en Argentina		2002
Bolivia	Encuesta Continua de Hogares		2005
Brazil	Pesquisa Nacional por Amostra de Domicilios	1995	2005
Chile	Encuesta de Caracterización Socioeconómica Nacional	1996	2006
Colombia	Encuesta de Calidad de Vida	1997	2003
Costa Rica	Encuesta de Hogares de Propósitos Múltiples	1994	2004
Dominican Republic	Encuesta Nacional de Fuerza de Trabajo	1996	2006
Ecuador	Encuesta de Condiciones de Vida	1995	2006
El Salvador	Encuesta de Hogares de Propósitos Múltiples	1998	2005
Guatemala	Encuesta Nacional sobre Condiciones de Vida	2000	2006
Honduras	Encuesta Permanente de Hogares de Propósitos Múltiples	1997	2005
Jamaica	Jamaica Survey of Living Conditions	1996	2002
Mexico	Encuesta Nacional de Ingresos y Gastos de los Hogares	1996	2006
Nicaragua	Encuesta Nacional de Hogares sobre Medición de Nivel de Vida	1998	2005
Panama	Encuesta de Niveles de Vida	1997	2003
Paraguay	Encuesta Permanente de Hogares	1999	2005
Peru	Encuesta Nacional de Hogares	1998	2006
Uruguay	Encuesta Nacional de Hogares Ampliada		2006
Venezuela, R. B. de	Encuesta de Hogares Por Muestreo	1995	2005

Source: The World Bank and Universidad Nacional de la Plata (CEDLAS) Socio-Economic Database for Latin America and the Caribbean.

a decade (1995–2005; table 2.1). The goal was to choose two comparable surveys for each country as close as possible to 1995 and to 2005. Together, the surveys represent nearly 200 million children ages 0–16 from 19 LAC countries.[8]

Coverage of Basic Opportunities

This section addresses the first component of the Human Opportunity Index, coverage of basic opportunities. It provides detailed information on five basic opportunities in the 19 LAC countries under consideration, without reference to the equity of their distribution, which is addressed in the following section.

For education, Latin America has registered, on average, an increase in both completing sixth grade on time and school attendance (table 2.2). By 2005, a simple average across countries of the probability of a 13-year-old child completing sixth grade was 68 percent, up from 57 percent in 1995, and 93 percent of children ages 10 to 14 were attending school, compared with 89 percent in 1995.[9]

The average probability of finishing sixth grade on time recorded impressive advances in several countries in the region, including Brazil, Colombia, El Salvador, Paraguay, and Peru, each of which expanded by 2 percentage points per year or more in a decade. These countries had very low initial levels of this indicator, and their efforts have put them closer to the leaders in the region. However, important differences persist across countries—in some, less than 60 percent of children finished sixth grade on time (Brazil, El Salvador, Guatemala, Honduras, and Nicaragua), compared with more than 80 percent in others (Argentina, Chile, Ecuador, Jamaica, Mexico, and Uruguay).

With regard to school attendance at ages 10 to 14, the expansion is less significant (only 0.4 percentage points growth per year over the decade), because the region had reached an already high level by the mid-1990s. However, dispersion across countries (that is, the difference between the lowest coverage and the highest coverage) has barely declined from 20 percentage points in 1995 to 18 percentage points in 2005, which suggests that no convergence is occurring and some countries still lag in this indicator.

The average growth in access to basic housing conditions was about 0.8 percentage points per year in water, sanitation, and electricity (table 2.3). These small increases are not because the region has reached high levels of coverage. On the contrary, average coverage in sanitation is only 54 percent, in water 75 percent, and in electricity 84 percent. These averages hide important differences. For instance, in Costa Rica, 98 percent of children lived in dwellings with access to clean water, whereas only 55 percent dwell similarly in El Salvador. Only 21 percent of children ages 0 to 16 in Nicaragua lived in dwellings with sanitation in 2005, compared with 92 percent in Costa Rica. Access to electricity is the most uniform across the region, with several countries reaching universal access (Chile) or nearly universal (Argentina, Costa Rica, Mexico, and República Bolivariana de Venezuela), while those with the lowest rates have at least two-thirds of the population covered (Bolivia, Honduras, Nicaragua, and Peru).

These figures only register average access to the selected basic opportunities in each country. They do not indicate whether children of a certain gender, location, or family structure have different access rates. Different access probability rates for children of different circumstance backgrounds would mean that the average rates hide important inequality in

Table 2.2 Coverage of Basic Opportunities in Education

Country	Sixth grade on time			School attendance (ages 10–14)		
	Circa 1995 (percent)	*Circa 2005 (percent)*	*Annual change*	*Circa 1995 (percent)*	*Circa 2005 (percent)*	*Annual change*
Argentina	—	85	—	—	96	—
Bolivia	—	78	—	—	95	—
Brazil	24	47	2.3	90	97	0.7
Chile	78	83	0.5	98	99	0.1
Colombia	63	76	2.2	89	91	0.3
Costa Rica	64	72	0.8	89	94	0.5
Dominican Republic	54	66	1.2	96	97	0.1
Ecuador	69	81	1.1	84	89	0.4
El Salvador	37	51	2.0	85	90	0.7
Guatemala	25	33	1.5	79	81	0.3
Honduras	43	54	1.3	78	84	0.8
Jamaica	89	88	−0.2	96	95	−0.2
Mexico	75	88	1.3	89	95	0.6
Nicaragua	33	44	1.6	81	88	0.9
Panama	75	77	0.3	92	94	0.3
Paraguay	53	66	2.3	93	92	−0.1
Peru	61	79	2.2	94	96	0.2
Uruguay	—	81	—	—	97	—
Venezuela, R. B. de	69	78	0.9	94	96	0.2
Average	**57**	**68**	**1.3**	**89**	**93**	**0.4**

Source: Authors' compilation based on data sources in table 2.1.

Note: — = Not available.

access to these basic opportunities. These differences have to be identified and measured so that corrective courses of action can be adopted. The next section turns to this task.

Measuring Inequality of Basic Opportunities for Children

This section addresses the second component of the Human Opportunity Index: the distribution of existing basic opportunities in a country that has not achieved universality. Basic opportunities are exogenous for children, even though they are endogenous to society.[10] Access to safe water and basic education, for example, are clearly not under the control of the child. Because lack of effort cannot justify children's lack of access to basic

Table 2.3 Coverage of Basic Opportunities in Housing Conditions

Country	Water			Sanitation			Electricity		
	Circa 1995 (percent)	Circa 2005 (percent)	Annual change	Circa 1995 (percent)	Circa 2005 (percent)	Annual change	Circa 1995 (percent)	Circa 2005 (percent)	Annual change
Argentina	—	93	—	—	82	—	—	99	—
Bolivia	—	64	—	—	32	—	—	68	—
Brazil	90	94	0.4	50	60	1.0	89	95	0.7
Chile	91	97	0.6	77	91	1.4	96	100	0.4
Colombia	80	82	0.3	62	64	0.2	91	93	0.3
Costa Rica	84	98	1.4	78	92	1.4	95	99	0.3
Dominican Republic	—	68	—	—	58	—	—	93	—
Ecuador	61	74	1.1	53	62	0.9	87	94	0.6
El Salvador	48	55	1.1	30	29	-0.2	75	84	1.2
Guatemala	62	70	1.3	22	34	2.0	66	75	1.4
Honduras	—	73	—	—	34	—	57	60	0.4
Jamaica	63	58	-0.9	47	46	-0.2	77	86	1.6
Mexico	80	89	0.9	41	55	1.3	94	99	0.5
Nicaragua	52	56	0.6	15	21	0.9	60	65	0.7
Panama	84	86	0.3	43	44	0.2	69	73	0.6
Paraguay	41	57	2.6	51	57	0.9	88	94	1.0
Peru	53	56	0.4	43	61	2.2	63	69	0.8
Uruguay	—	90	—	—	81	—	—	98	—
Venezuela, R. B. de	92	90	-0.2	83	86	0.4	99	99	0.0
Average	70	75	0.7	50	54	0.9	80	84	0.7

Source: Authors' compilation based on data sources in table 2.1.

Note: — = Not available.

63

goods and services, such access can be conceived of as the opportunities children are given. This makes indicators of opportunity empirically more tractable. The empirical analysis of inequality in those variables does not have to worry about disentangling the portion related to inequality in access to basic opportunities derived from circumstances from that related to any type of choice or effort.[11] For children, measurable inequality in access to basic goods and services related to circumstances such as gender and race *is* inequality in opportunity. On a completely level playing field, circumstances should play no role in the distribution of basic opportunities among children.

As discussed in chapter 1, the goal of equality of basic opportunities has two components: (i) ensuring that as many people as possible have access to basic opportunities, and (ii) ensuring that, in situations of limited available opportunities resulting from resource constraints, existing opportunities are fairly distributed, without any correlation with circumstances. The measure of inequality of opportunity constructed here (the D-index) estimates how fairly an existing set of limited (constrained) opportunities is distributed.

Building the D-Index

This measure of inequality of opportunity is a version of the dissimilarity index widely used in sociology and applied to dichotomous outcomes.[12] The D-index measures how dissimilar access rates are to a given service for groups defined by circumstance characteristics (for example, location, gender, parental education, and so forth) compared with the average access rate to the same service for the population as a whole. If the equal opportunity principle is consistently applied, an exact correspondence between population and opportunity distribution should be observed. That is, if half the population is in circumstance group A, 35 percent in group B, and 15 percent in group C, opportunities should be distributed in the same proportion. The D-index ranges from 0 to 1 (0 to 100 in percentage terms),[13] and in a situation of perfect equality of opportunity, D will be zero.

Access probability gaps are at the heart of the D-index (figure 2.1). The horizontal line located just above the 50 percent mark represents the average probability in the entire population that a child will complete sixth grade on time (the opportunity variable in this case), while the curved line represents the same outcome plotted by per capita income (the circumstance variable). The left-hand shaded portion represents poor income groups that have lower probabilities of finishing sixth grade than the population average, while the right-hand portion reflects wealthier children who have a higher-than-average probability of finishing on time. Access probability gaps are the absolute differences between group-specific access rates (p_i) and the overall average access rate ($\bar{p}$).

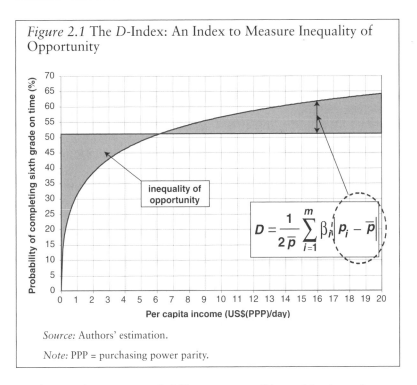

Figure 2.1 The *D*-Index: An Index to Measure Inequality of Opportunity

Source: Authors' estimation.

Note: PPP = purchasing power parity.

There can be as many probability gaps as possible combinations of group-defining circumstances. For example, 20 income groups, 7 family-size groups, and whether one is in a rural or urban setting together generate 280 probability gaps. If the years of schooling of parents, the presence of either one or two parents at home, and the gender of the child are added in, the total number of probability gaps would be a very large number. The *D*-index summarizes all those access probability gaps into a scalar measure by weighting them according to the population share in each circumstance group.[14]

In short, the *D*-index is a relative measure of the weighted average access probability gaps between different circumstance groups and the overall average access rate.[15] Thus, it can be interpreted as showing the fraction of all available opportunities that need to be reassigned from better-off groups to worse-off groups to achieve equal opportunity for all.[16]

National Estimates of Inequality of Opportunity among Children

Before moving on to combine the *D*-index estimates of unequal opportunity distribution with coverage levels to generate the Human Opportunity Index, we briefly review preliminary results on opportunity distribution alone. The *D*-index was applied to the 19 countries whose household surveys present nationally representative data, in most cases at two time

Box 2.1 Computing the *D*-Index Empirically

The *D*-index of inequality of opportunity could be estimated through a variety of parametric, nonparametric, or semi-parametric procedures. One could impose separability restrictions or consider interactions. In all cases, the three-step procedure described here would apply. Because this study applies this procedure to all Latin America and Caribbean countries with available data, and for several points in time, a standard specification that could be feasibly applied to all countries at all times is most desirable. This study's choice was a separable logistic model.

Given a random sample of the population, with information on whether child *j* had access to a given opportunity, and a vector of variables indicating his or her circumstances, one needs to follow three steps to estimate the *D*-index of inequality of opportunity: .

1. Estimate a separable logistic model on whether child *j* had access to a given opportunity as a function of his or her circumstances. The circumstances considered include parents' education, family per capita income, gender, family structure (number of siblings, single-parent household) and area of residence (urban versus rural). For education, age was also a variable used to predict the probability of completing each grade. The specification was chosen according to the needs of each circumstance: quadratic for years of education, logarithmic for real income, and categorical for age and the other dimensions. In all cases, the functions are linear in the parameters. From the estimation of this logistic regression one obtains coefficient estimates.

2. Given these coefficient estimates, obtain for each child in the sample the predicted probability of access to the opportunity in consideration, $\hat{p}_j$.

3. Compute
$$\bar{p} = \sum_1^n w_j \hat{p}_j \text{ and } \hat{D} = \frac{1}{2\bar{p}} \sum_{j=1}^n w_j \left| \hat{p}_j - \bar{p} \right|, \text{ where } w_j = \frac{1}{n}$$
or some other sampling weights.

Note: For a more complete discussion of the estimation procedures, see Barros, Molinas, and Saavedra (2008).

points, to analyze children's inequality of opportunity in education, electricity, and improved water and sanitation. The results are synthetic measures of the variation across circumstance groups of the way in which existing opportunities are distributed, depending on a child's born attributes and family background. In all cases, a lower score implies greater equity in the distribution of opportunity. The estimate can be interpreted as the share of opportunity that needs to be reallocated from more advantaged to less advantaged groups to achieve equality of opportunity.

Completing sixth grade on time is one of the indicators used to analyze inequality of educational opportunity. The average for 2005 of the *D*-index for the 19 countries considered is 11 percent, indicating that 11 percent of the opportunities of children to complete sixth grade on time need to be reallocated in these countries to eliminate the differences across the defined circumstance groups.[17] This number is lower than the average for 1995 (17 percent), indicating that the region has improved markedly in equality of opportunity of finishing primary education on time (table 2.4).

The degree of inequality of opportunity of finishing sixth grade on time, however, varies considerably across countries in the region, ranging from 3 percent or less in Argentina, Chile, and Jamaica to more than 20 percent in Brazil, Guatemala, and Nicaragua.[18] Another way to phrase this is that in Chile, better-off groups and worse-off groups are on average only 3 percent above or below the national average of finishing sixth grade on time, whereas in Guatemala this average distance is 27 percent.

School attendance rates for children ages 10 to 14, another educational indicator, show very low levels of inequality of opportunity. All countries with the exception of Honduras show a D-index of 5 percent or less in 2005. That is, 5 percent or less of total available opportunities would have to be reallocated among circumstance groups of children to equalize across all groups the probability of attending school. Over the previous decade, the level of inequality of educational opportunity for children declined from an average of 4 percentage points to an average of 3 percentage points. This low level of inequality is associated with the high levels of coverage, sometimes universal, that have been reached in the region since the mid-1990s (table 2.4).

Inequality of opportunity averages 12 percent in water, 26 percent in sanitation, and 10 percent in electricity in 2005 in the region. Again, these averages hide important cross-country differences. Inequality in access to sanitation ranges from more than 40 percent in Bolivia and the Central American countries of El Salvador, Guatemala, and Nicaragua, to 10 percent or less in Argentina, Chile, Costa Rica, Uruguay, and República Bolivariana de Venezuela. These wide differences across countries—up to 45 percentage points in sanitation—are smaller in the case of water (27 percentage points) and even less in electricity (26 percentage points). Inequality in access to water ranges from less than 5 percent in Argentina, Brazil, Chile, Costa Rica, Mexico, Panama, Uruguay, and República Bolivariana de Venezuela to more than 20 percent in Bolivia, Nicaragua, Paraguay, and Peru. Inequality in access to electricity ranges from more than 24 percent in Nicaragua and Honduras to zero in countries with universal coverage, such as Chile (table 2.5).

Between 1995 and 2005, opportunity inequality declined 0.4 percentage points a year in water and electricity, and 0.7 percentage points in sanitation. The slow improvement in water and in sanitation, despite high initial levels of inequality, indicates that advances in promoting equality of opportunity in these areas have been slow. Dispersion is even more striking in these cases. Some countries have made remarkable efforts, such as Guatemala, Mexico, and Peru, which have reduced inequality of opportunity by 1 percentage point per year or more for sanitation. However,

Table 2.4 Inequality of Opportunities (*D*-Index) in Education

Country	*Sixth grade on time*			*School attendance (ages 10–14)*		
	Circa 1995 (percent)	*Circa 2005 (percent)*	*Annual change*	*Circa 1995 (percent)*	*Circa 2005 (percent)*	*Ammual change*
Argentina	—	3	—	—	1	—
Bolivia	—	7	—	—	2	—
Brazil	36	20	−1.6	3	1	−0.2
Chile	6	3	−0.3	1	0	0.0
Colombia	20	11	−1.5	4	3	−0.1
Costa Rica	12	9	−0.3	5	2	−0.3
Dominican Republic	16	12	−0.4	1	1	0.0
Ecuador	11	7	−0.4	7	5	−0.2
El Salvador	25	15	−1.4	4	4	−0.1
Guatemala	37	27	−1.6	5	5	0.0
Honduras	20	17	−0.5	10	7	−0.4
Jamaica	3	2	−0.1	1	1	0.0
Mexico	10	5	−0.5	4	2	−0.2
Nicaragua	30	24	−0.8	6	4	−0.4
Panama	11	8	−0.4	3	3	−0.1
Paraguay	15	11	−0.7	2	3	0.1
Peru	16	9	−0.9	2	2	0.0
Uruguay	—	7	—	—	2	—
Venezuela, R. B. de	11	6	−0.4	2	1	−0.1
Average	17	**11**	−0.7	4	3	−0.1

Source: Authors' calculations.

Note: — = Not available.

some countries have recorded an increase in inequality in opportunities for sanitation (Jamaica). Paraguay and El Salvador have reduced inequality of opportunity in access to water by 1.8 and 0.8 percentage points per year, respectively.

Links between Inequality of Opportunity and Coverage

The results for inequality of opportunity described above mirror the numbers for coverage. That is, electricity is the most prevalent basic opportunity in the region, and also the least unequally distributed, whereas sanitation is the most unequally distributed as well as the least widespread. Are these two elements (coverage and inequality) inevitably connected? The correlation is high, but not perfect. Countries with high coverage are bound to have low inequality in access—if everybody has access there can be no group that is systematically without access. However, countries with low levels of coverage need not have high inequality. In fact, some countries have similar levels of average access but different levels of inequality. For instance, both El Salvador and Nicaragua have the same percentage of children with access to water (55 and 56 percent, respectively; table 2.3), but the former displays much less inequality than the latter (19 percent versus 28 percent; table 2.5). Going back to education, Peru and República Bolivariana de Venezuela have similar percentages of children finishing sixth grade on time (79 percent and 78 percent, respectively; table 2.2), but the former is more unequal than the latter (9 percent and 6 percent, respectively; table 2.4).

Nor do countries with higher levels of inequality produce higher reductions in it. For instance, Panama had an initial inequality index in sanitation of 35 percent while Mexico scored 33 percent (table 2.5). However, Mexico had a large reduction in inequality (1.2 percentage points a year) while Panama had a slower fall (0.6 percentage points). El Salvador and Nicaragua had similar levels of inequality in access to water (24 percent and 26 percent, respectively), but the former reduced its inequality at a rate of 0.8 points a year whereas the latter increased it at 0.3 percentage points.

Consequently, the data for the 19 countries, using the average prevalence ($\bar{p}$) and the D-index reveal three interesting patterns. First, countries with high average access rates also have very low D-indexes. Second, countries with lower average access rates have very high D-indexes. This need not necessarily be the case. One could imagine that a poor society concerned with equality and its available scarce basic goods would distribute them equally among different social groups. However, the pattern observed in Latin America and the Caribbean is that countries with low prevalence of an opportunity (generally poor countries) also have a very unequal distribution between circumstance groups. Third, despite the correlation between the indexes, in a few cases the rankings diverge, indicating that countries track their own paths with regard to equality of opportunity.

These examples indicate that changes in average access to a basic opportunity may be accompanied by different changes in inequality of access. Reducing inequality of access is not guaranteed for countries with low coverage, nor is it an immediate by-product of expansion in coverage. Hence, a simultaneous look at both average access and distribution of access is required, which is the role of the Human Opportunity Index.

The Human Opportunity Index

Most policy makers would prefer to have sufficient resources to provide basic opportunities to all children in society, no matter their background. This desire is seldom realistic, especially in developing countries with budget constraints. Policy makers are forced to make hard choices about how a limited set of opportunities is distributed in a society. The Human Opportunity

Table 2.5 Inequality of Opportunities (D-Index) in Housing Conditions

	Water			Sanitation			Electricity		
Country	Circa 1995 (percent)	Circa 2005 (percent)	Annual change	Circa 1995 (percent)	Circa 2005 (percent)	Annual change	Circa 1995 (percent)	Circa 2005 (percent)	Annual change
Argentina	—	4	—	—	8	—	—	1	—
Bolivia	—	20	—	—	42	—	—	22	—
Brazil	6	3	−0.2	25	19	−0.6	8	3	−0.5
Chile	7	2	−0.5	14	5	−0.9	3	0	−0.3
Colombia	15	12	−0.4	26	25	−0.2	6	5	−0.2
Costa Rica	5	1	−0.4	11	4	−0.7	2	1	−0.1
Dominican Republic	—	12	—	—	21	—	—	3	—
Ecuador	12	10	−0.2	24	21	−0.3	7	4	−0.3
El Salvador	24	19	−0.8	47	44	−0.4	14	9	−0.7
Guatemala	12	10	−0.2	51	41	−1.7	14	11	−0.6
Honduras	—	10	—	—	37	—	26	26	0.0
Jamaica	18	19	0.2	22	23	0.1	5	3	−0.3
Mexico	10	4	−0.6	33	21	−1.2	4	1	−0.3
Nicaragua	26	28	0.3	50	49	−0.1	24	24	0.0
Panama	9	6	−0.4	35	31	−0.6	23	19	−0.6
Paraguay	31	20	−1.8	30	26	−0.8	6	3	−0.5
Peru	25	22	−0.4	34	20	−1.7	26	22	−0.6
Uruguay	—	6	—	—	10	—	—	1	—
Venezuela, R.B.	5	4	−0.1	7	5	−0.2	1	1	0.0
Average	**15**	**12**	**−0.4**	**29**	**26**	**−0.7**	**11**	**10**	**−0.3**

Source: Authors' computations.

Note: — = Not available.

Index helps estimate how equitably access to basic opportunities is distributed throughout the population of children in a country, that is, whether the distribution of opportunities is associated with circumstances.

Combining Coverage Rates and Distribution in a Single Indicator

For a policy maker in a country without sufficient resources to immediately provide all basic opportunities to the population, the question arises: should policy try to minimize inequality of opportunity in a situation of limited total opportunities, or should it seek to raise the average access rate, notwithstanding distribution? To answer this question and set the stage for proposing a formal Human Opportunity Index for children, an example can be useful.

Consider four cases in a hypothetical country with a population of a quarter million families; the country is currently facing the threat of a pandemic disease affecting children. All households in this country have four children. The country is bilingual and evenly split between those who speak blue and those who speak red.

Equal deprivation (case 1). One million vaccines are needed for one million children, but none are available. The average access rate $(\bar{p})$ is zero and the D-index is also zero.[19]

Full coverage (case 2). The government has a budget for one million vaccines and all children are vaccinated. The average access rate is one (100 percent) and the D-index is zero.

Biased partial coverage (case 3). The budget can pay for only half a million vaccines. The government, which is run by the red-speaking people's party, decides to inoculate red-speaking children only. In this case, the average access rate is 0.5 (50 percent) and the D-index is also 0.5.

Equal partial coverage (case 4). The government has the same limited budget for vaccines (half a million vaccines) but decides to inoculate only two children per family. Only half of the children are vaccinated, regardless of their language. In this case, access is 0.5 and the D-index is zero.

How is a policy maker to decide between these situations? Clearly, case 2 (full coverage) is the best of the four cases, and case 1 (no coverage) is the worst. From a certain perspective, case 3 (biased partial coverage) would seem superior to case 1, because at least some of the population is covered, and those who are not covered are no worse off either way (a Pareto improvement). However, for a policy maker concerned with equitable distribution within society, case 3 is clearly worse than case 4 (equitable partial coverage), because, although the access rate is the same, the D-index is higher for case 3. The objective for this policy maker is to maximize the average access rate, $\bar{p}$, and reduce inequality of opportunities, D.

Let us further analyze the meaning of the average access rate, $\bar{p}$. Let H be the total number of opportunities available and N be the number of opportunities needed to ensure access for all. Then $\bar{p} = H/N$ can be reinterpreted as the percentage actually available of the total number of opportunities required for universal access. This interpretation of $\bar{p}$ clarifies both its strengths and its weaknesses. It demonstrates that $\bar{p}$ is certainly a measure of the stock of available opportunities, but it is completely insensitive to how these opportunities are allocated.

These observations provide clear direction for improving upon $\bar{p}$. A simple and intuitive improvement would be to modify the numerator so that only those opportunities allocated without any regard for circumstances are considered valid. Hence, if we let r denote the available opportunities allocated, respecting the principle of equal opportunity, then the desired function, O, can be expressed as $O = r/N$.

However, more specificity is required for r. One alternative is already available. Because the measure of inequality of opportunity, D, is the proportion of opportunities that must be reallocated for equality of opportunity to prevail, then $1 - D$ is the proportion properly allocated. Thus, $H(1-D)$ is the total number of opportunities allocated according to the principle of equal opportunity for all. Hence, one possibility is to let $r = H(1-D)$. In this case, the overall measure of opportunity, O, will be given by

$$O = \frac{r}{N} = \frac{H}{N}(1-D) = \bar{p}(1-D),$$

where $O \leq \bar{p} \leq 1$ and $O \leq D \leq 1$.

The level of opportunity measured by this index can be interpreted as the number of existing opportunities in a given society that have been allocated based on an equal opportunity principle. It is measured as a proportion of the total opportunities necessary for universal access. Those existing opportunities allocated in favor of specific circumstance groups, contrary to the mandate of the equal opportunity principle, are not counted in the level of opportunity of this society. Hence, another interpretation of the Human Opportunity Index is as the equal-opportunity-equivalent coverage of basic goods and services.

The Human Opportunity Index combines the two elements—coverage and inequality—in a single calculation. This function, inspired by Sen (1976), can provide a complete ordering of the four situations presented above. The equal deprivation situation ($O = 0$) is worse than the biased partial coverage situation ($O = 0.25$), which is worse than the equal partial coverage situation ($O = 0.5$), which is worse than the full coverage situation ($O = 1$). The two opposing forces that drive the Human Opportunity Index can be seen at work in the four cases. On the one hand, for a given level of the D-index, an increase in overall access to opportunities (a higher $\bar{p}$) raises the Human Opportunity Index, no matter how it is distributed. On the other hand, for a given level of access, lower equality of opportunity (a higher D-index) lowers the Human Opportunity Index. Going from equal partial coverage (case 4) to biased partial coverage (case 3) reduces the Human Opportunity Index from 50 percent to 25 percent. In this case, the egalitarian criterion kicks in: equally distributed opportunities keep the index at 50 percent, but if the government does not intervene to ensure equal distribution, the Human Opportunity Index falls to 25 percent.

The Human Opportunity Index is sensitive to allocations of opportunities to disadvantaged circumstance groups with respect to advantaged ones, but it is insensitive to the size of the population (if both coverage and inequality are kept constant). In addition, despite its distributive sensitivity, the index is Pareto-consistent: an increase in the number of opportunities available to any group will always increase the index. Its distributive sensitivity, however, implies that the impact will be greater if the increase benefits groups with below-average access to opportunities.[20]

Empirical Results from 19 LAC Countries

This section presents national estimates of the Human Opportunity Index, which expresses the interaction between total prevalence of opportunities and how they are distributed in two dimensions: education and housing conditions. Computations of the Human Opportunity Index are made for each country for each of the indicators within these dimensions (tables 2.6 and 2.7). For instance, with respect to finishing sixth grade on time, only 24 percent of all opportunities needed to ensure universal access to primary education are both available and allocated equitably in Guatemala, compared with 86 percent in Jamaica. This is the combination of both average coverage and distribution of access. In Guatemala in 2005, 33 percent of children had completed primary education on time ($\bar{p} = 0.33$; see table 2.2), or only 33 percent of the opportunities needed for universal coverage were available. Out of these, 27 percent (or 9 percentage points) were not allocated equitably (see table 2.4). As a consequence, only 24 percent (33 percent minus 9 percent) of the needed opportunities for universal coverage were available and were allocated equitably.[21] In Jamaica, however, 88 percent of children completed primary education on time (table 2.2), and only 2 percent of opportunities were not allocated equitably (table 2.4). Hence, 86 percent of needed opportunities for universal access were available and distributed fairly.

The Human Opportunity Index for education improved in the region for both indicators. The average of the index over all the countries for finishing sixth grade on time went from 49 percent in the mid-1990s to 62 percent in 2005 (table 2.6). For the same period, school attendance for those ages 10 to 14 increased from 86 percent to 90 percent. Likewise, the index for housing conditions rose for the three indicators considered. Equal opportunity in access to water increased from 61 percent to 67 percent, on average (table 2.7). In sanitation, the average grew from 38 percent to 43 percent, while in electricity it went from 72 percent to 78 percent.

Table 2.6 Human Opportunity Indexes in Education

Country	Sixth grade on time			School attendance (ages 10–14)		
	Circa 1995 (percent)	Circa 2005 (percent)	Annual change	Circa 1995 (percent)	Circa 2005 (percent)	Annual change
Argentina	—	82	—	—	95	—
Bolivia	—	73	—	—	94	—
Brazil	15	37	2.2	87	96	0.9
Chile	73	81	0.7	97	98	0.1
Colombia	50	67	2.9	86	88	0.4
Costa Rica	56	65	0.9	85	92	0.7
Dominican Republic	45	58	1.3	95	97	0.1
Ecuador	62	75	1.3	78	84	0.6
El Salvador	28	43	2.3	81	86	0.8
Guatemala	16	24	1.5	75	77	0.3
Honduras	35	45	1.3	70	78	1.1
Jamaica	87	86	−0.1	95	94	−0.1
Mexico	68	84	1.6	86	93	0.7
Nicaragua	23	33	1.5	76	85	1.2
Panama	67	70	0.6	89	91	0.3
Paraguay	45	59	2.4	91	89	−0.2
Peru	52	72	2.5	92	94	0.2
Uruguay	—	75	—	—	95	—
Venezuela, R. B. de	62	73	1.1	92	94	0.2
Average	**49**	**62**	**1.5**	**86**	**90**	**0.5**

Source: Authors' calculations based on household surveys.

Note: — = Not available.

Of interest is that those indicators with a higher regional average also show lower dispersion across countries. For instance, school attendance for those ages 10–14 averages 90 percent (the highest of all five indicators), and individual country indexes vary within a 22 percentage point range. Conversely, the index for sanitation averages 43 percent (the lowest) with country indexes varying nearly 80 percentage points. This means that some basic opportunities, such as late primary (or early secondary) school attendance and access to electricity, have advanced in almost every country of the region. However, sanitation and finishing sixth grade on time show large disparities from one country to another.

A brief perusal of the data leads to two main observations. First, countries can rank differently when measuring different opportunities. For instance, Jamaica performs highly for education but poorly for improved water and sanitation. Some countries, however, rank consistently across dimensions. Chile has good results in all five dimensions whereas Nicaragua has low

Table 2.7 Human Opportunity Indexes in Housing Conditions

Country	Water			Sanitation			Electricity		
	Circa 1995 (percent)	Circa 2005 (percent)	Annual change	Circa 1995 (percent)	Circa 2005 (percent)	Annual change	Circa 1995 (percent)	Circa 2005 (percent)	Annual change
Argentina	—	90	—	—	76	—	—	98	—
Bolivia	—	51	—	—	19	—	—	53	1.1
Brazil	85	91	0.7	37	49	1.2	81	92	0.6
Chile	84	94	1.0	67	87	2.0	93	99	0.5
Colombia	68	71	0.6	46	48	0.3	86	89	0.4
Costa Rica	80	97	1.6	69	88	1.9	93	98	—
Dominican Republic	—	60	—	—	46	—	—	91	0.9
Ecuador	53	66	1.2	40	49	0.8	81	90	1.6
El Salvador	36	45	1.3	16	16	0.0	65	76	1.6
Guatemala	54	63	1.3	11	20	1.6	57	66	0.3
Honduras	—	66	—	—	21	—	42	45	1.8
Jamaica	52	47	−0.9	37	36	−0.2	73	83	0.8
Mexico	72	85	1.3	28	43	1.5	90	98	0.6
Nicaragua	39	41	0.3	8	11	0.5	46	49	0.9
Panama	77	81	0.7	28	30	0.4	53	59	1.4
Paraguay	28	45	2.8	36	42	1.1	83	91	0.9
Peru	40	44	0.5	29	49	2.5	47	54	0.9
Uruguay	—	85	—	—	73	—	—	97	—
Venezuela, R. B. de	88	87	−0.1	77	82	0.5	98	98	0.0
Average	**61**	**67**	**0.9**	**38**	**43**	**1.0**	**72**	**78**	**0.9**

Source: Authors' calculations based on household surveys.

Note: — = Not available.

records in all. Second, some countries have made consistent progress in all categories while others demonstrate unbalanced performance over time. Countries like Brazil and Mexico have increased across all indexes, while other countries—Jamaica, Paraguay, Peru, and República Bolivariana de Venezuela—have stagnating or even receding indexes.

Summary Indexes

This section presents a summary index that incorporates all five indicators into two dimensions of children's opportunities—education and housing conditions. These two dimensions are then summarized in a single Human Opportunity Index. The overall Human Opportunity Index is a simple average of the country indexes along the two dimensions.[22] Each dimension has a summary index itself. For education it is the simple average of the two indicators, and for housing conditions it is the simple average of the three indicators.

The Human Opportunity Index can be read as that proportion of total available opportunities that has been distributed according to the principle of equality of opportunity. For example, if the Human Opportunity Index is 60 percent, it means that 60 percent of available opportunities in housing conditions or education are equally distributed among the population of children. Similarly, the summary index for each dimension equals the proportion of the available opportunities that are distributed according to the principle of equality of opportunity. For instance, a summary index in housing conditions of 60 percent means that 60 percent of the available opportunities for access to water, sanitation, or electricity are distributed equally across different circumstance groups of children.

The interplay between the scores of the education and housing indexes (table 2.8) and the overall Human Opportunity Index (table 2.9) is revealing. Chile ranks at the top of the Human Opportunity Index because it is a good performer in all dimensions (top place in both education and housing conditions). In the summary index for education, Chile and Jamaica have indexes of 90 percent, and in the summary for housing conditions, Chile and Costa Rica have indexes above 90 percent. At the other end of the spectrum, Bolivia, El Salvador, Guatemala, Honduras, Jamaica, Nicaragua, Panama, Paraguay, and Peru have housing conditions summary indexes of at most 60 percent. Only Nicaragua and Guatemala have such low indexes for education. Consequently, these two countries register a low score in the overall Human Opportunity Index. Jamaica stands out because of its top rank in education and low rank in water and sanitation. These extreme results lead the country to be placed in a middle position.

Just as interesting as the level of the Human Opportunity Index are its recent changes (figure 2.2): almost all countries in the region have recorded increases in the index for the period under study. Some countries have expanded remarkably—Brazil, El Salvador, Guatemala, Mexico, Par-

Table 2.8 Summary Opportunity Indexes for Education and Housing Conditions

Country	Opportunity index for education			Opportunity index for housing conditions		
	Circa 1995 (percent)	Circa 2005 (percent)	Annual change	Circa 1995 (percent)	Circa 2005 (percent)	Annual change
Argentina	—	89	—	—	88	—
Bolivia	—	83	—	—	41	—
Brazil	51	67	1.6	68	77	1.0
Chile	85	90	0.4	81	93	1.2
Colombia	68	78	1.7	67	69	0.5
Costa Rica	70	79	0.8	81	94	1.3
Dominican Republic	70	77	0.7	—	65	—
Ecuador	70	80	0.9	58	69	1.0
El Salvador	54	65	1.5	39	46	1.0
Guatemala	45	51	0.9	41	50	1.5
Honduras	52	62	1.2	—	44	—
Jamaica	91	90	−0.1	54	55	0.2
Mexico	77	88	1.2	63	75	1.2
Nicaragua	49	59	1.3	31	34	0.4
Panama	78	81	0.4	53	57	0.6
Paraguay	68	74	1.1	49	59	1.8
Peru	72	83	1.4	38	49	1.3
Uruguay	—	85	—	—	85	—
Venezuela, R. B. de	77	84	0.7	87	89	0.2
Average	**67**	**76**	**1.0**	**58**	**64**	**0.9**

Source: Authors' calculations based on household surveys.

Note: — = Not available.

aguay, and Peru have all increased the Human Opportunity Index by more than 1.2 percentage points yearly. It is particularly notable that countries like Brazil and El Salvador, which started from relatively low initial levels of the index (59 percent and 47 percent, respectively) are now among the fastest growers in the region. Other countries (Panama and Nicaragua) with similar initial conditions have not had comparable growth.

A similar comparison can be made of countries with high initial levels, such as Chile and República Bolivariana de Venezuela; both were above the 80 percent mark in the mid-1990s, but experienced different results over the period. Chile increased its Human Opportunity Index by 8 percentage points in a decade, but República Bolivariana de Venezuela by only 4 percentage points. These examples show there is room for policy options with regard to expansion of the index.

Table 2.9 Human Opportunity Index

Country	Human opportunity index		
	Circa 1995 (percent)	*Circa 2005 (percent)*	*Annual change*
Argentina	—	88	—
Bolivia	—	62	—
Brazil	59	72	1.3
Chile	83	91	0.8
Colombia	67	74	1.1
Costa Rica	76	86	1.1
Dominican Republic	—	71	—
Ecuador	64	74	0.9
El Salvador	47	55	1.2
Guatemala	43	50	1.2
Honduras	—	53	—
Jamaica	72	73	0.1
Mexico	70	82	1.2
Nicaragua	40	46	0.9
Panama	65	69	0.5
Paraguay	58	67	1.4
Peru	55	66	1.4
Uruguay	—	85	—
Venezuela, R. B. de	82	86	0.4
Average	63	70	1.0

Source: Authors' calculations based on household surveys.

Note: — = Not available.

Looking at the initial level of the Human Opportunity Index in 1995 and at the level of changes during 1995–2005, we could identify four "types" of countries. Some countries started with a low index and made significant improvements, like Brazil. Other countries started with a low index and made uneven progress, e.g., Nicaragua.[23] There are countries that started with a high index and made little progress, like República Bolivariana de Venezuela. However, the overall situation in this type of country might not be quite as worrisome because the original high level to some extent restricts their potential for growth. Nevertheless, some countries, despite a high initial level of the Human Opportunity Index, have managed to post a relatively high pace of growth, e.g., Costa Rica.

Summary and Conclusions

Equality of opportunity ensures that basic goods and services are distributed among children without correlation to circumstances such as gender,

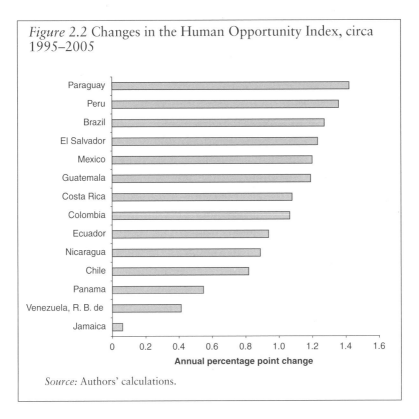

Figure 2.2 Changes in the Human Opportunity Index, circa 1995–2005

Source: Authors' calculations.

family background, or location. The Human Opportunity Index provides an instrument to gauge advances in equality of opportunity over time for a country and to compare performance across countries. It can be interpreted as a social welfare function that reacts to both changes in overall access to basic opportunities for children, as well as to their equitable distribution.

The Human Opportunity Index can help policy makers track progress toward providing a set of basic opportunities to all children within a society. The index indicates what portion of total available opportunities are allocated equitably, encompassing not only the coverage of a given basic opportunity, but also the way available resources are allocated. If policy makers seek to expand services without regard to distributional concerns, the index will grow slowly. However, pure redistribution of given resources would not suffice to accelerate the growth of social welfare. Only by combining expansion of coverage with equal allocation of opportunity will the growth of the Human Opportunity Index be maximized. Obviously, costs considerations are key in the allocation of resources, but that is beyond the scope of the discussion here.

Five basic opportunities are considered in this chapter: completion of sixth grade at age 13, school attendance for children ages 10 to 14, and access to water, sanitation services, and electricity for children ages 0 to 16. These five basic opportunities are aggregated into a summary index for education (the first two) and a summary index for housing conditions (the last three). The average of these two indexes constitutes an overall Human Opportunity Index that condenses into a single number the level of equality of opportunity in a country. The predetermined circumstances comprised gender, place of residence (urban or rural), years of schooling of the family head, family composition (single parent and number of children at home), and per capita income. Data from 36 nationally representative household surveys for 19 Latin American and Caribbean countries were used over a period of approximately a decade (1995–2005). These surveys represent nearly 200 million children in the region.

Most countries in the region show advances in the index for the period, although some registered setbacks. The main findings of the exercise are summarized in the following:

- The index for education, as calculated from surveys taken in or near 2005, ranges from a maximum of 90 percent for Jamaica and Chile to a minimum of about 50 percent for Guatemala. During the decade preceding 2005, Brazil, Colombia, and El Salvador registered the fastest increases in this index, above 1.5 percentage points a year, while Jamaica's decreased slightly.
- The index for housing conditions, again based on surveys taken in or near 2005, indicates that Argentina, Chile, Costa Rica, Uruguay, and República Bolivariana de Venezuela all have indexes above 85 percent. Bolivia, El Salvador, Guatemala, Honduras, Jamaica, Nicaragua, and Peru all rank low, with indexes below 50 percent. The largest changes for water and sanitation took place in Chile, Costa Rica, Guatemala, Mexico, Paraguay, and Peru with improvements of more than 1.2 percentage points.
- The Human Opportunity Index, which averages the indexes for education and housing conditions, is above the 80 percent mark for Argentina, Chile, Costa Rica, Mexico, Uruguay, and República Bolivariana de Venezuela, and below the 60 percent mark for El Salvador, Guatemala, Honduras, and Nicaragua. The larger advances in this index were observed in Brazil (1.3 percentage points per year); Mexico, El Salvador, and Guatemala (1.2 percentage points per year); and Paraguay (1.4 percentage points per year).

The compilation of statistical evidence for the region shows that the Human Opportunity Index has two salient regularities. First, countries with low coverage of a given basic opportunity also show large inequality in its distribution, which indicates that there is room for rapid expansion of the Human Opportunity Index through increasing the prevalence of basic opportunities while taking special care in the distribution of these increments. Second, heterogeneity is evident in the recent evolution of changes in the Human Opportunity Index. Comparing countries with similar initial positions illustrates that some countries have had remarkable increases while others have stagnated. This implies that there is margin for policy makers to identify areas of potential progress and lead advances in the Human Opportunity Index.

The countries, time periods, circumstance variables, and basic opportunities chosen for this study can be modified as necessary for future studies. Choices can be made according to the way in which a given society defines basic opportunities, the circumstance characteristics that might be most relevant in a country, and data availability. The selection of basic opportunities is open to debate and can be modified in other studies. The incorporation into the analysis of additional basic opportunities would provide a more complete and accurate portrait of a country's social reality. For instance, an index could incorporate other indicators, such as nutrition and immunization, to add a health dimension, and birth certificates to add a civil franchise dimension. Further possibilities for the index and its applications are discussed in the next chapter.

Notes

1. Mathematically, the Human Opportunity Index, O, will be given by $O = \bar{p} \times (1-D)$.

2. Several basic opportunities that might be of interest, such as preschool education or having a birth certificate, were not incorporated in the analysis because of lack of data from several countries.

3. This probability was computed by a logistic model conditioned on age and other control variables. For a formal treatment, see Barros, Molinas, and Saavedra (2008). A typical Latin American formal educational system starts at age six, with about six years of primary school and six years of high school. Most countries depart from this benchmark in different directions. "Completing sixth grade" means having completed six years of education on time in the first basic level of the country. In 10 countries of the region, this means completing primary education. But it is less than primary in other countries and more in Colombia. In most countries, basic education officially starts at age six (Brazil, Guatemala, and Nicaragua, start at seven), so by age 13, students that have survived in the system without repetition or interruption should have completed six years of basic education.

4. Anecdotal evidence indicates there were potentially large impacts on the quality of education among poor rural children in Arahuay (Peru) after machines from the One Laptop per Child project reached the local school (Bajak 2007). Without electricity in this rural village this project would not have been possible. The under-US$200 laptops are specially designed to educate children (ages 6–16 years) and to suit local language and customs, are loaded with copyright-free books, and allow children to master the Internet. Peru has bought more than 270,000 machines and Uruguay has ordered 100,000.

5. This does not include public well (*pilón, puesto público, pluma, llave pública*), truck (*camión cisterna*), rain, river or pond, and the like. The only exception is República Bolivariana de Venezuela, in which a public well is accepted by the study as an improved water system. This has a reason. In all surveys from 1995 on, general access to water systems from the public network was almost universal (between 90 and 93 percent) and public well access was almost 0 percent. But for the 2005 survey "Encuesta de Hogares Por Muestreo," the data are completely different. Public network connections represented only 73 percent of access and public wells represented 17 percent. Data from 2006 confirm that public network connections are available to over 90 percent of the general population, but that survey provides no way to create the urban dummy variable that is critically needed for this study.

6. Our definition of improved sanitation is stricter than that from other sources. For example, WHO-UNICEF's Joint Monitoring Programme for Water Supply and Sanitation considers different types of latrines to be improved sanitation, but they are excluded from our definition.

7. For education, gender refers to the child's gender; however, for water, sanitation, and electricity, gender refers to the gender of the household head.

8. Argentina has no nationally representative sample that includes rural areas, with the only nationally representative survey available to our knowledge being a special survey carried out by the World Bank to assess the effects of the 2002 economic crisis. Because national estimates and urban-only estimates are not strictly comparable, this chapter uses the results of the 2002 national survey for Argentina. However, the national estimates for 2002 give remarkably similar results to the urban-only estimates in 2003. Knowing that 2002 was an atypical year for Argentina, the results are to be interpreted with extreme caution.

9. Averages for the final period do not include Argentina and Uruguay, so that initial and final period averages are comparable. Besides, final period averages do not include Bolivia, the Dominican Republic, and Honduras for some indicators. This is due to lack of information in a given survey or comparability problems between surveys.

10. A more formal discussion of this procedure is presented in Barros, Molinas, and Saavedra (2008).

11. As an example, it is possible to assume that differences in access to sanitation among children that are related to circumstances are all inequalities in opportunity, because having or not having the "basic opportunity" is exogenous for the child. However, when an adult has or does not have access to sanitation, the outcome is partly related to differences in opportunity (low public sector investment) and partly related to the effort of the individual.

12. The methodological proposal relies heavily on traditional sociological and demographic studies in three areas: inequality of educational opportunities (see Boudon 1973 and Mare 1980), residential and occupational segregation (Duncan and Duncan 1955), and the measurement of the inequality of opportunity to survive (see, for instance, Koskinen [1985] and Barros and Sawyer [1993]).

13. For a formal proof of the range of the *D*-index, see Barros, Molinas, and Saavedra (2008).

14. Specific access rates are fitted for each individual pertaining to a given group. For details on the econometric methods used, see Barros, Molinas, and Saavedra (2008).

15. The sociological literature usually divides by either the proportion of a bad outcome $(1 - \bar{p})$ or by the product $\bar{p} \times (1 - \bar{p})$. These types of denominators tend to penalize growth of opportunities distributed at random. By dividing by $\bar{p}$, the measure exhibits some pro-growth bias. For further discussion, see Barros, Molinas, and Saavedra (2008).

16. The circumstances analyzed here—place of residence, gender, and several household characteristics—were used because comparable data were available from household surveys in all 19 countries of the LAC region. Should data become available on other potentially important circumstances, such as ethnicity or religion, for example, these can be incorporated into the index.

17. All averages across countries in this section refer to simple averages. Only countries with two data points are included in the average.

18. As complementary information, the study also calculated D-indexes for completion of third grade on time, school attendance for children ages 10–14, and literacy at age 15, circa 2005. The levels of inequality of opportunities for these complementary indicators are much smaller than the level for completion of sixth grade on time: only 1 percent on average across all countries regarding literacy at age 15, 3 percent for school attendance for children ages 10–14, and 8 percent for completing third grade on time, as compared to 12 percent in completing sixth grade on time. Nonetheless, the relative ranking of countries stays roughly similar

19. In a strict sense, D is not defined when $\bar{p} = 0$. A close substitute, $D1$, has to be used. More specifically,

$$D1 = \frac{1}{2} \sum_{i=1}^{m} \beta_i \mid p_i = \bar{p} \mid$$

and $D = (D1/\bar{p})$. For this example, $D1 = 0$. See Barros, Molinas, and Saavedra (2008) for more details.

20. For a formal derivation of these and other properties of the Human Opportunity Index, see Barros, Molinas, and Saavedra (2008).

21. Important improvements in education observed in Guatemala after 2006 could change this estimate.

22. Because the Human Opportunity Index is a simple average, the opportunities are assumed to be perfect substitutes within each dimension, and each dimension is a perfect substitute for the other.

23. Nicaragua shows very little progress in the Human Opportunity Index, even though important advances have been achieved in other fronts such as reducing the poverty gap, reducing infant and child mortality, and increasing access to paved roads.

References

Abou-Ali, Hala. 2003. "The Effect of Water and Sanitation on Child Mortality in Egypt." Unpublished. Environmental Economics Unit, Department of Economics, Göteborg University, Sweden.

Bajak, F. 2007. "In Peru, a Pint-Size Ticket to Learning: Officials Hope 270,000 Laptops for Poor Youngsters Improve Education System." *Washington Post*, December 30, A18.

Barros, Ricardo Paes de, and Diana Sawyer. 1993. "Unequal Opportunity to Survive: Education and Regional Disparities in Brazil." Texto para discussão No. 307, julho de 1993.

Barros, Ricardo Paes de, J. R. Molinas, and J. Saavedra. 2008. "Measuring Inequality of Opportunities for Children." Unpublished, World Bank, Washington, DC. www.worldbank.org/lacopportunity.

Boudon, R. 1974. *Education, Opportunity, and Social Inequality*. New York: Wiley.

Budlender, D., N. Chobokoane, and Y. Mpetsheni. 2001. *A Survey of Time Use: How South African Women and Men Spend Their Time*. Pretoria: Statistics South Africa.

Duncan, Otis, and Beverly Duncan. 1955. "A Methodological Analysis of Segregation Indexes." *American Sociological Review* 20 (2): 210–17.

Fuentes, Ricardo, Tobias Pfütze, and Papa Seck. 2006. "A Logistic Analysis of Diarrhea Incidence and Access to Water and Sanitation." Human Development Report Occasional Paper, UNDP, New York.

Galiani, Sebastian, Paul. J. Gertler, and Ernesto Schargrodsky. 2005. "Water for Life: The Impact of the Privatization of Water Services on Child Mortality." *Journal of Political Economy* 113: 83–120.

Gustavsson, M. 2007. "Educational Benefits from Solar Technology: Access to Solar Electric Services and Changes in Children's Study Routines, Experiences from Eastern Province Zambia." *Energy Policy* 35 (2): 122–29.

Koskinen, S. Time. 1985. "Trends in Cause-Specific Mortality by Occupational Class in England and Wales." Unpublished paper presented at IUSSP 20th General Conference, Florence, Italy.

Mare, R. D. 1980. "Social Background and School Continuation Decisions." *Journal of the American Statistical Association* 75: 295–305.

Kaufman, S., R. Duke, R. Hansen, J. Rogers, R. Schwartz, and M. Trexler. 2000. "Rural Electrification with Solar Energy as a Climate Protection Strategy." Research Report Number 9, Renewable Energy Policy Project, Washington, DC.

Rutstein, Shea O. 2000. "Factors Associated with Trends in Infant and Child Mortality in Developing Countries during the 1990s." *Bulletin of the World Health Organization* 78 (10): 1256–70.

Sen, A. 1976. "Real National Income." *Review of Economic Studies* 43: 19–39.

WHO (World Health Organization). 2002. *The World Health Report 2002: Reducing Risks, Promoting Healthy Life*. Geneva, Switzerland.

World Bank. 2006. *World Development Report 2006: Equity and Development*. Washington, DC: World Bank.

3

Uses and Policy Applications of the Human Opportunity Index

The Human Opportunity Index and its components outlined in the previous chapter are designed to describe and summarize the distribution of basic opportunities for children. Although itself a useful tool, the index and its components have a series of properties that can help diagnose the sources of inequality of opportunity. This chapter presents some applications and analyses of the properties of the Human Opportunity Index with a view to obtaining a better understanding of inequality and highlighting some of the ways the resulting information can be applied to designing effective policy.

The first section explains how the Human Opportunity Index can be used to identify the circumstances that most affect inequality of opportunity. In some countries, location is behind most differences in certain basic opportunities; in others, family background is more important. The second section describes how to interpret changes in the Human Opportunity Index over time, disentangling whether opportunity indexes are improving because of increases in coverage or because of better distribution (that is, improvement biased toward originally disadvantaged groups). The third and fourth sections illustrate how the index can be used to explore differences at the subnational level, and the use of additional basic opportunities. The fifth section explores the relationship between equal opportunity for children and macroeconomic performance, while the sixth section looks into some innovative policy experiences in expanding basic opportunities. The seventh section reviews ideas for possible future research using the Human Opportunity Index, and is followed by a summary section.

Estimating the Main Source of Inequality of Opportunity among Children

Any correlation of access to basic goods and services for children with circumstance groups signals inequality of opportunity. It also signals that public policies have not been effective in offsetting those systematic patterns. To level the playing field for children, policy makers need to know the inequality-of-opportunity profile for a given society to design effective public policies for reducing inequality of opportunity. This subsection seeks to determine (i) the main circumstances affecting inequality in a given opportunity, (ii) the relative effect on opportunity of a specific circumstance as compared with other circumstances, and (iii) the relative importance of a specific circumstance over time.

The dissimilarity index, or D-index, as discussed in the previous chapter, is a *synthetic* measure indicating how outcome probabilities depend simultaneously on all components of a defined set of predetermined circumstances. In addition to this synthetic measure, it is also possible to have *specific* measures that indicate the extent to which outcome probabilities depend on a specific circumstance. For policy design, it may be important to analyze how each circumstance contributes to overall inequality of opportunity. Moreover, a constant level of overall inequality of opportunity over time may hide important changes. For example, inequality of opportunity in education resulting from urban or rural location may be declining, while inequality of opportunity in education resulting from differences in a parent's education may be increasing.

To compute the synthetic D-index described in chapter 2, all circumstances are considered simultaneously. In this chapter, to compute a specific measure related to a particular circumstance—that is, specific D-indexes—the same formulation is applied but allowing only one circumstance to vary at a time, keeping all other circumstances at a fixed value. In other words, one could estimate how the outcome probability varies along a given circumstance (such as family per capita income), holding all other circumstances (such as parent's education, gender, and so forth) constant at their average values.[1]

A profile of inequality of opportunity can be defined by the relative size of each D-index to a specific circumstance considered in this study. That is, a specific D-index for each circumstance (for example, gender, parent's education, and so forth) is computed for a basic opportunity. Then these indexes are ranked by level, which allows sorting out which specific circumstances elicit larger inequality in a given basic opportunity.

A specific D-index can be computed for each of the six circumstances for each of the basic opportunities considered. Table 3.1 is an example of the results for completion of sixth grade on time for 19 countries in the Latin America and the Caribbean (LAC) region. Similar tables are computed for the other four basic opportunities (see tables A.1–A.3 in the appendix at the end of the book). The numbers in table 3.1 represent the proportion of the available opportunity (completion of sixth grade on time) that would have to be redistributed among children for equality of opportunity, if only one circumstance was considered. For example, for Brazil, the specific *D*-indexes calculated for each circumstance range from 2.7 percent for presence of parents to 11.7 percent for parent's education. That is, if the only circumstance considered is parent's education, 11.7 percent of available educational opportunities need to be reallocated to eliminate the differences in completing sixth grade on time across different groups. At the other end of the range, when considering only the location dimension (urban or rural), only 2.7 percent of available educational opportunities need to be reallocated in Brazil to eliminate the differences in completing sixth grade on time. In the specific case of Brazil, inequality of opportunity resulting solely from differences in parent's education is larger than inequality resulting from location, gender, presence of both parents—or from any other circumstance.

Table 3.1 *D*-Index for Completing Sixth Grade on Time, by Circumstance, circa 2005 (*percent*)

Country	Urban or rural	Parents' education	Per capita income	Number of siblings	Gender	Presence of parents
Argentina	0.1	2.9	0.2	0.8	0.6	1.5
Bolivia	1.5	4.3	1.8	1.5	0.7	1.3
Brazil	3.6	11.7	9.1	3.6	8.7	2.7
Chile	0.1	1.9	1.0	1.5	0.9	0.3
Colombia	5.3	5.0	1.4	2.5	1.3	0.3
Costa Rica	0.8	5.8	2.1	3.0	2.7	1.4
Dominican Rep.	1.4	8.3	4.1	2.2	5.3	0.5
Ecuador	0.0	3.9	2.1	1.8	0.3	0.5
El Salvador	5.0	9.1	3.6	5.2	3.2	0.8
Guatemala	9.0	20.6	5.6	6.8	2.2	1.0
Honduras	5.4	11.1	4.6	3.2	4.1	1.1
Jamaica	0.8	0.6	0.6	0.9	1.3	0.4
Mexico	0.4	3.3	0.2	1.2	0.7	0.3
Nicaragua	11.2	14.2	6.7	8.3	7.6	1.7
Panama	1.3	4.2	1.5	3.2	2.3	0.0
Paraguay	0.9	7.0	3.0	4.6	3.2	1.2
Peru	2.7	4.7	1.6	1.7	0.5	0.4
Uruguay	1.4	8.3	4.1	2.2	5.3	0.5
Venezuela, R. B. de	0.3	3.8	0.9	2.5	2.3	0.2

Source: Authors' computation.

Table 3.2 shows analogous results for one of the elements of housing conditions. The analysis of the specific D-indexes for sanitation shows that in most countries, the urban-rural division is clearly the dominant circumstance explaining inequality in children's access to sanitation, conditional on all other circumstances. Only in the few countries that already have high levels of coverage—Argentina, Chile, and República Bolivariana de Venezuela—is location not the dominant factor. Isolating all other factors, in Bolivia, El Salvador, Jamaica, and Nicaragua around 40 percent of the available opportunities in sanitation would have to be reallocated to ensure similar access across location groups. The next circumstances in importance are household per capita income and parent's education. Clearly, being born to a poor family is critical to a child's probability of having access to sanitation.

Profile of Children's Inequality of Educational Opportunity

This section summarizes the relative importance of each circumstance in explaining the inequality in the two indicators for educational oppor-

Table 3.2 D-Index for Probability of Access to Sanitation, by Circumstance, circa 2005 (*percent*)

Country	Urban or rural	Parents' education	Per capita income	Number of siblings	Gender	Presence of parents
Argentina	0.1	5.4	2.4	0.8	1.1	0.1
Bolivia	38.6	19.1	15.1	12.8	5.0	10.1
Brazil	12.4	6.7	8.4	0.2	1.3	0.6
Chile	3.5	1.1	1.1	0.1	0.1	0.2
Colombia	22.8	6.1	4.5	2.6	0.1	1.4
Costa Rica	0.7	1.3	1.1	0.2	0.1	0.0
Dominican Rep.	16.7	9.8	16.1	0.2	1.2	4.0
Ecuador	14.0	8.2	12.3	2.2	0.1	1.6
El Salvador	38.1	21.4	21.3	2.8	5.3	2.7
Guatemala	37.0	13.1	19.4	5.2	7.7	3.3
Honduras	29.3	15.6	15.6	1.4	1.3	1.7
Jamaica	44.2	11.3	1.2	15.5	20.6	10.3
Mexico	8.8	10.6	12.7	2.5	1.2	1.3
Nicaragua	44.7	22.3	22.7	1.3	0.3	8.6
Panama	21.5	15.1	17.6	3.6	1.3	7.1
Paraguay	25.2	10.6	13.0	4.4	0.9	3.6
Peru	37.9	11.3	23.7	0.6	0.9	2.1
Uruguay	5.9	3.2	7.6	0.4	0.5	0.4
Venezuela, R. B. de	2.7	3.7	1.9	0.6	0.5	1.6

Source: Authors' computation.

tunity. For completion of sixth grade on time, the most important circumstance variable is parent's education: for 17 out of 19 countries, the *D*-index specific to parent's education is the highest of all circumstances (table 3.3), followed by number of siblings (one of the top three circumstances for 14 out of 19 countries), and gender (one of top three in 9 of 19 countries). The presence of two parents at home had the lowest impact of all circumstances, ranking fifth or sixth in 17 out of 19 countries. Location (urban or rural) also ranks very low. For school attendance for children ages 10 to 14, the profile indicates that gender is the circumstance that elicits the largest inequality of opportunity in all countries. Parent's education follows in importance, ranked second among sources of inequality in 18 countries in the region.

The results indicate that parent's education defines an important divide in educational opportunity among children in Latin America and the Caribbean. Inequality in promotion and repetition rates, both of which affect timely completion, are strongly affected by parent's education. In addition, inequality in attendance between girls and boys is significant, indicating that gender is an important factor for inequality of opportunity. This information suggests that policy makers aiming to reduce inequality of opportunity indicated by repetition rates ought to devise policies that focus on children living in households where parents have low education levels. Similarly, in some countries, reducing inequality of opportunity in attendance rates according to gender requires a policy that addresses this

Table 3.3 Relative Importance of Six Circumstance Variables in Inequality of Educational Opportunity (*number of countries*)

Circumstance	Most important	2	3	4	5	Least important
Inequality in completion of sixth grade on time						
Area	1	3	3	1	6	5
Gender	1	2	6	4	5	1
Number of siblings	0	8	7	4	0	0
Parent's education	17	1	0	0	1	0
Per capita income	0	4	3	9	2	1
Presence of parents	0	1	0	1	5	12
Inequality in school attendance for ages 10–14						
Area	0	0	1	0	1	17
Gender	19	0	0	0	0	0
Number of siblings	0	0	0	2	16	1
Parent's education	0	18	1	0	0	0
Per capita income	0	1	11	6	1	0
Presence of parents	0	0	6	11	1	1

Source: Authors' computation.

divide by helping boys stay in school longer.[2] It is important to note, however, that the level of inequality manifested in these indicators is relatively
low. By contrast, the analysis does not find location to be an important
source of inequality of opportunity in either education indicator. This
implies that the rural areas are not significantly lagging in primary education attendance and repetition rates once other circumstances are taken
into account.[3]

The above analysis considers the region as a whole, but country-spe-
cific assessments can be obtained as well. For instance, when considering
inequality of opportunity in completing sixth grade on time in Colombia,
location is the largest source of inequality, not the smallest as in most
other countries (table 3.4).[4] Similarly, for Jamaica, although inequality
in opportunity is very low, gender is the most important divide, not parent's education as in most other countries. This highlights that policies to
reduce inequality of opportunity must be tailored to individual countries
so that the specific circumstances that generate inequality are correctly
identified and dealt with.

Profile of Inequality of Opportunity for Housing Conditions among Children

In contrast with educational opportunity, location is the most important
circumstance in explaining inequality of opportunity in housing conditions for children. Inequality indexes specific to area of residence are
among the top two largest for 18 countries with respect to access to water
and for 16 countries with respect to sanitation and electricity (table 3.5).
Without a doubt the urban-rural divide is the most important circumstance in explaining inequality of opportunity in basic housing conditions.
Conversely, demographic characteristics such as gender of the household
head, number of siblings, and presence of parents are among the least
important circumstances for all three indicators.

These results are inherent to the nature of these infrastructure services.
Once water, sanitation, or electricity services are provided to an entire
region, it is more likely that every household has access to them, regardless
of demographic characteristics. Still, economic conditions may sometimes
preclude a household from connecting to public or community water and
sanitation systems. The clear policy implication for the region as a whole
from these results is that location differences in access to water, sanitation,
and electricity are the key circumstance behind inequality of opportunity
in housing conditions among children.

However, a caveat similar to that in the previous section can be raised
here with respect to the particular conditions of each country. Table 3.6
shows the relative importance of each circumstance by country for sanitation. For countries in which rural areas are relatively small, geographic
conditions less harsh, or public services have expanded significantly in

Table 3.4 Profile of Inequality of Opportunity for Sixth Grade Completion on Time: Relative Importance of Six Circumstance Variables by Country

Country	Most important	2	3	4	5	Least important
Argentina	parents' education	presence of parents	siblings	gender	per capita income	location
Bolivia	parents' education	per capita income	location	siblings	presence of parents	gender
Brazil	parents' education	per capita income	gender	siblings	location	presence of parents
Chile	parents' education	siblings	per capita income	gender	presence of parents	location
Colombia	location	parents' education	siblings	per capita income	gender	presence of parents
Costa Rica	parents' education	siblings	gender	per capita income	presence of parents	location
Dominican Rep.	parents' education	gender	per capita income	siblings	location	presence of parents
Ecuador	parents' education	per capita income	siblings	presence of parents	gender	location
El Salvador	parents' education	siblings	location	per capita income	gender	presence of parents
Guatemala	parents' education	location	siblings	per capita income	gender	presence of parents
Honduras	parents' education	per capita income	siblings	gender	location	presence of parents
Jamaica	gender	siblings	location	per capita income	parents' education	presence of parents
Mexico	parents' education	siblings	gender	location	presence of parents	per capita income
Nicaragua	parents' education	location	siblings	gender	per capita income	presence of parents
Panama	parents' education	siblings	gender	per capita income	location	presence of parents
Paraguay	parents' education	siblings	gender	per capita income	presence of parents	location
Peru	parents' education	siblings	location	per capita income	gender	presence of parents
Uruguay	parents' education	gender	siblings	per capita income	location	presence of parents
Venezuela, R. B. de	parents' education	siblings	gender	per capita income	location	presence of parents

Source: Authors' computation.

Note: At the time this book was written, the needed variables for Haiti, the poorest country in the region, were unavailable. However, a study by Demombynes and Leon (2008) using Demographic and Health Surveys shows that key circumstances do affect primary educational attainment on time (see box 3.1).

Box 3.1 Preliminary Evidence from Haiti

Data from the Demographic and Health Surveys for Haiti allow a succinct preview of inequality of opportunity to be made. Although these surveys are not fully comparable to the Living Standards Measurement Study surveys and labor surveys used for other countries analyzed in this book, they permit a preliminary comparison with other countries in the region.

School attendance for children ages 6 to 14 has increased in Haiti. The proportion of urban children attending school rose from 86.4 percent to 91.2 percent between 1995 and 2005. In the same period school attendance in rural areas grew even more rapidly, from 67.0 percent to 79.3 percent. This growth, however, has been accompanied by concerns about educational quality because there is evidence of crowded schools, high rates of repetition, and over-age attendance (attending school when older than the prescribed age). The public sector has been unable to grow to meet the demand for education; instead, private schools represent the largest share of school growth in the country. Uniquely among Latin American countries, Haiti has a system in which only 20 percent of primary-school-age students are enrolled in public schools, with the remainder enrolled in a mixture of religious, for profit, and nongovernmental organization–funded schools.

In a recent study of Haiti, Demombynes and De Leon (2008) used a probabilistic model to show that gender of the child and dwelling location (urban or rural) do not play a significant role in explaining over-age attendance at school for children ages 6 to 14. These two variables were not significant in either of the two years under study (1995 and 2005). Conversely, economic status of the household (as measured by a composite index of assets) and the presence of both parents at home showed significant negative impacts for both years. That is, the absence of one or both of the parents increases the probability of children attending school above the prescribed age. Similarly, children living in households with lower economic status are more likely to attend school over age. Total years of education in the household showed a significant negative impact in the initial year, but not in the most recent year.

This evidence shows that Haiti is similar to other countries in the region in that gender and location are not important sources of inequality of opportunity in schooling. In contrast, presence of both parents has a significant influence in over-age school attendance in Haiti whereas this variable is among the least important in the region for explaining both the probability of completing sixth grade on time and school attendance for ages 10–14. Furthermore, parent's education, which is the most important variable in explaining inequality of educational opportunity for children in the region, does not appear to have a regular impact in Haiti (as measured by total years of education in the household). Instead, economic status is the relevant variable in Haiti whereas family per capita income has little importance for explaining inequality of educational opportunity in the region.

The importance of economic status for explaining over-age school attendance indicates that this circumstance constitutes a significant source of inequality of opportunity in Haiti. Policies that either provide funds for children to attend private schools or expand the supply of public schools could be a step toward reducing inequality in educational opportunity in Haiti.

Table 3.5 Relative Importance of Six Circumstance Variables in Inequality of Opportunity for Housing Conditions

Circumstance	Most important	2	3	4	5	Least important
Access to water						
Area	17	1	0	0	0	1
Gender	0	0	2	4	8	5
Number of siblings	0	1	2	4	3	9
Parents' education	1	8	8	0	0	2
Per capita income	1	9	7	0	2	0
Presence of parents	0	0	0	11	6	2
Access to sanitation						
Area	14	2	2	0	0	1
Gender	0	1	1	4	3	10
Number of siblings	0	0	1	7	8	3
Parents' education	3	4	11	1	0	0
Per capita income	2	12	4	0	0	1
Presence of parents	0	0	0	7	8	4
Access to electricity						
Area	14	2	1	1	0	0
Gender	0	1	1	6	8	3
Number of siblings	0	0	5	5	3	6
Parents' education	3	7	6	3	0	0
Per capita income	2	9	6	0	1	1
Presence of parents	0	0	0	4	7	8

Source: Authors' computation.

rural areas, the location divide is not important. For Argentina, Costa Rica, Uruguay, and República Bolivariana de Venezuela, socioeconomic conditions such as parent's education and family per capita income are more important as determinants of inequality of opportunity in access to basic housing conditions (table 3.6).

Explaining Changes in the Human Opportunity Index over Time

As shown in chapter 2, the Human Opportunity Index can vary, and has varied, significantly over time in different countries. Because the Human Opportunity Index takes into consideration both average coverage and inequality of access to a given basic opportunity, a policy analyst may wonder about the specific source of the change in the index. If it improved, is it because coverage rose, or because inequality declined, or a combination?

Table 3.6 Profile of Inequality of Opportunity for Access to Sanitation: Relative Importance of Six Circumstance Variables by Country

Country	Most important	2	3	4	5	Least important
Argentina	parents' education	per capita income	gender	siblings	presence of parents	location
Bolivia	location	parents' education	per capita income	siblings	presence of parents	gender
Brazil	location	per capita income	parents' education	gender	presence of parents	siblings
Chile	location	per capita income	parents' education	presence of parents	siblings	gender
Colombia	location	parents' education	per capita income	siblings	presence of parents	gender
Costa Rica	parents' education	per capita income	location	siblings	gender	presence of parents
Dominican Rep.	location	per capita income	parents' education	presence of parents	gender	siblings
Ecuador	location	per capita income	parents' education	siblings	presence of parents	gender
El Salvador	location	parents' education	per capita income	gender	siblings	presence of parents
Guatemala	location	per capita income	parents' education	gender	siblings	presence of parents
Honduras	location	per capita income	parents' education	presence of parents	siblings	gender
Jamaica	location	gender	siblings	parents' education	presence of parents	per capita income
Mexico	per capita income	parents' education	location	siblings	presence of parents	gender
Nicaragua	location	per capita income	parents' education	presence of parents	siblings	gender
Panama	location	per capita income	parents' education	presence of parents	siblings	gender
Paraguay	location	per capita income	parents' education	siblings	presence of parents	gender
Peru	location	per capita income	parents' education	presence of parents	gender	siblings
Uruguay	per capita income	location	parents' education	gender	siblings	presence of parents
Venezuela, R. B. de	parents' education	location	per capita income	presence of parents	siblings	gender

Source: Authors' calculations.

94

One property of the Human Opportunity Index is that changes are additively decomposable, which means that the foregoing question can be easily answered. Any change in the index can be attributed either to an increase in the coverage rate, $\bar{p}$ (scale effect), or a reduction in the index of inequality of opportunity, D-index (distributional effect). A simple exercise to decompose the sources of the evolution of the Human Opportunity Index consists of computing the change the index would have if one of its components (either coverage or inequality) were held constant. Holding each component separately constant allows one to total the change in the index as a sum of changes in coverage only (the scale effect) and changes in inequality of opportunity only (the distribution effect). See box 3.2 for a formal treatment.

Children's Educational Opportunity

The average change in the Human Opportunity Index in educational opportunity differs by indicator. The completion of sixth grade on time

---

Box 3.2 Decomposing Changes in Inequality of Opportunity

Consider two years: *initial* and *final*. Any change in the Human Opportunity Index O could be decomposed into a scale effect, $\Delta_{\bar{p}}$, and a distributional effect, Δ_D, as follows:

$$change = O^{final} - O^{initial} = \Delta_{\bar{p}} + \Delta_D,$$

where the scale effect, $\Delta_{\bar{p}}$, and the distributional effect, Δ_D, are defined as follows:

$$\Delta_{\bar{p}} = \bar{p}^{final}(1 - D^{initial}) - \bar{p}^{initial}(1 - D^{initial})$$

and

$$\Delta_D = \bar{p}^{final}(1 - D^{final}) - \bar{p}^{final}(1 - D^{initial}).$$

This decomposition allows the analyst to hypothesize the change in O if either coverage or inequality had not changed at all. In real life situations, both variables change over time, interacting in such a manner that, in practice, one variable cannot move without affecting the other. In general, it is difficult to observe improvements in the distribution of existing opportunities in a country without also observing expansion of coverage.

Source: Barros, Molinas, and Saavedra 2008.

increased by 1.5 percentage points per year between 1995 and 2005, while the Human Opportunity Index for school attendance for children ages 10 to 14 increased by only 0.5 percentage points per year. The levels for each index in 2005 were 62 percent and 90 percent, respectively (see table 2.6).

As the data in chapter 2 show, these average growth numbers hide important differences in the performance of each country. The level of children's educational opportunity has increased for most countries in the region, although at different speeds according to indicator and country. However, three notable regularities are apparent. First, in almost every country, the scale effect represents the largest share (about two-thirds) of total change. That is, extension in overall coverage of educational opportunity, and not a more equitable distribution of opportunity, is the main force driving equality of opportunity in education across the region (figure 3.1).[5] Another notable finding is that countries with the largest expansion in coverage of an educational opportunity also show the largest distributional effect, which implies that educational opportunity has been growing for the poorest segments of the population and that improvements in equity are easier in contexts of expansion.

Second, three countries (Brazil, El Salvador, and Mexico) register changes above the average in both education indicators, suggesting that the two indicators move together in these countries and implying that these countries are making significant efforts to expand educational opportunity. In contrast, Peru and Paraguay have recorded important advances in completion of sixth grade on time, but not in attendance rates for ages 10 to 14. This means that enrollment in late primary (or lower secondary) is not accompanying the improvements in efficiency of the system in primary. A third group of countries have below-average changes in both indicators. Some of these countries, such as Chile, Jamaica, and República Bolivariana de Venezuela, already have very high coverage of primary education, so any further advances must rely on expansion of secondary education. Others, like the Dominican Republic, Guatemala, and Nicaragua, have low levels of coverage in completion of sixth grade on time and have not recorded significant advances in this area.

A third point is that the size of the change in the Human Opportunity Index does not depend on its initial level. For instance, Brazil and Guatemala had similar and very low initial levels for completing sixth grade on time, but Brazil improved faster. Similarly, Mexico and Panama started from relatively high levels for completing sixth grade on time, but the former had a much larger increase than the latter. These changes in the Human Opportunity Index can be depicted graphically (figure 3.2).[6] The vertical axis of figure 3.2 represents equality of access to the opportunity, while the horizontal axis stands for average access to the basic opportunity (coverage). Gray dotted curved lines are combinations of equality and coverage that render the same level of the Human Opportunity

Figure 3.1 Decomposition of Changes in Human Opportunity Indexes for Education

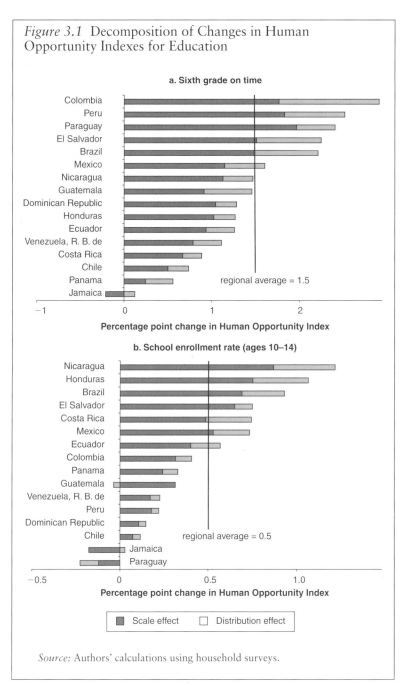

Source: Authors' calculations using household surveys.

Index, or "iso-opportunity curves." Figure 3.2 shows the initial and final levels of the Human Opportunity Index for the four countries discussed here, as well as the changes in both coverage (scale effect) and equality (distribution effect) that led to the overall change.[7] Guatemala and Brazil both start at very low levels of the Human Opportunity Index (around 15 percent), but Brazil ends much higher than Guatemala (37 percent compared with 24 percent) thanks to both larger scale and distributional effects. A similar process can be seen for Mexico in comparison with Panama.

The notable examples of Brazil and Mexico with regard to educational opportunity may be the result of the well-known programs Bolsa Escola and Oportunidades, which have successfully increased schooling of the poorest segments of society. These programs are renowned for focusing on expanding educational opportunities through both supply and demand actions among the children of the poorest families, which directly promotes equality of opportunity.

Another interesting comparison is between Paraguay and El Salvador. The two countries experienced similar expansion in coverage of completion of sixth grade on time (around 14 percentage points in 6–7 years), but El Salvador reduced inequality in distribution by 10 percentage points, whereas Paraguay reduced it by only 4 percentage points (figure 3.3). Consequently, the increase in El Salvador's Human Opportunity Index

Figure 3.2 Changes in the Human Opportunity Index for Completion of Sixth Grade on Time: Brazil, Guatemala, Mexico, and Panama

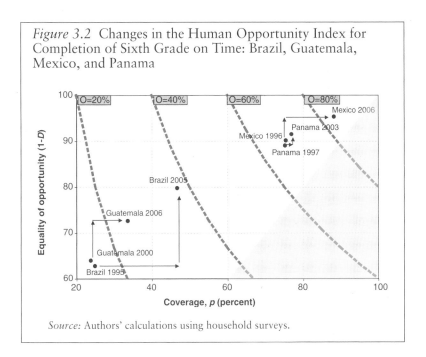

Source: Authors' calculations using household surveys.

Figure 3.3 Changes in the Human Opportunity Index
for Completion of Sixth Grade on Time: El Salvador and
Paraguay

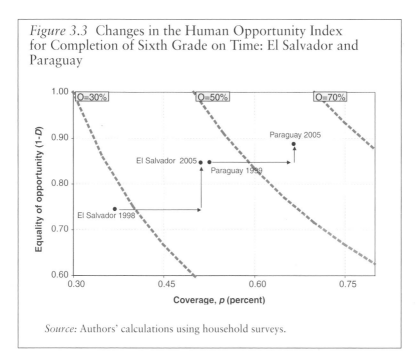

Source: Authors' calculations using household surveys.

(16 percentage points) was larger than Paraguay's (14 percentage points).[8]
The message complements that of figure 3.2: countries with similar expansions in coverage may have different distributional effects and therefore different changes in the Human Opportunity Index. To achieve a larger increase in the index, expansions in coverage must be accompanied by reductions in inequality of opportunity.

Children's Opportunities in Housing Conditions

The average yearly increase in the Human Opportunity Index was 0.9 percentage points in access to water, 1.0 percentage points in access to sanitation, and 0.9 percentage points in access to electricity. These are similar changes despite wide disparities in initial levels: the resulting average indexes in 2005 are 43 percent for sanitation, 67 percent for water, and 78 percent for electricity, with wide cross-country disparity in access to these three basic opportunities.

Both the size of the changes and the decomposition into scale and distributional effects show a more varied pattern for housing conditions opportunity than for educational opportunity (figure 3.4).[9] First, a few countries recorded declines in access to opportunities in housing conditions. Jamaica and República Bolivariana de Venezuela show small

Figure 3.4 Decomposition of Changes in the Human
Opportunity Indexes for Housing Conditions

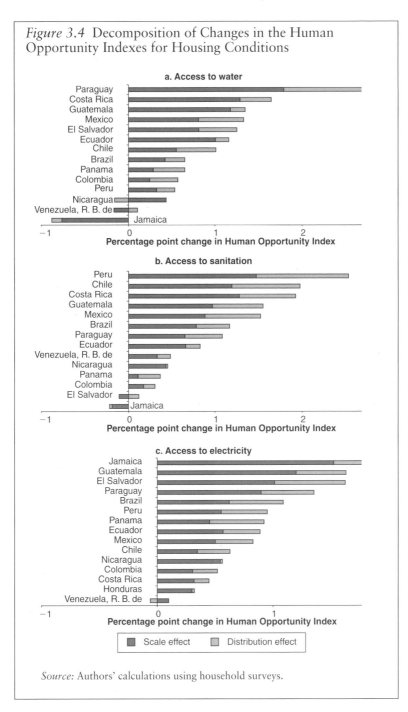

Source: Authors' calculations using household surveys.

declines in access to clean water; Jamaica registered small declines for sanitation, and no country shows a fall in children's access to electricity. These drops may have occurred because the expansion of coverage in basic opportunities in housing conditions did not keep pace with the growth of families with children. Second, contrary to the results of the analysis of educational opportunity, there are cases here where the distributional effect is as large as or larger than the scale effect, for instance, in Panama, for all three housing conditions indicators.

Again, the decomposition into scale and distributional effects allows for interesting analyses. For example, El Salvador, Guatemala, and Nicaragua all expanded overall access to water (between 4 and 8 percentage points for the periods considered), but their performance in reducing inequality of access is very different. El Salvador reduced inequality by 6 percentage points, whereas Guatemala only reduced it 1 percentage point. Nicaragua even had an increase in inequality, of 2 percentage points (figure 3.5 and table 2.5). These cases illustrate that expanding coverage is not enough for increasing children's oppotunities rapidly. Equal opportunity in access to water, measured by the Human Opportunity Index, increased at more similar rates in El Salvador than in Guatemala (table 2.7), despite the latter having a faster expansion of overall

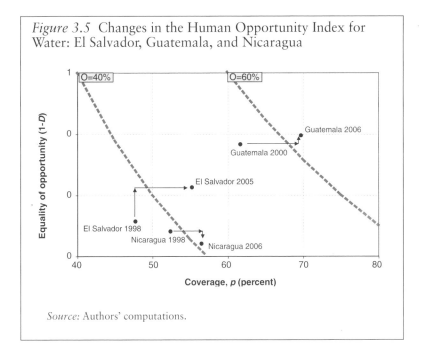

Figure 3.5 Changes in the Human Opportunity Index for Water: El Salvador, Guatemala, and Nicaragua

Source: Authors' computations.

coverage. Nicaragua's score could have increased more if its expansion in coverage had been accompanied by a reduction in inequality of access. These countries' experiences underscore that expansions in coverage need to pay heed to alleviation of existing inequalities.

A similar comparison can be made between Ecuador and Paraguay with regard to access to sanitation (figure 3.6). Both countries start with similar average access levels (around 52 percent) and both have similar annual growth rates in the scale effect (see figure 3.5b). However, Paraguay's growth was accompanied by a larger reduction in inequality of access.

The examples need not be limited to countries with low opportunity levels. Brazil and Jamaica, both with Human Opportunity Index scores in electricity above the 75 percent mark, vary with respect to relative scale and distributional effects (figure 3.7). For their respective periods, Jamaica expanded coverage slightly more than Brazil (8 versus 7 percentage points), but the latter reduced inequality in access more than the former (5 versus 2 percentage points). Decreasing inequality of opportunity through a larger distributional effect—that is, decreasing the D-index—is important to greater expansion of the Human Opportunity Index. Box 3.3 discusses the forces behind changes in the D-index over time.

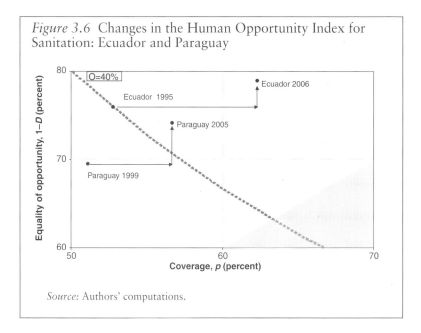

Figure 3.6 Changes in the Human Opportunity Index for Sanitation: Ecuador and Paraguay

Source: Authors' computations.

Figure 3.7 Changes in the Human Opportunity Index for Electricity: Brazil and Jamaica

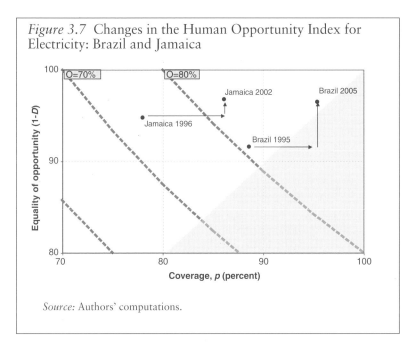

Source: Authors' computations.

Box 3.3 Decomposing Changes in Inequality of Opportunity over Time

Researchers or policy makers may want to further decompose the Human Opportunity Index's inequality component to estimate its main determinants. The degree of inequality of opportunity for children, as measured by the D-index, has three immediate determinants: (i) the absolute gap between a group's specific coverage and the overall mean, (ii) the group-specific shares in the total population, and (iii) the overall coverage rate. The inequality of basic opportunity can change if and only if at least one of these three determinants changes. For a formal treatment, see Barros, Molinas, and Saavedra (2008).

Usually one associates inequality of opportunity with coverage gaps between circumstance groups. The greater the coverage gaps, the greater the inequality of opportunity. The effect of changes in coverage gaps on changes in inequality of opportunity can be termed the "gap effect." Hence, changes in this component most closely reflect changes in the actual distribution of basic opportunities in each society.

The overall coverage rate translates an absolute index of inequality into a relative index. It is essential to isolating changes in scale. The effect

(*Box continues on the following page.*)

Box 3.3 Decomposing Changes in Inequality of Opportunity over Time *(continued)*

of changes in the overall coverage rate on changes in the level of inequality of basic opportunity will be called the "scale effect."

Finally, the group's specific shares in the total population capture the distribution of individuals across circumstance groups. The group's relative size in the population serves as the weight of a weighted average to calculate the *D*-index, and variations in levels of inequality of basic opportunities can, as a result, be caused to some extent by changes in these weights. Hence, the effect of changes in the group's specific shares on changes in the inequality of basic opportunities will be referred to as the "composition effect."

For the 16 countries in the study with at least two observations, the decomposition of the changes in the *D*-index for completion of sixth grade on time yields the following results: the scale effect was the largest effect in 10 countries, while the gap effect was the largest in 3 countries—Chile, Ecuador, and Jamaica. The composition effect was predominant in the remaining three countries.

Different Performances within and across Countries

The Human Opportunity Index furthers reporting and the analysis of advances in equality of opportunity in several ways. The overall index presented in chapter 2 combines different basic opportunities so that the level and progress of a country can be judged with a single measure. However, this overall index can hide important variations in access to basic opportunities within and across countries. In fact, the results show that some countries perform well in the overall measure, but may perform very differently when analyzing the different basic opportunities. For instance, the data across the 10-year period show that Chile is among the top performers in the region in the overall Human Opportunity Index, with high levels in all the opportunities considered here, while Honduras ranks low in all opportunities. Brazil ranks in the middle, but with a heterogeneous performance; equality of opportunity in Brazil in access to electricity is similar to Chile's (both above 90 percent), while its equality of opportunity in access to completion of sixth grade on time is equivalent to that of Honduras (figure 3.8). Other countries, such as Peru and Colombia, also show very sharp differences both in the level and in the changes of the index across the different opportunities.

The index can also be applied at the subnational level to analyze differential progress in opportunities. Within a country, too, the Human

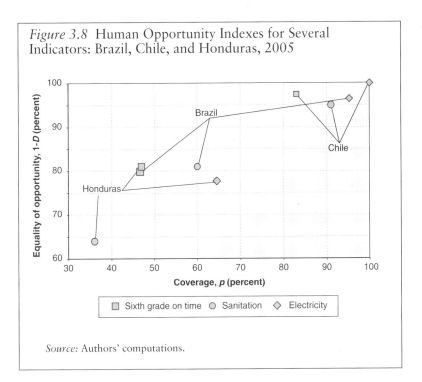

Figure 3.8 Human Opportunity Indexes for Several Indicators: Brazil, Chile, and Honduras, 2005

Source: Authors' computations.

Opportunity Index may hide enormous differences across regions, states, or municipalities. For instance, an analysis for Brazil shows the stark differences across the country (figure 3.9). Some states in Brazil have an index well above the national average (for example, Santa Catarina, São Paulo, and Paraná), whereas others are well below the average (for example, Sergipe, Alagoas, and Piaui). This disparity across states is even more notable if the states' indexes are compared with the average indexes of other countries in the region (figure 3.9). No Brazilian state has equality of opportunity in completion of sixth grade on time as high as the average for Chile (LAC's best performer in this indicator), although Santa Catarina is close; while some of the poorest states, mostly in the northeast, rank below the country average for Guatemala, the LAC country with the lowest index in this basic opportunity. An analysis of the different states shows that the poorest states are also those in which opportunities are distributed more inequitably. Hence, Brazil, usually characterized as one of the most unequal countries in the region, is also a country with a high degree of inequality of opportunity, within states and across states. It is encouraging for Brazilians, however, that it shows one of the largest increases in the Human Opportunity Index for education over the decade 1995–2005 (table 2.8).

Figure 3.9 Human Opportunity Index: Completion of Sixth Grade on Time in Brazil by State, 2005

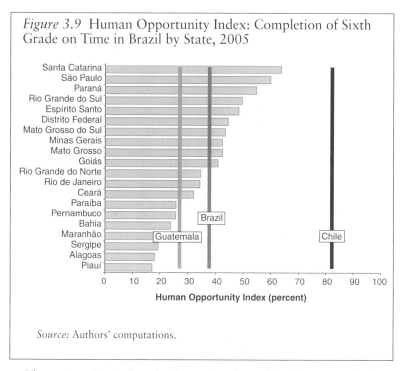

Source: Authors' computations.

The main point is that the diagnosis of equality of opportunity in a given country needs to take into consideration all observed heterogeneity. Policy makers should then make better decisions about the allocation of scarce resources into programs that aim to increase equality of opportunity in basic services for children. Differences arising from circumstances across regions need to be carefully considered so that policies that target the sources of inequality of opportunity can be implemented.

Considering Additional Basic Opportunities

The basic opportunities for this study were chosen because they are critical for the development of a person and are exogenous to personal effort and choice, and because comparable data for the largest possible number of countries were available. When studying a specific country, these conditions can be modified as much as called for by the characteristics of the country. Every country has unique requirements regarding circumstances important to explaining inequality of opportunity. Likewise, a country's level of development may cause certain opportunities to be considered basic, even though they are either not affordable for or of interest to other countries. The study of equality of opportunity has to take into consideration variations among countries in both relevant circumstances and pertinent basic opportunities. The analytical instruments presented in this book permit research into other opportunities, should a country consider them germane.

In addition to the importance of a good or service for a child's development, this book assumes that universality of these basic opportunities is technologically feasible. An additional key implicit consideration is that social consensus has been reached that universality in the provision of these goods or services is a valid social goal. These goals will vary from society to society and with the course of development. In the same way that some Millennium Development Goals, such as universal primary education, are not a useful goal for many middle-income countries because they have already surpassed, or are close to surpassing, that goal, some basic opportunities are not relevant for some countries. Chile serves as an example. Chile has already achieved universal or nearly universal school attendance at ages 10 to 14, and as seen in figure 3.10, is close to reaching this goal for children age 6. Finishing 8th, 10th, and 12th grades on time still needs some additional effort to reach universality, while considerably more work is required to reach universal access to other basic opportunities, such as computer and Internet access. A key point is that such an analysis requires that society consider these to be fundamental tools for

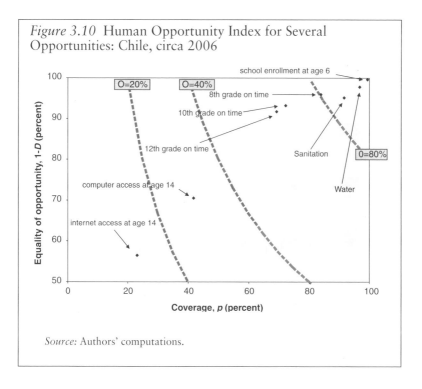

Figure 3.10 Human Opportunity Index for Several Opportunities: Chile, circa 2006

Source: Authors' computations.

learning and for participating in modern society, and basic opportunities for all children, and that society further agree to allocate the resources needed to accomplish universal access. In the course of development, other goods and services will become basic opportunities with the goal of universality. In many countries, educational and health services that foster early childhood development are gradually being considered targets for universality, as are higher levels of secondary education or specific standards in education. Universal access to institutional births and primary health care could also be in the set of basic opportunities to which this framework could be applied.

The Human Opportunity Index and Economic Performance

From a policy point of view, it is useful to know if the Human Opportunity Index correlates with other measures of economic performance and is somehow influenced by them, or if it has its own dynamics. The evidence indicates that the Human Opportunity Index is negatively related to per capita income inequality as measured by the Gini coefficient (table 3.7). The negative correlation coefficient is 0.46 and significant. This provides evidence that an index that measures how unequally opportunities are allocated is measuring something other than income inequality.[10] For example, it might happen that a country, say Chile, has high market returns to education, which induces more able individuals to invest in additional education, and has higher market returns to talent than other economies given an economic structure that encourages innovation; in such a case, market incomes could be more unequal than in other economies, despite the fact that the country has made more progress in providing opportunities to its children. It could also be that current market income inequalities are reflecting past inequality of opportunity. In any case, it is clear that inequality of opportunity is related to, but is different—conceptually and empirically—from inequality of outcomes.

There is a small, negative correlation of the Human Opportunity Index with the poverty headcount, showing that they, too, measure different things. Countries with high monetary poverty incidence may or may not show high inequality of opportunity. This is consistent with the argument that complete measures of poverty should incorporate other indicators of well-being. In contrast, the Human Opportunity Index shows a robust and highly significant association with real GDP, with a correlation of 82 percent.

Moreover, the association between GDP and the Human Opportunity Index seems to build over time. There is a weak, positive association between the index and average GDP growth over a recent five-year period, whereas the association with long-term growth in GDP (proxied

Table 3.7 Correlation between Human Opportunity Index (circa 2005) and Other Economic and Social Indicators

Variable	*Correlation with Human Opportunity Index*
GDP per capita (constant 2000 US$)	0.82***
Gini coefficient	−0.46**
Welfare index[a]	0.81***
Poverty headcount at US$2/day	−0.38*
GDP growth (annual %) (last 5 years)	0.302
GDP growth (annual %) (last 20 years)	0.57*
Expenditure per student, primary (% of GDP per capita)	0.81***
Net migration (% of population), controlling for GDP[b]	0.51*

Source: Authors' calculations using country surveys, World Development Indicators, and governance indicators.

Note:

a. Sen's Welfare Index = $Y \times (1 - G)$, where Y is income per capita and G is the income inequality coefficient.

b. Net migration = (Immigrants − emigrants)/population.

* Correlation is significant at the 10 percent level.

** Correlation is significant at the 5 percent level.

*** Correlation is significant at the 1 percent level.

by the average annual growth of the last 20 years) is stronger: a significant correlation of 0.57, versus a nonsignificant one of 0.30 for the five-year period. One can conclude that increases in the Human Opportunity Index and the universalization of opportunities come as part of the development process. It requires sustained, long-term growth, accompanied by the right combination of policies for the provision of these services.

Other indicators of social performance display interesting relationships. Additional correlations were estimated using expenditures in education, showing, as would be expected, high and significant correlations, suggesting that public expenditures do matter in increasing opportunities. Finally, the correlation with net migration is positive and significant (0.51). This correlation controls for the level of income. Even though causality should be further explored, this suggests that countries with more-equal opportunities receive more migrants—for a given level of income, countries that provide more opportunities, and provide them more equitably, discourage people from leaving and encourage people to come.

Policy Experiences

It is beyond the scope of this book to link the specific results reported in the previous sections to actual policy measures adopted by countries. However, the goal of providing basic services following the principle of equality of opportunity calls for policies focusing on children whose circumstances make them less likely to have access to basic education and housing conditions. Experiences in the provision of basic opportunities show that although there are difficulties, it is possible to target services to children in specific circumstances to avoid inequality of opportunity.

Education in Brazil

Since the mid-1990s, access to basic educational opportunities in Brazil has improved sharply. This exceptional performance is confirmed by the two indicators used in this study: completion of sixth grade on time and school attendance of children 10 to 14 years old. In fact, when the Latin American countries are ranked by their improvement in educational opportunities, Brazil is either the best or the second best in the region (see figure 3.1).

This accelerated progress was not due to exogenous factors but was the result of public policies especially designed for this goal. Traditionally, Brazil has faced two major educational problems: (i) very high repetition rates, mainly at the lower primary educational level; and (ii) learning deficiencies revealed by a high percentage of children with low scores on standardized tests. Reducing repetition rates and improving student performance have been the two main educational challenges for the country. The policies implemented over this period fostered educational opportunities through a well-balanced use of three complementary pillars: (i) improvement in the availability and quality of school inputs, (ii) direct action to reduce repetition, and (c) conditional income transfers to families aimed at giving them effective conditions and incentives to maintain their children's attendance in school.

The first pillar of the country educational policy was an impressive and comprehensive increase in resources for schools. The FUNDEB Fund[11] was designed to ensure a minimum level of resources per student to all municipalities in the country. Additionally, a program was created to provide monetary resources directly to schools, while further federal programs were implemented to ensure basic infrastructure and equipment in schools in poor areas to improve school management and to strengthen teachers' qualifications.[12] Most of these programs were part of FUNDESCOLA,[13] a fund partially financed by the World Bank. In addition, programs devoted to providing school lunches, textbooks, and transportation for children in primary schools were improved and modernized.[14] Together these programs have improved the quality of schools, particularly in poor areas, and as a consequence have fostered learning and contributed to reducing repetition rates. Moreover, by improving the quality of education and the perceived benefits from attending school, the programs provide extra incentive for parents to keep their children in school.

For decades, extremely high repetition rates in Brazil precluded the educational advancement of many children. Moreover, repetition clogged the educational system, limiting the availability of vacancies for children not yet in school. Given the importance of lowering repetition rates in Brazil, several programs were implemented under the second pillar to directly improve grade promotion. Examples are the adoption of automatic grade progression, the organization of schools in cycles combining multiple series (in most states, first and second grades were combined in an initial cycle, reducing repetition at the end of first grade), and the introduction of accelerated classes (to complete more than one grade in a given school year). These modifications in the organization of schools led to important reductions in grade repetition. Hence, they served both to open vacancies for new students and to provide incentives for those already in school to stay.

In addition to these improvements in school resources and school functioning, policies under the third pillar were devoted to giving students from disadvantaged backgrounds better conditions for benefiting from educational opportunities and additional incentives for attending schools. A system of conditional cash transfer programs was introduced to improve equity in educational access. At the federal level, available programs were consolidated and expanded to constitute the Bolsa Família program. These programs were vital to the accelerated educational progress of the country. The income transfers gave families the resources to help keep their children in school and to allow them to effectively benefit from available educational opportunities.

In sum, the unprecedented educational progress in Brazil since the mid-1990s was the result of a well-designed and well-balanced set of public policies. First, several policies were designed and implemented to improve school quality and hence school attractiveness. Second, school rules were modified to foster promotion and to avoid unnecessary retention. These changes opened vacancies, allowing a greater number of children to attend school, and gave extra incentives for parents to keep their children in school. And third, these policies were complemented by a comprehensive conditional cash transfer program, giving poor children better conditions for attending school and for benefiting from education.

Access to Water in Paraguay

Paraguay has the fourth-lowest coverage of improved access to water among the 19 LAC countries considered in this book. However, it registered the greatest increase in the Human Opportunity Index pertaining to water over the 1995–2005 period. As noted in chapter 2, location of residence is the most important circumstance associated with children's inequality of opportunity in access to water in the region. In Paraguay—with the fourth-largest rural population among the countries considered—the coverage rate in rural areas was less than half the urban coverage. This section describes some features of water provision policy in rural Paraguay that may have contributed to this increase in the Human Opportunity Index for water.

The most interesting feature in water provision in rural Paraguay is a participative policy-making process that encompasses the central government, local government, community user groups, associations of user groups, and the private sector. SENASA, the National Environmental Sanitation Service, is the government rural water agency. In rural areas, potable water supply services are provided by water user associations, or *Juntas*, that are created with SENASA's support (Sotomayor et al. 2008). SENASA is responsible for providing technical assistance and coordinating and executing the necessary investments for the provision of potable water service in rural areas. Notably, SENASA is no longer a service provider, but rather a facilitator.

Once the technical studies and designs of a proposed water system are available, SENASA seeks community support for the project. The beneficiaries participate from the beginning of the water project via the community *Junta*. The assets of a water project are immediately delivered to the *Junta* for operation and maintenance. Community meetings, open to all, are held to discuss the pros and cons of a project and the requirement for community inputs such as cash and in-kind contributions. The *Junta* signs a contract with SENASA defining (i) the community contribution in the form of cash, labor, land, or materials; (ii) the portion of funds provided by SENASA that must be repaid and conditions for repayment; (iii) the need to contribute to a fund for the replacement of equipment and instruments; (iv) the responsibility of the community to take over maintenance and operation of the system once completed and the estimated amount this will cost; and (v) the obligation of the *Junta* to create an administration for the operation and maintenance of the system. This approach has operated for several years in hundreds of communities.

The rapid expansion of *Juntas* in Paraguay made possible the construction of new water systems in rural areas. However, the expansion tested the limits of SENASA's capacity for providing follow-up and support services to the *Juntas*. To face this challenge, SENASA developed the model of associations of *Juntas* to support the provision of technical assistance. SENASA is expected to participate directly in supporting *Juntas* only in the event of major problems.

The private sector is increasingly involved in the provision of water in rural Paraguay. SENASA expanded beyond its partnerships with local communities to include small periurban private water providers known as *aguateros,* which operate mainly in the greater metropolitan region of Asunción. *Aguateros* have constructed piped water supply systems with no public financing over the last decades in urban areas. Their systems average about 300 connections, and, according to a 2002 survey, 90 percent of their customers were satisfied with the service they provided (Drees-Gross et al. 2005). *Aguateros* operate where water resources are abundant and they can select customers based on their capacity to pay the full costs of providing the service.

To expand partnerships with the private sector, SENASA piloted the first minimum subsidy bidding in the rural water sector worldwide. Three rounds of bidding were organized in 2002, 2004, and 2005 targeted to *aguateros* expanding their services to rural areas. The subsidy allocation is provided per new connection made in the service area. In the first round of bidding, the subsidy was fixed at US$150 per connection and the selection criterion was the connection cost for the end consumer. The lowest bid was extremely competitive, requiring a community commitment ranging from US$50 to US$67 per connection in four communities (Drees-Gross et al. 2005).

The winning consortium hired poor residents during construction, mostly to dig pipe trenches, paying them with cash and with vouchers to reduce their connection fees. In addition, many residents opted to pay the connection fee in installments at a reasonable interest rate. After the second round of bidding, *aguateros* had to compete on the amount of subsidy they would request from the government. With this system, the bidding risk was shifted from the community to SENASA. Connection cost per household was fixed at US$80, and a predetermined tariff level was established. The maximum connection subsidy was capped to prevent excessive costs to SENASA. *Aguateros* were required to provide service to any household willing to pay the connection charge in a defined service area for 10 years. This subsidy scheme has been a success: communities are satisfied because service has expanded rapidly and their contributions to the costs of expansion have declined—and this innovative partnership takes the initial financial pressure off the government.

The partnership among the government rural water agency, local user groups, associations of user groups, and private firms in the provision of water in rural Paraguay provides an example of how institutional arrangements designed to foster synergies among several stakeholders may prove quite successful in expanding children's access to opportunities.

Electricity in Brazil, Chile, and Honduras

As with water supply, inequality of opportunity in electricity is most often associated with location of residence. The urban-rural divide explains the greatest proportion of inequality of opportunity among children in Latin America, which points to the importance of rural electrification policies. The natural questions are which communities get connected and which criteria are used to select communities.[15] In general, countries use two different criteria. The first is to bring on to the grid communities that will be most cost effective to connect, which means communities closer to the actual grid, with relatively large populations (and hence a sizeable market for power consumption), or with productive potential. The second criterion includes communities according to indications of social need, such as poverty and exclusion, irrespective of small population. The Northeast Rural Poverty Alleviation Project in Brazil, for example, adopted the social-allocation criterion for rural electrification. A combination of both approaches can also be adopted, as in the Chilean Territorial Development Project or in the Rural Infrastructure Project of Honduras, where both poverty incidence and productive potential were considered for including communities in the program.

Two additional factors need to be considered once a town gets electricity service. First, extending the service to the poorest communities should not put undue strain on the utility's finances; otherwise, the service can be discontinued or suffer from regular disruptions. Second, having a connection in town does not guarantee that all households get the service. International experience shows that between 15 and 20 percent of households in communities with more than 10 years of access are without connections. Connection fees and tariffs are other important barriers that prevent poor households from accessing the service. These two factors, if not dealt with properly, could keep poor children from having equal access to electricity, even after the town has access to the service. A policy maker must ensure that promoting connections for the poor is done in a way that keeps a utility company's finances sound.

To accomplish this, mechanisms have been successfully implemented whereby public funding is provided to private firms that competitively bid for these funds (for instance, in the state of Ceará, Brazil). In other cases, public utilities provide the service with subsidized tariffs. However, it is well known that subsidies to electricity providers or consumers go disproportionately to the better-off because the nonpoor spend a larger share of their total budgets on electricity than do the poor. Connection subsidies or connection microloans for either grid or off-grid facilities are more likely to go to the poor and help them access the service.

The experiences illustrate that policies that target poor, distant communities in the rural sector and policies that help poor households get connected will promote the expansion of electricity service among children in a way that maximizes improvement in the Human Opportunity Index.

Chile Grows Up with You: An Integrated Social Protection System for Children from Conception to Pre-Kindergarten

Chile displays the highest Human Opportunity Index among the 19 countries analyzed in this book. It consistently provided high levels of relatively equitably distributed opportunities for education and housing to children during 1996–2006. This good performance is consistent with a process of consensus building around long-term policies that gradually integrate sectoral policies pertaining to children and focus on segments of more vulnerable children.

One of the latest initiatives, started in 2007, is an integrated social protection system for children from conception to pre-kindergarten, called *Chile Crece Contigo* (MIDEPLAN 2007). This system, known as CCC, complements an ambitious conditional cash transfer program called *Chile Solidario*. It is a product of the interministerial committee that attempted to operationalize the proposals of a presidential advisory committee. This advisory committee comprises 14 interdisciplinary experts on medicine, economics, sociology, psychology, and public policy and is committed to children's welfare and opportunities. To generate inputs to their work, the advisory committee conducted a wide consultation process. CCC is an initiative that advances the *National Policy toward Children and Adolescence 2001–2010*, established in 2000. This national policy has undergone a national consultation process involving governmental and nongovernmental institutions. The Policy draws on the International Convention on Children's Rights, ratified by Chile in 1990.

KEY FEATURES OF *CHILE CRECE CONTIGO*
The main objective of the system is to equalize opportunities. It is recognized that currently in Chile the family socioeconomic background at birth is one of the best predictors of adults' socioeconomic levels. Supporting people since the beginning of their life is in line with the Chilean Government's priority to reduce inequality gaps currently observed in the country (MIDEPLAN 2007).

Chile Crece Contigo attempts to provide children with universal access to basic services to ensure adequate development at the first stage of their life cycle. Before the age of 4, basic skills such as language, social ability, emotional control, and cognitive capabilities are acquired. The first six years of life are the most important in a person's development process.

Given the multidimensionality of early childhood development, a wide and well-coordinated network of public initiatives is needed. The system aims at increasing coordination and catalyzing synergies for supporting each child according to his or her specific needs. Early detection of child developmental challenges as well as identification of biological, psychological, and social risk factors is needed to support effective intervention to equalize opportunities. This requires timely, simultaneous, and coordinated support of several initiatives focusing on children. Effective coordination requires good management systems at the local level, a priority of CCC.

This social protection system supports all children according to their specific needs through four lines of action: (i) providing targeted support for children of households at the bottom 40 percent of income distribution or with other special vulnerability conditions, (ii) monitoring child development from the first prenatal checkup to enrollment in school, (iii) making educational programs available to all citizens, and (iv) improving maternity and paternity laws.

For children from households at the bottom 40 percent of income distribution that do not belong to the contributory social security system, CCC guarantees automatic access to a family subsidy for all pregnant women and children from birth to age 18. By 2010, CCC will make available for free, quality child care to all children whose parents work, are students, or seeking work. CCC facilitates the access of families in this population segment to current public initiatives such as the social protection program *Chile Solidario*, accelerated study programs, labor market insertion support, housing improvement programs, mental health care programs, domestic violence prevention programs, legal assistance, and others (MIDEPLAN 2007).

The CCC system ensures that each pregnant woman has access to all relevant information any parent and family member should be aware of regarding pregnancy and childbirth, as well as relevant Labor laws. The CCC system organizes workshops on childbirth and child care and promotes active parenting. It also organizes visits by health professionals to households with either pregnant women with any identified risk factor or children with some developmental risk factors. The CCC system focuses on early detection of children with any developmental lag, emphasizing children up to two years old. Once identified, the children are supported accordingly to overcome this lag.

Educational programs aimed to all citizens are provided on subjects such as children's development of physical, cognitive, and social skills at different stages of their life cycle. These educational programs use a variety of channels such as TV, radio, and Web sites (e.g., www.crececontigo.cl). In addition, the system is promoting several improvements of maternity and paternity laws, such as (i) automatic transfer to postbirth any unused prebirth leave in case of early delivery; (b) right of working women to breastfeed their children, regardless of whether there is a child care center in their workplace; and (c) extension of maternity leave of to up to one year in case of birth of a child with disability.

The management of the CCC system emphasizes local delivery of public services and, as a result, CCC has developed a territorial network of system management. It supports municipalities' efforts to strengthen their management capabilities, maintains an online information system to monitor children's development, and certifies the quality of service providers.

Further Policy Considerations

This book focuses on the measurement of the equality of distribution of basic opportunities and thus provides a tool to facilitate benchmarking and assess progress. It does not dwell on how to make progress. But a better understanding of progress and of patterns of inequality are critical for policy design. Historical conditions, ethnic fragmentation, and harsh geography may all be reasons why certain groups have fewer opportunities than others, and may explain the patterns observed in this report. Sokoloff and Engerman (2000), for instance, posit that colonial heritage precluded quick growth of primary education in Latin American until the mid-20th century, when national governments started expanding the service. In contrast, in North America, primary education was funded and organized at the local level and universality became a goal in the 19th century. Alesina and Easterly (1999) showed that local investment in public goods, including education, is smaller in communities with higher ethnic fragmentation. Geography also has a large role in explaining differences in access to public goods (see Escobal and Torero [2004] for an example for Peru).

The importance of these factors will vary across countries. The improvements observed during the last decades, and as reported here since the mid-1990s, show that countries are increasing the level and improving the distribution of resources, and that a process of equalization of opportunities is starting to level out differences. But differences persist, and understanding why certain groups' interests have not been properly represented politically in the allocation of resource is critical to preventing their children from receiving fewer opportunities.

An important consideration for equality of opportunity is the way in which countries organize themselves for effective provision of key services. That was the topic of *World Development Report 2004: Making Services Work for Poor People* (World Bank 2003). How effective a society is in organizing itself to provide services equitably will depend on the availability of the right technology, resources, and administrative capabilities at different government levels, as well as on political economy considerations. Countries organize themselves very differently to provide these goods and services. Even if the rich can find private alternatives, for the poor the provision of public goods is critical for access to basic opportunities.

Public goods provision is, however, not necessarily equal to public sector provision. As discussed by Besley and Ghatak (2006), some sort of government intervention might be critical because the private sector by itself will not provide the optimal level of a public good—but this does not imply direct public sector involvement in the activity itself. The design of a system to effectively provide public goods, including an adequate regulatory framework, could entail a partnership between the public sector and the private sector, as well as the involvement of a "third sector" comprising nongovernmental organizations and community organizations. Regardless of the arrangement and roles of the different sectors, the incentive structure the government puts in place, and the accountability mechanisms for providers, has to be defined to ensure that no group is discriminated against and that the poor are adequately served.[16] In that regard, decentralization can contribute to the effectiveness of policies aimed at improving equality of opportunities, because it can increase the accountability of service providers to citizens and it can increase the decision-making capabilities of local authorities with better information.

The geographical consideration merits an additional discussion. As seen above, for basic opportunities such as water, sanitation, and electricity, the geographical dimension is a critical aspect of inequality of opportunity in many countries in the region. Hence, equalization of opportunities as a policy objective is also at the heart of countries' interest in dealing with spatial variations in welfare—the topic of the *World Development Report 2009* (WDR). To address spatial disparities, that report discusses the use of spatially connective policies (roads and telecommunications, for example) and spatially focused policies (local investment incentives, for example), depending on the characteristics of the country. However, a key pillar of a development strategy aimed at reducing spatial disparities is what the 2009 WDR calls *spatially blind policies*. A key trait of many policies in this group is a focus on providing portable human capital, such as health and education, that people will carry with them whenever economic incentives and opportunities promote their relocation from backward to leading areas. This set of policies readily relates to the emphasis on equality of opportunity discussed in this book. A key message of the WDR is that it is economically inefficient for governments to try to ensure that all economic opportunities are equalized throughout a country; the economic map of a country can and should be heterogeneous because the viability or profitability of economic activities will depend on market conditions; but, critically for policy and for this book, the basic opportunities map should look homogeneous. For instance, job opportunities cannot be equal in every location in a country, but there should be equal opportunity in access to potable water and sanitation in every location in a country— itself a tall order. A government should aim to implement policies that guarantee that a child's birthplace does not have an impact on his or her chances to succeed in life.

One program in this category is the conditional cash transfers that have been popular and highly successful in a number of countries. In Brazil, Bolsa Família, discussed above, improved education and health outcomes. Transfers given in exchange for school attendance and health checks not only provide direct assistance through cash, but also ensure that children improve their portable human capital and opportunities in the future. These programs have been subject to rigorous evaluation, and experiences like Bolsa Família in Brazil, Oportunidades in Mexico (Behrman, Sengupta, and Todd 2005), Familias en Accion in Colombia (Attanasio, Fitzsimons, and Gomez 2005) and Bono de Desarollo Humano in Ecuador (Schady and Araujo 2008) show that these inteventions have improved educational attainment and, in some cases, nutritional status among poor children. Any policy aimed at improving children's access to basic services will fall into this category.

Future Developments for the Human Opportunity Index

A limited number of circumstances were selected for this regional study's first description of inequality of opportunity for children. A more complete set of circumstances needs to be developed to build a more thorough understanding of the problem. For instance, race and ethnic characteristics are likely to be important circumstances that influence the probability of accessing some basic opportunities. However, because of lack of comparable data, these circumstances have not been taken into consideration here. Similarly, other forms of location differences, such as state, municipality, or even neighborhood, can be important for diagnosing the source of inequality of opportunity. If the analysis is restricted to urban areas, dropping the circumstance of location of residence, more countries (Argentina and Uruguay) can be included in the analysis over time (Barros et al. 2008).

The number and choice of basic opportunities can also be modified. Only variables related to two basic dimensions of opportunity (education and housing conditions) are included here, mostly because of the availability of relatively comparable information from different household surveys for a large number of countries. It is foreseeable that access to health care and other basic opportunities, such as civil franchise, need to be included in future versions of the index, if comparable and accessible data become available. For instance, data on nutritional indicators for children, such as body weight or body-mass index, as well as vaccination records, would be informative, as would be variables that approximate the quality and level of access to health infrastructure, such as likelihood of institutional birth. Preschool attendance or other interventions to foster early childhood development would enhance the educational dimension. For civil franchise, one could seek data on children's possession of birth certificates, school grade records, identification documents, and the like. The housing dimension could benefit from data on waste disposal.

Special efforts to collect more detailed data on the situation of children are needed for promoting an equal opportunity agenda. The region has advanced in the collection of statistics but there is room for improvement, especially with regard to children and youth.

The Human Opportunity Index presented in this and the preceding chapter can be enhanced in several ways. The current version provides a first look at the situation of the equal opportunity principle among children in the region. Future versions of the index can provide a more thorough description of the problem by considering more circumstances and basic opportunities to permit a better understanding of the problem and more effective policy recommendations.

Summary

The Human Opportunity Index can serve as a useful diagnostic tool for policy analysis. Its flexibility for application to different circumstances, opportunities, and population groups makes it a suitable point of reference for gauging advances in the provision of equal opportunity for all. The index makes it possible to compute the origin of changes in equality of opportunity, tracing its sources to expansions in coverage and reductions in inequality. It can also identify the circumstances that are the main barriers to equality of opportunity. The application of these properties to multiple population groups and diverse basic opportunities can provide a road map for policy makers devising the expansion of basic opportunities as part of the development process.

Equalization of opportunity is part of the development process. Empirically, the Human Opportunity Index is strongly associated with GDP and with long-term growth. In a complex interaction, growth generates the resources to expand basic opportunities, and basic opportunities are critical for individual development—to build human capital and for long-term growth. Latin America as a whole has made progress since the mid-1990s toward the objective of providing more opportunities and disproportionally increasing the access of disadvantaged groups, thus reducing the role of exogenous circumstances like location, gender, and family background. But coverage in most cases is far from universal, and location, gender, and family background still matter and have a substantive role in precluding many children from access to opportunities. Despite progress in the region, the playing field is far from level. According to the analysis presented here, the urban-rural divide is still critical in many respects, and it is the most important circumstance in explaining inequality of opportunities in access to water, sanitation, and electricity. The basic opportunity map of the countries is very heterogeneous.

Despite tremendous progress in access to opportunity in education, family background is still a strong factor that influences children's possibilities of accessing high-quality primary education, or even attending early secondary school; the root causes of low intergenerational mobility are still powerful. In fact, the analysis of educational opportunities reported here show that gender and parent's education are the main sources of inequality in school attendance for children ages 10–14, while parent's education and income are the major sources of inequality in access to quality primary education, as proxied by completing sixth grade on time.

But progress in opportunities in the region is encouraging. The improvements observed in basic opportunities in Latin America have been the result of expansions in coverage in all cases. However, countries' patterns of increases in coverage differ; in some cases, expansion has entailed large reductions in inequality of opportunity, whereas in others inequality reduction has been modest. There are some policy experiences—SENASA for water in Paraguay, the Chilean Territorial Development Project for electricity, and educational policies in Brazil—that show that coverage can be expanded while emphasizing distributive considerations. Cash transfer programs that provide portable human capital have also been critical to progress in countries such as Brazil and Mexico.

The reviewed policy initiatives show that the seeds to universalize opportunity are there. Latin America—so unequal in outcomes—is moving toward less inequality of opportunity.

Notes

1. Alternatively, instead of imagining that all other circumstances are being held constant, one may imagine that the impact of all other circunstances has been eliminated. Hence, all remaining variation in access to the service would be exclusively related to the selected circumstance. For more methodological details, see Barros, Molinas, and Saavedra (2008).

2. In several LAC countries, primary school dropout is a problem mainly among boys, particularly in countries of the Caribbean.

3. This analysis does not address issues of relative educational quality in rural and urban areas.

4. Similar tables to table 3.4 for school attendance for ages 10–14, access to water, and access to electricity are presented in the appendix. See tables A.4–A.6.

5. The data for figure 3.1 are presented in table A.7 in the appendix.

6. The Brazilian and Mexican surveys are 10 years apart whereas the Guatemalan surveys are only 6 years apart (see table 2.1), but their different performance is not proportionate to the different elapsed periods. (See also figure 3.1a.)

7. The figure has a nonfeasible area to the right of the diagonal defined by $x = y$ (shaded triangle). This is because inequality of distribution depends on the extent of coverage. In the case of full coverage, there is no inequality of distribution so O equals 1 (that is, both coverage and equality of distribution equal 1). But if, for instance, coverage equals 80 percent, the maximum possible inequality in distribution (as measured by D) is 20 percent, so equality ranges from 80 percent to 100 percent. For a formal proof, see Barros, Molinas, and Saavedra (2008).

8. The initial situation in each country should also be taken into account. El Salvador started with an inequality level of 25 percent, whereas Paraguay started with only 15 percent. In relative terms, the reduction of inequality was larger in El Salvador than in Paraguay.

9. A table with the data for figure 3.4 is presented in table A.8 in the appendix.

10. Inequality of opportunity, the D-index, is positively related to the Gini coefficient, as expected, but the correlation is low: between 0.21 for education and 0.30 for water and sanitation.

11. Fundo de Manutenção e Desenvolvimento da Educação Básica e de Valorização dos Profissionais da Educação.

12. Programa Dinheiro Direto na Escola provides monetary resources directly to schools. Basic infrastructure and equipment are provided under Programa de Adequação do Prédio Escolar and Programa de Melhoria da Qualidade do Equipamento Escolar. School management is improved under Plano de Desenvolvimento da Escola. Teachers' qualifications are strengthened under Pro-Formação and Programa de Gestão e Aprendizagem Escolar.

13. Fundo de Fortalecimento da Escola.

14. Lunches are provided under Fundo de Fortalecimento da Escola, textbooks under Programa Nacional do Livro Didático, and transportation under Programa Nacional de Apoio ao Transporte Escolar.

15. This section is based on World Bank Independent Evaluation Group (2008).

16. A case in point is that of equity effects of privatization of utilities in Latin America during the 1990s. The evidence is mixed. Mackenzie and Mookherjee (2003) found some positive effects in access and service quality among the poor, while Estache at al. (2001) showed positive effects in access rates to electricity services among the poor in Chile. However, there is evidence also of a reduction in the level of regional cross-subsidies in water concessions in Argentina, harming rural and smaller towns (Campos et al. 2003).

References

Alesina, Alberto, & Reza Baqir, and William Easterly. 1999. "Public Goods and Ethnic Divisions." Policy Research Working Paper Series 2108, World Bank, Washington, DC.

Attanasio, Orazio, Emla Fitzsimons, and Ana Gomez. 2005. "The Impact of a Conditional Education Subsidy on School Enrolment in Colombia." Centre for the Evaluation of Development Policies, The Institute for Fiscal Studies, London.

Barros, R., S. Freije, J. Molinas, and J. Saavedra. 2008. "Inequality of Opportuniy for Children in Urban Latin America and the Caribbean." Unpublished, World Bank, Washington, DC. www.worldbank.org/lacopportunity.

Barros, R., J. Molinas, and J. Saavedra. 2008. "Measuring Inequality of Opportunities for Children." Unpublished, World Bank, Washington, DC. www.world bank.org/lacopportunity.

Behrman, J., P. Sengupta, and P. Todd. 2005. "Progressing through Progresa: An Impact Assessment of a School Subsidy Experiment in Mexico." *Economic Development and Cultural Change* 54 (1): 237–75.

Besley, Timothy, and Maitreesh Ghatak. 2006. "Public Goods and Economic Development." In *Understanding Poverty*, ed. A. Banerjee, R. Benabou, and D. Mookherjee. New York: Oxford University Press.

Campos, Javier, Antonio Estache, Noelia Martin, and Lourdes Trujillo. 2003. "Macroeconomic Effects of Private Sector Participation in Infrastructure." In *The Limits of Stabilization*, ed. William Easterly and Luis Servén,. Washington, DC: World Bank and Stanford Social Sciences, an imprint of Stanford University Press.

Demombynes, G., and G. De Leon. 2008. "Schools in Haiti: Trends and Determinants 1995–2005." Unpublished, World Bank, Washington, DC.

Drees-Gross, F., J. Schwartz, M. A. Sotomayor, and A. Bakalian. 2005. "Output-Based Aid in Water: Lessons in Implementation from a Pilot in Paraguay." *OBApproaches*, Note Number 07, World Bank, Washington, DC.

Escobal, Javier, and Máximo Torero. 2003. "Adverse Geography and Differences in Welfare in Peru." United Nations University, World Institute for Development Economics Research, Helsinki, Discussion Paper 2003/73.

Estache, Antonio, Andrés Gómez-Lobo, and Danny Leipziger. 2001. "Utilities Privatization and the Poor: Lessons and Evidence from Latin America." *World Development* 29(7): 1179–98.

McKenzie, David, and Dilip Mookherjee. 2003. "Distributive Impact of Privatization in Latin America: An Overview of Evidence from Four Countries." *Economia* 3(2): 161–218.

MIDEPLAN. 2007. "Chile crece contigo: Sistema de Proteccion Integral a la Primera Infancia." Ministerio de Planificacion: Secretaria Ejecutiva de Proteccion Social. http://www.crececontigo.cl/upfiles/userfiles/file/Documento_Chile_Crece_Contigo.pdf.

Schady, Norbert, and Maria Caridad Araujo. 2008. "Cash Transfers, Conditions, and School Enrollment in Ecuador." *Economía* 8 (2): 43–70.

Sokoloff, Kenneth L., and Stanley L. Engerman. 2000. "History Lessons: Institutions, Factor Endowments, and Paths of Development in the New World." *Journal of Economic Perspectives* 14 (3): 217–32.

Sotomayor, M. A., et al. 2008. "Paraguay: Fifth Rural Water Supply and Sanitation Draft Project Appraisal Document." Unpublished, World Bank, Washington, DC.

World Bank. 2003. *World Development Report 2004: Making Services Work for Poor People*. Washington, DC: World Bank.

World Bank Independent Evaluation Group. 2008. *The Welfare Impact of Rural Electrification: A Reassessment of the Costs and Benefits. An IEG Impact Evaluation*. Washington, DC: World Bank.

4

Inequality of Economic Opportunity in Seven Latin American Countries

This chapter uses a "top-down" approach that decomposes total outcome inequality into two components, one resulting from circumstances beyond the control of the individual, and a residual component that captures rewards to effort as well as luck. The first component can be presented as an indicator of the level of inequality of opportunity, a measure of the *opportunity share of overall inequality*. This is a "consequential" approach, in which inequality of opportunity is defined by the importance of unequal outcomes across groups defined by circumstances. This decomposition is applied to income, consumption, and labor earnings. Chapter 5 uses the same methodology to investigate educational achievement.

Measuring Inequality of Economic Opportunity

To measure inequality of opportunity for a certain outcome, total inequality in the outcome can be decomposed into two parts: one resulting from circumstances beyond individual control and a second part resulting from unequal individual effort and luck.[1] Unequal outcomes resulting from circumstances are generally considered socially unacceptable or, at the very least, undesirable. This chapter reports the results of this decomposition of unequal outcomes for three different indicators of economic welfare: labor earnings, household income per capita, and household consumption expenditure per capita. The rationale for using three variables is to capture the differentiated impacts they have on household welfare and, thereby, gain a more complete understanding of inequality of opportunity.[2]

Methodology

The approach is conceptually simple. First, six variables related to circumstances exogenous to the individual were identified from the most comprehensive data sets available: gender, race or ethnicity, birthplace, the educational attainment of the mother, the educational attainment of the father, and the main occupation of the father. These variables are discussed in more detail below. Then the sample was partitioned (in each country) into groups or "cells," such that all individuals in any given cell have exactly the same combination of circumstances. The resulting subgroups are known in the literature as "types." These cells are then compared with one another. The difference in outcomes between cells can be attributed to inequality of opportunity, while the differences within cells can be considered the result of effort or luck.

Next, an inequality measure was chosen that satisfied two properties:

- It had to be *decomposable*, in the sense that the value of the index for some population is exactly equal to the sum of the value of the index across types (that is, computed over group means) and the (appropriately aggregated) value of the index within all types.
- It had to be *path independent*, in the sense that the decomposition must yield the same result whether the direct or the residual approaches discussed above were used. In other words, the decomposition is invariant on whether within-group inequality is eliminated first and the between-group component computed second, or the reverse.

There is a single index that satisfies both of these requirements: the mean log deviation, or Theil-L index.[3] Because this measure happens to be a member of the generalized entropy class of measures, when its parameter goes to zero, it is also known as E(0). The decomposition can change for other generalized entropy inequality measures that are path-*dependent*, but the discussion in this chapter is confined to E(0).

Caveats

Two potential caveats with estimation should be mentioned. First, finely partitioning the sample into many cells can lead to sample-size restrictions common to most nonparametric methods. Even being parsimonious in subdividing the sample by parental education or occupation, or birthplace, the partition still results in 216 cells. This leads to a nontrivial number of cells with a small number of observations, leading to large sampling variances in mean estimation. This can create an upward bias in the estimate of between-group inequality and decrease precision. To address this problem, the nonparametric approach was complemented with a parametric estimation procedure proposed by Bourguignon, Ferreira, and Menéndez (2007). Both sets of results are reported here. The main conclusion is that with the exception of Mexico, the parametric and nonparametric estimation results are very close, which reinforces confidence in the estimates.

The second caveat is that although the six variables employed in this chapter are a richer set of circumstances than those used in any previous study known to the authors, it is still possible to think of other relevant variables that are not observed. A "true" measure of inequality of opportunity would require using all relevant circumstance variables to partition the population into types. But this is, of course, extremely unlikely to be feasible in practice for any conceivable data set, and it is certainly impossible for the seven countries examined here. The empirical estimates defined in this chapter—regardless of whether parametric—should therefore be interpreted as lower-bound estimates of inequality of opportunity; including any additional circumstances would cause each cell to be further subdivided. This cannot lower the between-group inequality share and, unless the additional element is orthogonal to the measure of advantage, will raise it. Similarly, in the parametric case, adding another independent circumstance variable to the right-hand side of the reduced-form regression must reduce the variance of the residual and increase the variance of observed circumstances.[4]

A specific—and controversial—example of a circumstance omitted from the set of variables is innate talent. To the extent that genetic or otherwise predetermined differences in skill, strength, and physical and intellectual capacity are correlated with observed circumstance variables (such as family background), these differences are captured by our lower-bound measure of inequality of opportunity. But most variance in innate talent is likely to be uncorrelated with observed characteristics such as parental education, race, or gender and hence is not captured by this decomposition. While views differ on whether talent should be treated as a circumstance, as noted above, the resulting decomposition without including it can be considered a lower-bound estimate of inequality of opportunity related to circumstances. Hence, whichever side of the debate one is on, it can be assumed that including talent as a variable would increase the resulting inequality of opportunity.

Uses for Policy

The decomposition generates two different kinds of output that may be useful to policy makers. The first, of course, is simply a lower-bound measure of the degree of inequality of opportunity in a society. It is not a perfect measure—it provides an assessment of the inequality associated with a set of only six observed circumstances. But it is informative, and can be presented either as an indicator of the *level of inequality of opportunity*, or as a measure of the *opportunity share of overall inequality*. Both numbers are discussed below for the seven countries for which data were available. If estimated repeatedly over time, these indicators can provide governments and other social actors with a useful diagnostic of the way in which the distribution of opportunity is evolving in their countries.

This chapter also reports on a second output from the decomposition, which may be even more useful for policy making. Because the decomposition relies on the levels of mean advantage (mean income, for example) for each group, it is possible to rank all types (or circumstance groups), from least to most advantaged—an opportunity profile of the population. Such a profile can be used to focus on the bottom of the distribution of advantage, but because types vary widely in population share, comparing the single most-disadvantaged type across countries is less than ideal. Instead, the chapter reports advantage levels for the bottom types accounting for 10 percent of the population in each country. This minimum level of advantage is informative because, like an income-based poverty measure, it contains information on both the level and distribution of advantage. It is, in fact, the concept by which Roemer (2006) suggested that the rate of economic development should be measured.[5] Policy makers can learn much about who has the fewest opportunities in their countries merely by looking at the circumstance types included. The set of circumstances for groups with the fewest opportunities constitutes an opportunity-deprivation profile that identifies those groups least able to share in national prosperity, as defined by predetermined characteristics they inherited through no fault of their own.

The Data

This study was based on data from seven nationally representative household surveys: the Brazilian Pesquisa Nacional por Amostra de Domicílios (PNAD) 1996; the Colombian Encuesta de Calidad de Vida (ECV) 2003; the Ecuadorian Encuesta Condiciones de Vida (ECV) 2006; the Guatemalan Encuesta Nacional sobre Condiciones de Vida (ENCOVI) 2000; the Mexican Encuesta Nacional sobre Niveles de Vida de los Hogares (MxFLS) 2002; the Panamanian Encuesta de Niveles de Vida (ENV) 2003; and the Peruvian Encuesta Nacional de Hogares (ENAHO) 2001.[6]

These surveys afford the most internationally comparable set of indicators on which to base the estimates of inequality of opportunity for the region. Together, these surveys are representative of more than half of the Latin American population. In all countries, the sample is restricted to individuals ages 30 to 49, which encompasses the cohorts with the highest proportion of employed persons.[7] Sample sizes for each survey, both before and after excluding observations with missing data, are reported in table 4.1.

The surveys contain information on a common set of circumstances: (i) three variables related to family background—father's and mother's

Table 4.1 Survey Characteristics

Survey information	Brazil	Colombia	Ecuador	Guatemala	Mexico	Panama	Peru
Survey and year Sample selection criteria	PNAD 1996 age 30–49 and head or spouse	ECV 2003 age 30–49	ECV 2006 age 30–49	ENCOVI 2000 age 30–49	MxFLS 2002 age 30–49	ENV 2003 age 30–49	ENAHO 2001 age 30–49 and head or spouse
Original sample size	85,692	22,517	12,650	6,956	8,631	6,339	13,947
Observations with both earnings and circumstance data	50,560	16,575	9,671	4,661	4,478	4,127	9,830
Share of original sample	0.590	0.736	0.765	0.670	0.519	0.644	0.704
Observations with income and/or consumption and circumstance data	71,688	22,436	12,643	6,865	6,726	5,653	13,649
Share of original sample	0.837	0.996	0.999	0.984	0.779	0.889	0.979

Source: Authors' compilation.

education and father's occupation during respondent's childhood; (ii) ethnicity (or race); and (iii) birthplace (or type of area of birth). The only exception is that the father's occupation variable is missing for Colombia and Peru. The results in this chapter explicitly note the implications of this exception by comparing the country rankings with those in an alternative set of decompositions that ignore the father's occupation variable for all countries.

Gender is also used as a circumstance variable in the analysis of earnings. Parental education variables are coded into three categories: (i) no education (or unknown); (ii) primary (incomplete or complete, depending on the country), and (iii) complete primary or secondary (or higher). Father's occupation is recoded into two categories: agricultural workers and others. Ethnicity (coded in two categories) is captured either by self-reported ethnicity or by the ability to speak an indigenous language. Birthplace is coded in three broad regions (one being generally the capital area), but is captured by the type of area (urban or rural) for Panama.[8]

The number of categories for each circumstance variable was reduced to no more than three to restrict the number of circumstance-group cells with no or very few observations. This step is important because the nonparametric analysis relies on the quality of the estimates for conditional means in these cells, and their sampling variation may be very high for cells containing few observations. As indicated earlier, that may artificially increase the estimated between-group inequality, thus inducing an overestimation of inequality of opportunity.

Turning to the advantage variables, labor earnings are measured on an individual basis as monthly earnings from all occupations, including the monetary value of various in-kind payments. There are, however, some methodological differences across surveys that may affect comparability. The main example is differences in the reference period for the earnings of self-employed workers, which is the month in Brazil, Colombia, and Peru; a period that depends on the frequency of payments in Panama; and the year elsewhere.

Family income and consumption are measured using per capita household income (from all sources) and per capita aggregate household consumption, respectively. Aggregates for family income (generally constructed by survey providers) are computed as the sum of all household members' individual incomes, and include all labor earnings as well as any other income from assets, pensions, and transfers. The reference period for other incomes again differs somewhat across surveys. Incomes from family (agricultural or nonagricultural) businesses are included.

Consumption expenditure data are available for six of the seven countries; Brazil is the exception. The reference period is the year, but some expenditure is measured on a weekly or monthly basis. Consumption aggregates do differ across surveys in some respects. In particular, income and consumption are adjusted for differences in the local cost of living in most Living Standard Measurement Study (LSMS) data sets (Ecuador, Guatemala, and Panama, but not Colombia) and in the Peruvian ENAHO. LSMS surveys (Colombia, Ecuador, Guatemala, and Panama) and the Peruvian ENAHO also include imputed rents for owner-occupied housing in both consumption and income aggregates, whereas the MxFLS and the PNAD do not.

Inequality of Opportunity for Earnings

Latin America is well known for having one of the highest levels of earnings inequality in the world, with mean log deviations (Theil indexes in parentheses) ranging from the lowest level of 0.572 (0.485) in Panama to the most unequal score of 0.786 (0.790) in Guatemala.[9] Of this inequality, the data and the parametric and nonparametric techniques described above find that between one-fifth and one-third can be explained by the unequal opportunity associated with six circumstance characteristics: gender, ethnicity, parental education levels, father's occupation, and birthplace (figure 4.1).[10]

This decomposition of earnings inequality generates two closely related measures of inequality of opportunity. One is simply the level of inequality attributable to circumstances—that is, the height of the bottom (parametric) or bottom plus middle (nonparametric) portions of the bars in figure 4.1. The nonparametric level estimates for earnings range from a mean log deviation of 0.123 in Colombia to 0.230 in Guatemala.[11]

Another measure is the share of the total area accounted for by the black and dark gray areas—earnings inequality that is accounted for by these six circumstances. For this sample of countries, the share measure of (nonparametrically estimated) inequality of opportunity is Brazil (35 percent), Guatemala (29 percent), Ecuador (26 percent), Panama (25 percent), Mexico (23 percent), Peru (21 percent), and Colombia (20 percent). The differences between Guatemala, Mexico, Ecuador, and Panama are statistically insignificant.[12]

Opportunity shares are systematically, but not substantially, lower for the parametric estimates in all countries. The difference is only 3 percent (and statistically insignificant) for Brazil. In the other countries the differences are larger but either borderline significant or insignificant at the 5 percent confidence level. This is consistent with the caveat (discussed above) that the large sampling variance within cells with few observations may cause an upward bias in the nonparametric estimates.[13]

Of interest is the fact that a ranking of the countries by the level of inequality of opportunity is strikingly different from the overall earnings-inequality ranking. In particular, Brazil, which has only the fifth highest earnings inequality, has the second highest level of inequality of opportunity and by far the largest opportunity share of that inequality (refer to table 4.5).

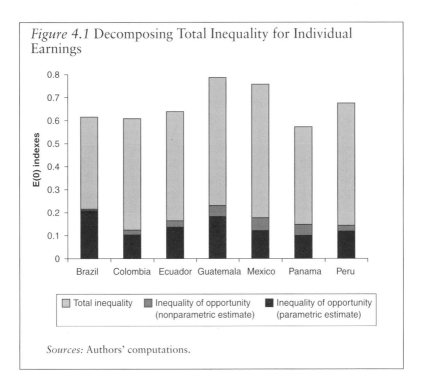

Figure 4.1 Decomposing Total Inequality for Individual Earnings

Sources: Authors' computations.

Such rerankings suggest that inequality of opportunity and inequality of outcomes really do measure different aspects of distribution in a society.

Estimates for the partial share of earnings inequality accounted for by each circumstance variable indicate that family background variables are systematically most important (figure 4.2).[14] This is particularly true for mother's education, which is associated with between 9 percent and 12 percent of total inequality. The relative shares of inequality associated with ethnicity and birthplace vary between countries, with ethnicity being more important in Mexico and Brazil (explaining between 5 percent and 7 percent of inequality) and the birthplace having more effect in Brazil, Mexico, Panama, and Peru (explaining 4–6 percent of inequality). Inequality of opportunity related to gender ranges from a low of 0–1 percent in Colombia and Panama to a high of 5 percent in Guatemala. In Brazil, Ecuador, and Mexico, gender accounts for 3–4 percent of overall inequality.

As elsewhere in this book, this section compares measures of inequality of opportunity across countries for a single time. But what about the dynamics? Is inequality of opportunity stable or volatile? Does it move in parallel with overall outcome inequality, or independently? While repeated cross-sections with the required information for Latin America are hard to find, one study, Cogneau and Gignoux (Forthcoming), used four special

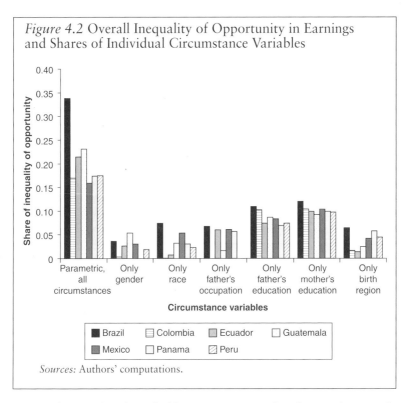

Figure 4.2 Overall Inequality of Opportunity in Earnings and Shares of Individual Circumstance Variables

Sources: Authors' computations.

waves of a Brazilian household survey over two decades to ask precisely these questions (box 4.1).

Inequality of Opportunity for Household Income and Consumption

Important as earnings may be as an indicator of economic advantage, any discussion of economic opportunity must also consider the distribution of household welfare, as measured by income or consumption, or both, per capita. Overall household income inequality is generally very high in this sample of countries (table 4.2). In all six countries for which consumption data are available, consumption inequality is considerably lower than either income or earnings inequality.[15] This is consistent with the widely accepted view that income and earnings are not as accurately measured as consumption expenditures (particularly in standard income surveys of self-employed farmers or informal sector workers), and that consumption is likely to be closer than current income to permanent income (provided households have access to some consumption-smoothing mechanisms).[16]

Box 4.1 Inequality of Opportunity Dynamics: Earnings in Brazil, 1976–96

How does inequality of opportunity vary over time, as structural and macroeconomic factors change? Do inequality of opportunity and outcome inequality follow parallel or divergent trends? What effect does an expansion in schooling have on changes in economic opportunities? These were questions addressed by Cogneau and Gignoux (Forthcoming) in their study of the evolution of inequality of opportunity in the distribution of earnings in Brazil between 1976 and 1996.

In 1976, 1982, 1988, and 1996, in addition to the regular information on birthplace and ethnicity, the Brazilian National Household Surveys (PNAD) also asked questions on family background. Using these samples (restricted to employed men between 40 and 49 years old), Cogneau and Gignoux decomposed total earnings inequality into a share attributable to four predetermined circumstances and a residual component. These decompositions are very similar to those presented in this book.

Overall, levels of inequality and inequality of opportunity in earnings displayed a similar historical path, including a peak in the late 1980s at the apex of hyperinflation and a subsequent decline (see table below). Nevertheless, overall inequality rose slightly from the beginning to the

Inequality of opportunity in earnings over two decades in Brazil

	1976		1982	
Overall inequality				
Gini index	0.570	(0.009)	0.585*	(0.004)
Theil index	0.625	(0.027)	0.687	(0.017)
Inequality of opportunity				
Theil index with 9 groups	0.212	(0.021)	0.222	(0.009)
Share of overall inequality	0.339		0.323	
Theil index with 128 groups	0.254	(0.023)		
Share of overall inequality	0.406			

Source: PNAD surveys, *Instituto Brasileiro de Geografica e Estatistica.*

Note: Inequality of opportunity indexes calculated for men ages 40 to 49, based on either 9 or 128 groups of social origins constructed from four variables regarding the father's level of education (four categories), the father's occupation (four), birthplace (four), and color (two). The 128-group categorization is not available in 1982 because no information on birthplace was collected.

* Indicates significance at 5 percent compared with the previous year; bootstrapped standard errors, obtained using 100 replications, in parentheses.

end of the period, while inequality of opportunity posted a slight drop. Even though indexes of inequality of opportunity at the end of the period (1996) are not significantly different from the indexes at the beginning of the period (1976), they decline slightly, and significantly, from 1982 and 1988 to 1996. Because overall earnings inequality rose over the period, even though the levels of inequality of opportunity were largely stable, the inequality-of-opportunity share in total inequality fell from the mid-1970s to the mid-1990s.

Unequal access to education was one of the main channels explaining the effects of circumstances such as family background on labor market outcomes. Moreover, educational policies may be the main public intervention for fostering equal opportunity. Cogneau and Gignoux (Forthcoming) found that educational inequality increased for the older cohorts (the ones going to school in the 1940s and 1950s) and then diminished for the younger ones (at school in the 1960s and 1970s), and that these educational changes contributed to the subsequent increase (in the 1980s) and decrease (1990s) of inequality in economic opportunity. Moreover, changes in educational intergenerational mobility were limited over the period and did not significantly affect earnings inequality.

	1988		*1996*	
	0.623*	(0.005)	0.599*	(0.005)
	0.772*	(0.018)	0.719	(0.028)
	0.239	(0.013)	0.173*	(0.008)
	0.310		0.241	
	0.280	(0.012)	0.213*	(0.009)
	0.363		0.296	

A decomposition parallel to the one undertaken for earnings allows an estimation of the share of inequality in household per capita income (figure 4.3) and consumption (figure 4.4). Gender is now excluded from the set of circumstance variables because these indicators (income and consumption) are defined at the household level, and the gender of the household head is endogenous (and thus not a circumstance). Endogeneity arises both because in some countries reported headship is an interviewee choice and because household formation (for example, whether one marries) is endogenous. Thus, five circumstances are used (race, father's and mother's education, father's occupation, and birthplace) as they pertain to the reported head of the household.[17] Income results are reported for all six countries, but consumption data was not available for Brazil.

The nonparametric estimates of inequality of opportunity levels for household incomes range from 0.121 in Ecuador to 0.231 in Guatemala. The opportunity shares of inequality range from 21 percent in Mexico to 37 percent in Guatemala. Although the levels are broadly similar, the shares tend to be higher for incomes than for the corresponding estimates for earnings in most countries.[18] This tendency could be because, in addition to earnings capacity, circumstances may affect three other important household income determinants: capital incomes or transfers; the choice of one's partner; and the composition of the rest of the household (including, most important, the number of children).

Parametric and nonparametric estimates are generally closer for both income and consumption than they are for earnings, and the differences are

Table 4.2 Gini Coefficient and Mean Log Deviations for the Distributions of Income and Consumption per Capita

Inequality measures	Brazil	Colom- bia	Ecuador	Guate- mala	Mexico	Panama	Peru
Income per capita							
Gini coefficient	0.6	0.555	0.487	0.577	0.587	0.566	0.55
Mean log deviation	0.695	0.559	0.417	0.619	0.711	0.63	0.557
Consumption per capita							
Gini coefficient	—	0.506	0.455	0.49	0.593	0.459	0.45
Mean log deviation	—	0.449	0.354	0.409	0.635	0.381	0.351

Source: Authors' calculations based on samples of individuals ages 30 to 49 from the following household surveys: Brazilian PNAD 1996, Colombian ECV 2003, Ecuadorian ECV 2006, Guatemalan ENCOVI 2000, Mexican MxFLS 2002, Panamanian ENV 2003, and Peruvian ENAHO 2001.

Note: — = Not available.

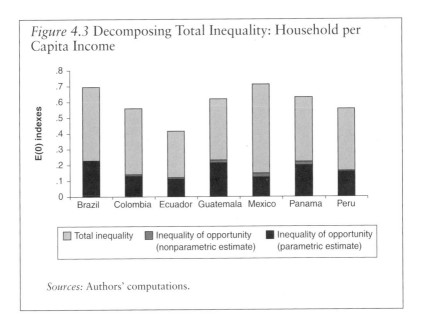

Figure 4.3 Decomposing Total Inequality: Household per Capita Income

Sources: Authors' computations.

seldom statistically significant.[19] This convergence likely reflects, once again, the fact that the proportion of cells with very few observations is lower for the income and consumption samples than for the earnings samples.

While overall inequality is lower in consumption distribution than in income distribution, the opposite is true for estimates of inequality of opportunity. The opportunity shares of inequality are systematically higher for all six countries (20–30 percent), regardless of estimate method (figure 4.4). This supports the hypothesis that earnings and income-based measures of inequality of opportunity tend to underestimate permanent income inequality of opportunity.[20] The nonparametric estimates of inequality of opportunity for consumption expenditures are 27 percent in Colombia and Mexico, 34 percent in Ecuador, 35 percent in Peru, 42 percent in Panama, and 52 percent in Guatemala.

Turning to the analysis of individual circumstance variables, parental background characteristics are once again associated with the largest share of inequality of opportunity (figure 4.5). The share of inequality related to mother's education is as high as 25 percent in Guatemala and higher than 15 percent in most countries. The share of inequality associated with the other variables is usually higher than for earnings, with the same ranking of each circumstance (parental background most important, followed by ethnicity or birthplace). Both ethnicity and birthplace are particularly important in Guatemala and Panama, and birthplace is important in Peru.

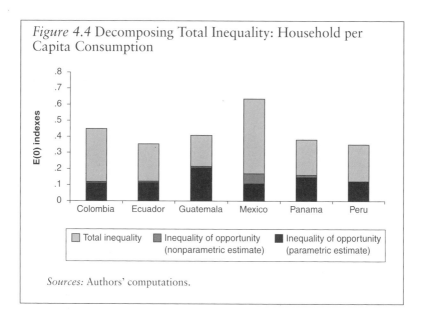

Figure 4.4 Decomposing Total Inequality: Household per Capita Consumption

Sources: Authors' computations.

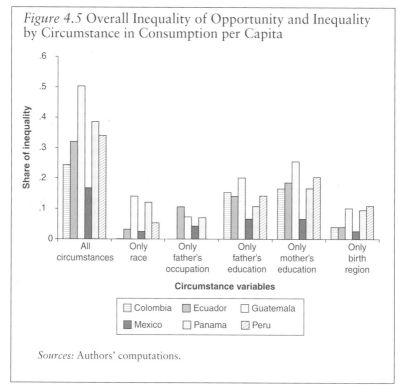

Figure 4.5 Overall Inequality of Opportunity and Inequality by Circumstance in Consumption per Capita

Sources: Authors' computations.

The Opportunity Profile: Identifying the Most-Disadvantaged Groups

The analysis has so far focused on measures of overall inequality of opportunity in each country. But the partition of the population into types used for the decompositions reported above can also be used to identify individually the groups that are the most disadvantaged in the distribution of opportunity in each society. This section of the chapter seeks to identify the most-disadvantaged groups and the extent of the disadvantages they face. The type's mean outcomes are used as the ranking criterion for the type-specific opportunity sets.[21] All types, in each country, are ranked in increasing order of mean outcome, and the most-disadvantaged groups are identified as the bottom m groups of that country's opportunity profile, where the population share over m sums to 10 percent.

The analysis thus targeted the groups with combinations of circumstance types that were worst off in per capita consumption (per capita income in the case of Brazil, where consumption information was not available), that cumulatively totaled the most-disadvantaged 10 percent of the population (table 4.3). The number of disadvantaged groups varies across countries: 5 in Guatemala and Peru, 6 in Brazil, 16 in Ecuador, 20 in Mexico, and 25 in Panama. Some represent large populations—more than 2 million for two groups in Brazil—while others represent only a few hundred individuals. For instance, the group of black and mixed-raced individuals, born in the North or Northeast regions, whose fathers were uneducated agricultural workers and whose mothers did not go to school, form the most-disadvantaged type and accounts for 6.8 percent of the population in Brazil. This table thus provides a profile of opportunity deprivation, highlighting those groups of individuals most affected by circumstance in their economic outcomes.

This is not the same as a poverty profile because it does not rank individuals or households by their income levels, but only by types. Individuals from very disadvantaged backgrounds who have escaped poverty through their own efforts or luck are included. Individuals from more advantaged backgrounds, who did poorly either through bad luck or poor performance, are not. This is not, therefore, the sort of profile to be used for targeting remedial transfers intended to alleviate the hardships of those with very low consumption levels. It is, instead, the sort of profile to be used to identify broad groups, defined by economically exogenous characteristics that are, on average, not sharing in social prosperity. Both profiles are useful and informative, but serve different purposes.[22]

A number of common trends are salient. First, members of ethnic minorities form the vast majority of the population in these disadvantaged groups. In two out of seven countries, these groups are composed exclusively of members of these minorities: black and mixed race in Brazil, and native

Table 4.3 Characteristics of the Most Economically Disadvantaged Groups (*percent*)

Characteristic	Brazil	Colombia	Ecuador	Guatemala	Mexico	Panama	Peru
Member of ethnic minority	100	33	61	100	65	76	100
Father's occupation in agriculture	88	—	93	100	94	84	—
Father's occupation not in agriculture	12	—	7	0	6	16	—
Father without education	89	77	87	99	72	58	100
Father's education primary	10	23	11	0	16	37	0
Father's education secondary	0	0	2	0	11	5	0
Mother without education	91	96	98	99	94	93	99
Mother's education incomplete or complete primary	9	4	1	0	5	6	0
Mother's education complete primary or secondary	0	0	1	1	1	2	1
Regions with the largest share of most-disadvantaged individuals (and share in percent)	Northeast and north regions (100%)	Peripheral departments (65%)	Coastal and insular regions (51%), highlands and Amazonia regions (48%)	North and northwest departments (99%)	South-central and south regions (68%)	Rural areas (96%)	South and coastal departments (58%), inland departments (42%)

Source: Authors' calculations based on samples of individuals ages 30 to 49 from the following household surveys: Brazilian PNAD 1996, Colombian ECV 2003, Ecuadorian ECV 2006, Guatemalan ENCOVI 2000, Mexican MxFLS 2002, Panamanian ENV 2003, and Peruvian ENAHO 2001.

Note: — = Not available.

speakers of indigenous languages in Guatemala. In four of the five remaining countries, ethnic minorities are still a majority: 76 percent of native speakers of indigenous languages in Panama and 56 percent in Peru; 65 percent of self-reported indigenous ethnicity in Mexico; and 61 percent of self-reported indigenous, black, or mixed-race ethnicity in Ecuador. Colombia is the only country in the sample in which ethnic minorities are not the majority in the most-disadvantaged groups, but even there, the proportion of members of minorities, 15 percent, is still higher than in the total population.

Second, family background is strongly associated with membership in the most-disadvantaged groups. In the five countries for which this information is available, no less than 84 percent of those in the most-disadvantaged groups are daughters and sons of agricultural workers, and this proportion reaches 100 percent in Guatemala. Almost the same holds true for parental education. In six out of seven countries, more than 80 percent of individuals in the most disadvantaged groups are daughters and sons of women who did not go to school—99 percent in Guatemala, 98 percent in Ecuador, 94 percent in Mexico, 93 percent in Panama, 91 percent in Brazil, and 82 percent in Peru. Colombia is once again the exception, with a little more heterogeneity—the proportion is "only" 58 percent. Similar results hold for father's education, although less strongly, in Ecuador, Mexico, Panama, and Peru.

Third, a majority of disadvantaged individuals are often natives of the same geographic regions. In Brazil, all persons included in this profile were born in the northeast or north regions; in Guatemala, 99 percent in a north or northwestern department; in Panama, 97 percent in a rural area (the geographical regions are not identified for this country). Colombia, Ecuador, Mexico, and Peru have more heterogeneity in the geographic origins of individuals in the most-disadvantaged groups: in Mexico, 68 percent were born in the south-central and southern regions and 31 percent in the southern region; in Colombia, 65 percent in one of the country's outlying departments; in Peru, 59 percent in the southern and other coastal departments and 40 percent in the other inland (Sierra and Selva) nonsouthern departments; and in Ecuador, 51 percent in the Costa and Insular regions and 48 percent in the Sierra and Amazonia regions.

These findings suggest that the most-disadvantaged types, from the perspective of equality of opportunity, can be easily identified by a common set of characteristics. In the seven Latin American countries examined here, the most-disadvantaged types tend to be members of ethnic minorities, or to hail from agricultural families with low levels of education, living in poor regions.

A similar exercise offers a portrait of the most-advantaged groups in all seven countries (table 4.4). These are the members of types accounting for 10 percent of the population, starting from the type with highest mean consumption and working down. Almost no members of ethnic minorities belong to the most-advantaged groups, except in Colombia, where members of minorities form 6 percent of these types.[23] There are also

Table 4.4 Characteristics of the Most Economically Advantaged Groups (*percent*)

Characteristic	Brazil	Colombia	Ecuador	Guatemala	Mexico	Panama	Peru
Member of ethnic minority	0	4	0	0	1	0	0
Father's occupation in agriculture	3	—	6	8	0	1	1
Father's occupation not in agriculture	97	—	94	92	100	99	99
Father without education	3	0	0	1	0	0	0
Father's education primary	30	12	0	6	0	0	0
Father's education secondary	66	87	100	94	100	100	100
Mother without education	1	0	0	0	8	0	0
Mother's education incomplete or complete primary	35	1	10	20	4	0	0
Mother's education complete primary or secondary	64	99	90	80	88	100	100
Regions with the largest share of most-advantaged individuals (and share in percent)	Southeast, center-west and south (46%), Sao Paulo and federal district (44%)	Central departments (37%), Bogota and islands (32%)	Pichincha and Azuay provinces (44%)	Guatemala city, northeast and El Peten (67%)	Federal district and north (88%)	Cities and intermediate urban centers (99%)	Lima, Callao and Arequipa departments (96%)

Source: Authors' calculations based on samples of individuals ages 30 to 49 from the following household surveys: Brazilian PNAD 1996, Colombian ECV 2003, Ecuadorian ECV 2006, Guatemalan ENCOVI 2000, Mexican MxFLS 2002, Panamanian ENV 2003, and Peruvian ENAHO 2001.

Note: — = Not available.

few children of agricultural workers (8 percent in Guatemala, 6 percent in Ecuador, 3 percent in Brazil, 1 percent in Panama, almost none in the other countries) or of parents with no education (almost no individuals with noneducated mothers in Brazil, Ecuador, Guatemala, and Panama, and less than 10 percent in Colombia, Mexico, and Peru).

The geographic origins of individuals in the most-advantaged groups tend to be more varied than those of individuals in the disadvantaged groups. In general, it appears that good opportunities are not as geographically concentrated as lack of opportunity. Still, a majority among the advantaged were born in the capital city or one of the richer regions: 44 percent from São Paulo and the Distrito Federal in Brazil; 31 percent from Bogotá and 46 percent from the central departments in Colombia; 44 percent from Quito and Cuenca provinces in Ecuador; 67 percent from Guatemala City and northeastern and El Petén departments in Guatemala; 88 percent from the federal district or a northern department in Mexico; 99 percent from an urban center in Panama; and 46 percent from the Lima, Arequipa, or Callao departments in Peru.

Another way to examine relative advantages is to compare the mean levels of consumption of the most-disadvantaged and -advantaged groups as proportions of the national means (figure 4.6).[24]

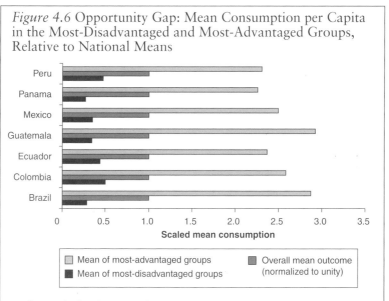

Figure 4.6 Opportunity Gap: Mean Consumption per Capita in the Most-Disadvantaged and Most-Advantaged Groups, Relative to National Means

Source: Authors' computations.

Note: Mean outcome of 10 percent most-disadvantaged and 10 percent most-advantaged groups, scaled by the overall mean. The partition for Brazil is based on income data because consumption data were not available.

The levels of welfare attained by the 10 percent of the population in the most-disadvantaged groups lie between 27 percent (Panama) and 50 percent (Colombia) of the mean national level of welfare. At the opposite end, the levels of welfare of the 10 percent of the population in the most-advantaged groups lie between 230 percent (Panama and Ecuador) and 290 percent (Brazil and Guatemala) of the national mean level of welfare. The comparison indicates that a larger disadvantage of economic opportunities for the low-opportunities groups is generally associated with a larger advantage for the high-opportunities groups. Nevertheless, this relationship is not systematic: in Panama, the relative disadvantage of the worst-off group is higher than in other countries, whereas the relative advantage of the better-off group is not. The opposite situation is found in Colombia.

Summary

This chapter describes the results of a comparative assessment of inequality of economic opportunity in seven Latin American countries. The analysis was top-down: total inequality in earnings, income, and consumption was decomposed into a share resulting from observed predetermined circumstances—associated with inequality of opportunity—and a second share encompassing effort, talent, and luck. The predetermined circumstances considered were mother's education, father's education, father's occupation, race or ethnicity, and birthplace. In the analysis of labor market earnings, gender was added.

Inequality of economic opportunity was found to account for between one-fifth and one-third of overall earnings inequality, as lower-bound estimates. Inequality of earnings opportunity in the seven Latin American countries considered was highest in Brazil and lowest in Colombia. The ranking for share of inequality of opportunity was quite distinct from the ranking in overall earnings inequality (table 4.5). Inequality of opportunity for household welfare was generally greater than for earnings. When household welfare is measured by household income per capita, lower-bound estimates range from 21 percent in Mexico to 37 percent in Guatemala. When household consumption per capita is used, the share of total inequality is even higher than for income: 27 percent in Colombia and Mexico, 34 percent in Ecuador, 35 percent in Peru, 42 percent in Panama, and 52 percent in Guatemala.[25]

The share for inequality of opportunity of income tended to be higher than for earnings, while estimates for consumption were higher than for income or earnings in every country, and by virtually every method. This finding lends support to the notion that measurement error and transitory components add to the non-circumstance-driven variance in the earnings and income measures. The consumption-based measure might, therefore, be preferable, if one is interested in inequality of opportunity for long-term welfare, or permanent income.

The rankings depicted in table 4.5, summarizing the main findings described in the chapter, must be interpreted with care for two reasons. First, many differences in rank across countries are not statistically significant. For instance, the differences in shares of inequality of opportunity in earnings between Ecuador and Panama, or between Mexico, Peru, and Colombia, are not significant. Neither are the differences in shares of inequality of opportunity in consumption per capita between Peru and Ecuador, or between Mexico and Colombia. Second, the comparability of earnings, income, and consumption across countries is plagued by discrepancies originating from differences in the welfare aggregate and other aspects of survey methodology.

That being said, it is interesting to note that country rankings for outcome inequality and for inequality of opportunity are never the same. As expected, there is a fairly high rank correlation between outcome inequality and the level of inequality of opportunity in all three measures. When inequality of opportunity is expressed as a share of outcome inequality, however, the correlation is considerably weaker. For per capita income, for instance, Mexico appears to be the most outcome-unequal country, but the least opportunity unequal. Guatemala, which is the most opportunity unequal, has the fourth highest level of outcome inequality. The correlation between outcome rankings and opportunity-inequality rankings is a little higher for earnings, but even there, differences are substantial: Brazil has the fifth-highest level of overall observed earnings inequality, but appears to be the most opportunity unequal.

These low correlations suggest that inequality of opportunity, measured in this way, really picks up something quite different from outcome inequality. There may be a positive correlation between inequality of outcomes and of opportunities, and indeed the mechanisms of intertemporal reproduction of inequality would lead one to expect this.[26] But they are different concepts.

Also reassuring in this regard is the close rank correlation between income and consumption for the measures of inequality of opportunity for household welfare. Among the six countries for which data are available for both concepts, the opportunity share ranking differs only for one pair of countries—whereas Colombia appears to be the least opportunity unequal when consumption is used (below Mexico), the order is reversed for income. Both concepts yield precisely the same ranking over the other four countries: most opportunity unequal is Guatemala, followed by Panama, Peru, and Ecuador.[27] In fact, that reranking vanishes when the father's occupation variable is omitted from the analysis so that, when the set of circumstances is made as comparable as possible for this sample of countries, the share measures of inequality of opportunity yield precisely the same country ranking for income and consumption.

Table 4.5 Inequality of Economic Opportunity: Country Rankings

Indicator	Brazil	Colombia	Ecuador	Guatemala	Mexico	Panama	Peru
Earnings							
Overall inequality	0.617	0.608	0.638	0.786	0.756	0.572	0.675
Rank	5	6	4	1	2	7	3
Levels of inequality of opportunity	0.215	0.123	0.164	0.230	0.177	0.140	0.143
Rank	2	7	4	1	3	6	5
Share of inequality of opportunity	0.349	0.203	0.256	0.293	0.234	0.245	0.212
Rank	1	7	4	2	5	3	6
Per capita income							
Overall inequality	0.695	0.559	0.417	0.619	0.711	0.63	0.557
Rank	2	5	7	4	1	3	6
Levels of inequality of opportunity	0.228	0.140	0.121	0.231	0.148	0.218	0.163
Rank	2	6	7	1	5	3	4
Share of inequality of opportunity	0.329	0.25	0.29	0.373	0.208	0.346	0.292
Rank	3	6	5	1	7	2	4
Per capita consumption							
Overall inequality	—	0.449	0.354	0.409	0.635	0.381	0.351
Rank		2	5	3	1	4	6
Levels of inequality of opportunity		0.119	0.122	0.214	0.17	0.159	0.122
Rank		6	4	1	2	3	4
Share of inequality of opportunity		0.265	0.344	0.524	0.267	0.417	0.348
Rank		6	4	1	5	2	3

Source: Authors' calculations based on samples of individuals ages 30 to 49 from the following household surveys: Brazilian PNAD 1996, Colombian ECV 2003, Ecuadorian ECV 2003, Guatemalan ENCOVI 2000, Mexican MxFLS 2002, Panamanian ENV 2003, and Peruvian ENAHO 2001.

Note: — = Not available. Inequality measured by the mean log deviation. Inequality of opportunity shares are nonparametric estimates.

Across all indicators of economic welfare, the circumstances that had the greatest impact on opportunity shares were family background variables: education levels of both parents (with the mother's having a stronger effect) and occupation of the father. Race or ethnicity and birthplace had smaller effects, but they were still sizable, particularly in Central American countries. Indeed, the importance of an indigenous background in Guatemala and Panama help account for the overall higher levels of inequality of opportunity in those countries.

Finally, opportunity-deprivation profiles identify the most-disadvantaged types in each country and describe their aggregate characteristics. As expected, the most-disadvantaged groups can generally be identified as members of ethnic minorities, daughters and sons of agricultural workers, with low levels of education and generally living in specific poor regions. The circumstances most important in ranking groups at the very bottom of the opportunity scale are not necessarily the same as those accounting for the largest shares of inequality in the overall decomposition. In particular, race and ethnicity are more important determinants of severe opportunity deprivation than of opportunity shares of overall inequality. Family background variables, like parental education and occupation, are salient for both.

Notes

1. This chapter is based on Ferreira and Gignoux (2008). The reader is referred to that work for technical details.

2. There are two additional steps in the mapping from household income or consumption to individual welfare that are overlooked here by using income or consumption per capita. First, an extreme assumption is made about the inexistence of economies of scale in consumption within the household. Second, an assumption is made that household resources are shared equally, which may well not be the case.

3. Among inequality measures anchored by the arithmetic mean income (which includes almost all measures ever used in practice) and that satisfy the Pigou-Dalton Transfer Principle (which requires that inequality fall if a richer person transfers one unit to a poorer person), only the mean log deviation is decomposable and path independent. This result was established by Foster and Shneyerov (2000), and first applied in the context of inequality of opportunity by Ferreira and Gignoux (2008).

4. A possible misunderstanding would be to argue that, because certain omitted circumstances might be negatively correlated with the observed circumstances, the parametric measure need not be a lower bound. It is, of course, possible that the share of inequality attributed to a specific set of (observed) circumstances is overestimated. This might happen if omitted circumstance variables are negatively correlated with observed ones. But the R^2 of the relevant regression cannot fall by including these other circumstance variables, so the estimate *is* a lower-bound for the share of inequality attributed to *all* circumstances (rather than to the observed subset), analogous to the nonparametric case.

5. Reviewing the *World Development Report 2006*, Roemer proposed that "the rate of economic development should be taken to be the rate at which the mean advantage level of the worst-off type grows over time" (Roemer 2006, 243).

6. For a comprehensive discussion of the data set and variables for this methodology, see Ferreira and Gignoux (2008). PNAD and ENAHO are original national household surveys, MxFLS is a Rand-type survey, and the others are Living Standards Measurement Study surveys.

7. Employment rates for men and women, respectively, ages 30 to 49, are 0.90 and 0.55 in Brazil, 0.91 and 0.62 in Colombia, 0.97 and 0.72 in Ecuador, 0.96 and 0.51 in Guatemala, 0.96 and 0.46 in Mexico, 0.91 and 0.53 in Panama, and 0.94 and 0.72 in Peru. For Brazil and Peru, the sample is further restricted to household heads and spouses because the family background information was collected only for these individuals.

8. Ferreira and Gignoux (2008) contains tables that describe the specific definitions of the circumstance variables in each survey and the corresponding descriptive statistics.

9. The differences between Brazil, Colombia, and Ecuador, and between Ecuador and Peru, are insignificant at the 5 percent level on the basis of the bootstrapped standard errors.

10. Ferreira and Gignoux (2008) also contains each individual estimate (and bootstrapped standard errors) for two alternative nonparametric estimators, the parametric estimate, and three different generalized entropy measures.

11. These results should be interpreted as lower-bound estimates for inequality of opportunity for earnings among the population of employed workers. The unemployed and those outside the labor force are excluded from the analysis, and extrapolation of these shares to the overall population would imply a sample selection bias.

12. The precision of each estimate, using bootstrapped standard errors, is documented in Ferreira and Gignoux (2008). If the father's occupation variable is omitted in all countries to make the set of circumstance variables more comparable, Mexico's opportunity share drops below Peru's and Colombia's (although the differences between them remain insignificant).

13. Given the methodological trade-offs between parametric and nonparametric methods, which are discussed in greater detail in Ferreira and Gignoux (2008), we recommend that (i) where possible, surveys that might be used to estimate inequality of opportunity should use larger sample sizes; and (ii) where that is not possible, researchers should report both parametric and nonparametric estimates to get a sense of the plausible range of true inequality of opportunity.

14. These are estimated through the parametric method and are essentially estimates of the share of inequality attributable to an individual variable (for example, place of birth) when controlling for all other observed determinants.

15. With the exception of Mexico.

16. See, for example, Deaton (1997) on both of these reasons to prefer consumption to income data in assessing the distribution of welfare in developing countries.

17. A separate set of regressions was run on the same data, but without including father's occupation, and the differences in results were statistically insignificant in all cases.

18. The reverse is true only in Brazil and Mexico, where the differences are small (and in the Mexican case, statistically insignificant).

19. Mexico is once again an exception, probably because the Mexican survey does not include imputed rent for owner-occupied housing and does not adjust for spatial differences in the cost of living. Moreover, the MxFLS has a small sample,

and correspondingly large sampling weights, which may affect the precision of nonparametric estimates.

20. This point is analogous to the well-known fact that intergenerational mobility estimates are much higher when based on single-period wages for parents and children, than when based on longer earnings histories. See, among others, Solon (1999) and Mazumder (2005).

21. A stochastic dominance approach would be more satisfactory but would provide only a partial and incomplete ranking and would suffer from sample-size limitations. Note also that other first-order moments, such as the median or another quantile, could alternatively be used. Ferreira and Gignoux (2008) lists the most-disadvantaged groups in each country by their defining characteristics, as well as their mean per capita consumption (in levels and as shares of the national means) and population share.

22. Identifying the overlap between the two profiles would be an interesting subject for further analytical work.

23. Nevertheless, in both Guatemala and Panama, the groups with the highest mean income are formed of native speakers of indigenous languages. However, these groups represent only a very small share, much less than 1 percent, of the population in advantaged groups.

24. An attempt to present similar results in comparable currency units (rather than in relation to national means) was foiled by difficulties with purchasing power parity (PPP) exchange rates and the national Consumer Price Indexes used to deflate national currencies back to 1993, which is the year for which the latest consumption PPPs are available.

25. These indexes are a little smaller for the parametric estimates, but with the exception of Mexico, the differences are not statistically significant. Consumption data for Brazil are not available.

26. See Bourguignon, Ferreira, and Walton (2007) for a discussion.

27. Brazil, for which there are no consumption data, lies between Panama and Peru in the income-based ranking.

References

Bourguignon, François, Francisco Ferreira, and Marta Menéndez. 2007. "Inequality of Opportunity in Brazil." *Review of Income and Wealth* 53 (4): 585–618.

Bourguignon, F., F. Ferreira, and M. Walton. 2007. "Equity, Efficiency and Inequality Traps: A Research Agenda." *Journal of Economic Inequality* 5 (2): 235–56.

Cogneau, D., and J. Gignoux. Forthcoming. "Earnings Inequalities and Educational Mobility in Brazil over Two Decades." In *Poverty, Inequality and Policy in Latin America, CESifo Seminar Series*, ed. S. Klasen and F. Nowak-Lehmann. Cambridge, MA: Massachusetts Institute of Technology (MIT) Press.

Deaton, A. 1997. *The Analysis of Household Surveys: A Microeconometric Approach to Development Policy*. Baltimore: The John Hopkins University Press.

Ferreira, Francisco H. G., and Jérémie Gignoux. 2008. "Inequality of Economic Opportunities in Latin America." www.worldbank.org/lacopportunity. Washington, DC: World Bank.

Foster, J., and A. Shneyerov. 2000. "Path Independent Inequality Measures." *Journal of Economic Theory* 91 (2): 199–222.

Mazumder, Bhakshar. 2005. "The Apple Falls Even Closer to the Tree Than We Thought: New and Revised Estimates of the Intergenerational Inheritance of Earnings." In *Unequal Chances: Family Background and Economic Success*, ed. S. Bowles, H. Gintis, and M. Groves. Princeton, NJ: Princeton University Press.

Roemer, John E. 2006. "Economic Development as Opportunity Equalization." Cowles Foundation Discussion Paper No. 1583, Yale University, New Haven, CT.

Solon, Gary. 1999. "Intergenerational Mobility in the Labor Market." In *Handbook of Labor Economics*, ed. Orley Ashenfelter and David Card. Amsterdam: North-Holland.

5

Inequality of Opportunity in Educational Achievement in Five Latin American Countries

This chapter presents estimates of inequality of opportunity for educational achievement in several Latin American countries, using a technique similar to that in the previous chapter.[1] Inequality of opportunity in the acquisition of education is as important as inequality of opportunity in economic welfare, for several reasons. First, education is one of the main determinants of individual earnings and welfare. Inequality of educational opportunity thus may very well translate into inequality of economic opportunity. Second, education has considerable intrinsic value, and inequality of opportunity in its acquisition may therefore be considered unfair in its own right. Third, education is related to other intrinsically valued individual capabilities, such as participation in political institutions. Finally, through a number of these channels, inequality of educational opportunity may also engender economic and institutional inefficiencies.[2]

Measuring Inequality of Educational Opportunity

This chapter examines inequality of opportunity for educational achievement for 15-year-old children in five Latin American countries (as well as nine European and North American nations). These measures are estimated using internationally comparable data on standardized test scores for reading and mathematics from the Program for International Student Assessment (PISA). Educational achievement measured by test scores is likely to be a better measure of human capital than educational attainment, measured by years of schooling or completed levels of education, because of the considerable heterogeneity in the quality of education across schools.

Methodology

The measures of inequality of opportunity in educational achievement reported in this chapter are based on the same kind of decomposition performed for economic outcomes in chapter 4. Total observed inequality is decomposed into two parts: one resulting from circumstances beyond the control of the individual, and the second related to efforts made in the acquisition of education, as well as luck, measurement error, and those components of innate talent that are uncorrelated with the observed circumstances. The data contain five circumstance variables: the gender of the child, father's and mother's levels of education, father's main occupation, and the type of area where the child's school is located. With the notable exception of race (not available in the PISA data), these are the same variables that were used for the measurement of inequality of economic opportunity.

However, the methodological parallel with chapter 4 is not perfect. An additional difficulty arises when performing these decompositions for education data. The test score variables that measure educational achievement are standardized, so that their mean and standard deviations have arbitrary values (the mean and standard deviation for the set of Organisation for Economic Co-operation and Development [OECD] countries were fixed at 500 and 100, respectively). This standardization implies both a translation of the mean and a rescaling of the dispersion. And no inequality measure is capable of deriving from a distribution so transformed, the inequality of the original distribution.[3] Nevertheless, a measure of inequality of opportunity in achievement, formulated as a share of total inequality, can be constructed and is unaffected by the standardization of test scores. This technique is used for the estimations in this chapter; the functioning and limitations of the technique are explained in more detail in Ferreira and Gignoux (2008).

Caveats

The same potential caveats discussed in chapter 4 apply to the measurement of inequality of educational opportunity. In particular, nonparametric estimates require large samples. Because the PISA samples are not so large, there is a trade-off in the definition of the circumstance categories. More categories would better capture the effects of various circumstances on achievement, but more categories would also imply that some "cells" (groupings of individuals with the same circumstances, or "types") are empty, or contain only a few observations. Cells with few members raise a problem because the conditional mean outcomes for these types are imprecisely estimated. Partitioning the sample into many cells can therefore bias the estimate of the share of inequality of opportunity upward. The nonparametric measures are, therefore, complemented with the same parametric estimation procedure performed in chapter 4, but for E(2) rather than E(0).[4]

As in chapter 4, the existence of omitted, unobserved circumstance variables requires that the measures of inequality of opportunity be interpreted as lower-bound estimates of the true shares. If some previously unobserved circumstance were to somehow become observable, the share of unequal opportunity accounted for by circumstances might rise, but would never fall. Also as before, the parametric decompositions permit identifying the partial contribution of each individual circumstance variable to inequality of opportunity. Because the sample size is twice as large for reading as for mathematics (see below), the parametric decomposition yields lower estimates of inequality of opportunity than the nonparametric decomposition for achievement in mathematics, but the two sets of estimates are much closer for achievement in reading.

The Data

This study used a set of internationally comparable surveys of educational achievement from PISA, sponsored by the OECD. The data come from the unit-record PISA 2000 surveys, and were collected in five Latin American countries. These five surveys are a subset of the first wave of PISA surveys, which were conducted in 43 countries in all, including 29 OECD countries. The surveys were fielded at schools in Brazil and Mexico (and most other OECD countries) in 2000, and in Argentina, Chile, and Peru in 2001 (table 5.1).

The samples of examinees are representative of the populations of 15-year-olds attending school. The samples are not, therefore, representative of the total population of 15-year-olds in each country because dropouts are not covered. Moreover, children attending the lowest grades

Table 5.1 PISA Survey Dates, Coverage Rates, and Sample Sizes

Indicator	Argentina	Brazil	Chile	Mexico	Peru
Year of survey	2001	2000	2001	2000	2001
Coverage rate (percent)	77	69	82	45	50
Sample sizes					
Reading	3,983	4,893	4,889	4,600	4,429
Mathematics	2,230	2,717	2,721	2,567	2,460

Source: OECD *Programme for International Student Assessment (PISA).*

(below grade 7) were not surveyed in Argentina (excluding 4 percent), Brazil (16 percent), or Peru (10 percent). Coverage rates (expressed as ratios of the population represented by the survey to the total population of 15-year-olds) vary considerably across countries, as shown in table 5.1. Because of this selection issue, the international comparisons of inequalities in observed test scores should be interpreted with care—they are not assessments of the entire educational system, but only of the distribution of achievement conditional on having remained in the system.

In each country, all children in the sample took a test in reading. Additionally, about half of the sample took a test in mathematics, and the other half took a test in science (table 5.1). This chapter considers only reading and mathematics test scores. All surveys contain information on a common set of five circumstances: the gender of the child, mother's and father's education, father's occupation, and the location of the school. Parental education is measured by the highest level of education completed and is coded into three categories: (i) no education, primary education, or unknown level; (ii) lower secondary education or upper secondary; and (iii) college education. Father's occupations are aggregated into three categories: (i) legislators, senior officials and professionals, technicians and clerks; (ii) service workers, craft and related trades workers, plant and machine operators and assemblers; and (iii) skilled agricultural and fishery workers, elementary occupations,[5] or unknown occupation.

School location is not as predetermined (that is, economically exogenous) as place of birth. However, as any migration that takes place between birth and test-taking at age 15 likely reflects the decision of the parent rather than the child, it is reasonable to consider school location exogenous. School location is, therefore, used as a proxy for the person's inherited spatial endowment, and it is recoded using three categories: (i) villages or small towns (less than 15,000 inhabitants); (ii) towns (between 15,000 and 100,000 inhabitants); and (iii) cities (larger than 100,000 inhabitants).[6] School location information was not collected in Peru. As in chapter 4, when presenting the results, the chapter compares the country rankings with those in an alternative set of decompositions in which the school location variable is ignored for all countries.

The test score variables used to measure achievement are constructed from student answers to a series of test items, by means of an adjustment based on item response theory (IRT). Achievement (or cognitive skill) is treated as an unobserved or latent trait. IRT attempts to determine how much of this unobservable trait each examinee possesses. Because this trait cannot be measured directly, IRT seeks to infer it from a set of responses to test items. IRT methods consist of modeling the item responses as the outcome of two sets of independent parameters, one describing the items and the other the examinee's skills. The technical details are discussed in Ferreira and Gignoux (2008).

Inequality of Opportunity in Educational Achievement

Inequality in both access to and attainment of education in Latin America, whether measured by years of schooling or completed levels of education, has been amply documented.[7] However, inequality in educational achievement, as measured by student performance on comparable tests, has traditionally received less attention, largely because of data scarcity.[8] Although standardized test score data pose challenges for the measurement of total inequality in education, because of the lack of a metric for achievement, they provide insight into the extent of inequality of opportunity in the acquisition of education.

The distributions of test scores for reading, conditional on father's occupation (figure 5.1) and school location (figure 5.2), are obtained using nonparametric kernel density estimates, and provide a disaggregated description of the link between these two circumstances and achievement. Groups of children from more privileged family backgrounds have significantly higher densities at high achievements (figure 5.1), and students in larger cities have significantly higher densities at high achievements (compared with students in rural areas and small towns) in Mexico and to a lesser extent in Chile (figure 5.2). This exploratory analysis suggests that differences in achievement associated with parental occupation are strong in all five countries, and that differences associated with school location, an imperfect proxy for place of residence, vary across countries and are more pronounced in Mexico.

Although informative, a comparison of conditional density functions does not provide a synthetic measure of inequality of opportunity in the acquisition of education. Figure 5.3, by contrast, decomposes total inequality in achievement in reading scores into the share accounted for by the five circumstance variables analyzed, and a second share accounted for by effort, skill, or luck. The first set of bars on the left side of figure 5.3 gives the nonparametric estimate of the share of inequality of educational opportunity within total inequality for Argentina (28 percent), Brazil (22 percent), Chile (24 percent), Mexico (27 percent), and Peru (23 percent). However, these estimates are not as precise as the estimates of the extent of inequality of economic opportunity: on the basis of bootstrapped standard errors, there are no significant differences in these shares across the five countries. When excluding the school location variable estimates for countries where this information is available (all but Peru), the results are Argentina (23 percent), Brazil (18 percent), Chile (22 percent), and Mexico (21 percent). The differences between these estimates are not statistically different either.

The second set of bars gives the parametric estimates, computed using the same set of five circumstance variables. These estimates are approximately 20–30 percent lower than the nonparametric estimates in most

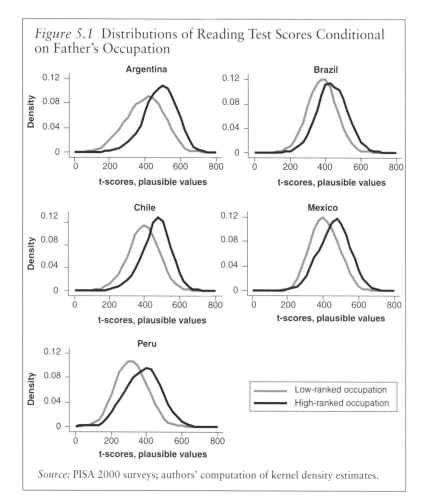

Figure 5.1 Distributions of Reading Test Scores Conditional on Father's Occupation

Source: PISA 2000 surveys; authors' computation of kernel density estimates.

cases. The difference can be the result either of problems with the functional form assumptions inherent in parametric estimation (which might reduce its ability to capture between-group inequalities), or of small-sample biases that increase spurious sampling variation in nonparametric decompositions. Thus, the parametric measures might be interpreted as reasonable "lower-bound" estimates of the plausible shares of inequality related to these five circumstances, while the nonparametric estimates might be seen as reasonable "upper-bound" estimates. In short, the data suggest that between 14 percent and 28 percent of inequality in reading achievement in a group of five Latin American countries can be accounted for by the set of five circumstances: gender, education level of mother and of father, father's occupation, and geographic location of school.

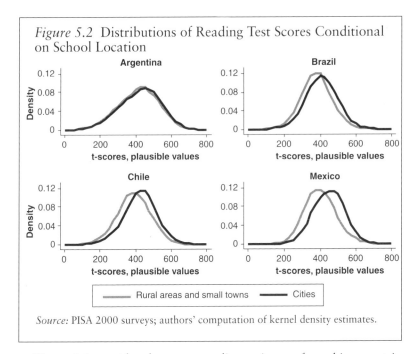

Figure 5.2 Distributions of Reading Test Scores Conditional on School Location

Source: PISA 2000 surveys; authors' computation of kernel density estimates.

Figure 5.4 provides the corresponding estimates for achievement in mathematics; the nonparametric estimates of the opportunity shares are Argentina (29 percent), Brazil (24 percent), Chile (23 percent), Mexico (27 percent), and Peru (17 percent). Once again, no cross-country differences are statistically significant, except for Peru, which is not fully comparable because of the lack of information on school location in this country. When excluding the school location variable, the estimates are Argentina (23 percent), Brazil (19 percent), Chile (19 percent), and Mexico (21 percent), with all differences insignificant. The differences with the parametric estimates are somewhat larger in this case, which is explained by the smaller samples available for achievement in mathematics. The results suggest that the range for the share of inequality in achievement accounted for by gender, family background, and spatial location is between 17 percent and 29 percent in these Latin American countries.

Figure 5.4 also gives the partial shares of inequality in achievement accounted for by each circumstance variable considered separately. These are estimated parametrically, and capture inequality of opportunity attributable to each individual variable while controlling for the others. The results are very similar for achievement in reading and mathematics. The main result is that family background variables, particularly father's occupation and mother's education, are the most important, and are associated with between 5 percent and 14 percent of total inequality in outcomes for educational achievement.

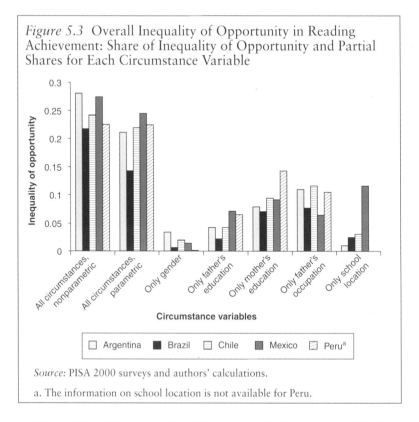

Figure 5.3 Overall Inequality of Opportunity in Reading
Achievement: Share of Inequality of Opportunity and Partial
Shares for Each Circumstance Variable

Source: PISA 2000 surveys and authors' calculations.

a. The information on school location is not available for Peru.

The ranking of these variables differs across the five countries. Mother's
education explains a significantly higher share of inequality in Chile, Mexico,
and Peru than in the other two countries, while father's occupation explains a
significantly higher share in Argentina and Chile than in Mexico. The shares
of inequality accounted for by gender and school location are generally less
important, accounting for less than 3 percent of total inequality. An important exception is Mexico, where school location accounts for a larger share
of inequality of opportunity than in any other country, accounting for as
much as 12 percent of inequality in reading and 9 percent in mathematics.

Comparing Inequality of Opportunity in
Latin American and OECD Countries

While the numbers presented in the previous section are themselves interesting and policy relevant, comparisons with other countries could shed
further light on inequality of educational opportunity in LAC. Are the

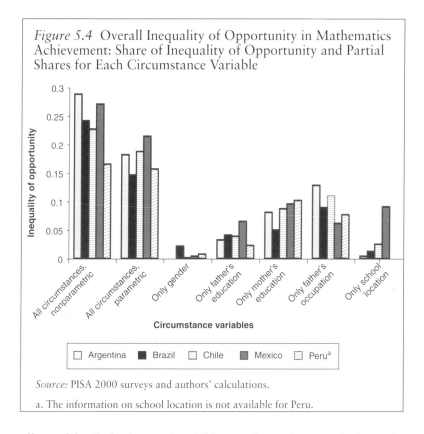

Figure 5.4 Overall Inequality of Opportunity in Mathematics Achievement: Share of Inequality of Opportunity and Partial Shares for Each Circumstance Variable

Source: PISA 2000 surveys and authors' calculations.

a. The information on school location is not available for Peru.

effects of family background variables, gender, and geography larger in Latin America than in Europe or North America? Very little evidence is available to answer this question, in large part because the specifics of each country's educational system make cross-country comparisons difficult.[9] The internationally comparable PISA surveys, which took place in five Latin American nations and 38 other countries, including the United States, Canada, and most of Europe, offer unique conditions for such an international comparison. All these surveys applied the same methodology, and the same information on family background and location was collected in all participating countries.

These data were used to estimate the level of inequality of opportunity for education for a set of nine European and North American countries—Canada, Finland, France, Germany, Italy, Spain, Sweden, the United Kingdom, and the United States—for the purpose of comparison with Latin America.[10] Using a parametric decomposition, the share of inequality in achievement in reading accounted for by circumstance is estimated to range from 12 percent in Canada to 27 percent in Germany (figure 5.5),

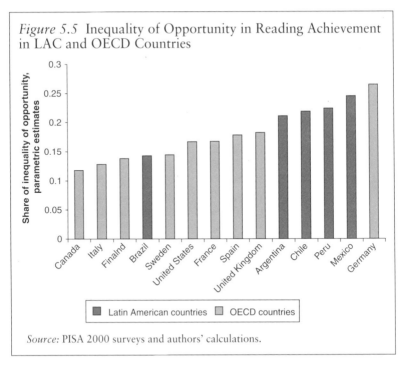

Figure 5.5 Inequality of Opportunity in Reading Achievement in LAC and OECD Countries

Source: PISA 2000 surveys and authors' calculations.

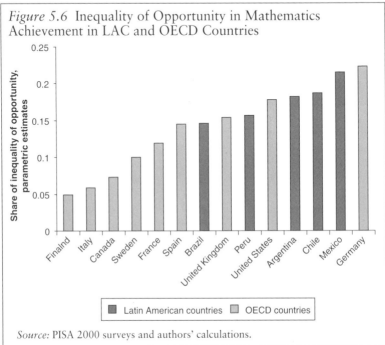

Figure 5.6 Inequality of Opportunity in Mathematics Achievement in LAC and OECD Countries

Source: PISA 2000 surveys and authors' calculations.

and in mathematics from 5 percent in Finland to 22 percent in Germany (figure 5.6). As can be seen in the figures, the estimates for Latin American countries are higher than average, but well within the OECD range. They are smaller in Canada, Scandinavian countries (Finland and Sweden), and Italy; intermediate in France, Spain, the United Kingdom, and the United States; and higher in Germany. For more complete results, see Ferreira and Gignoux (2008).

Compared with industrial countries, the median Latin American country seems to be more opportunity unequal, with about 20 percent of total inequality accounted for by circumstances. In the typical industrial country, that number is 15 percent. In Germany and the United States, relative levels of inequality of opportunity are comparable with (or above) those observed in Latin America. However, in absolute terms, Peru and Argentina have the highest estimated levels of inequality of opportunity, and the five Latin American countries have higher levels of inequality of educational opportunity than all OECD countries, with the exception of Germany (figures 5.7 and 5.8).[11] In Europe and North America, parental occupation and education account for almost all the inequality of opportunity, whereas gender and geography appear to have almost no effect; see tables in Ferreira and Gignoux (2008).

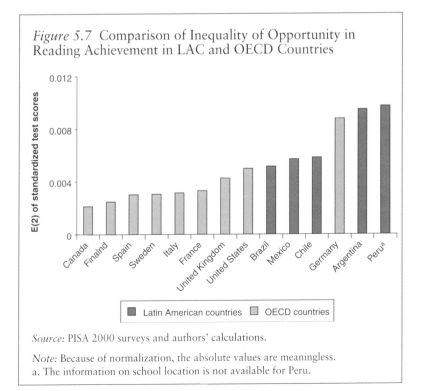

Figure 5.7 Comparison of Inequality of Opportunity in Reading Achievement in LAC and OECD Countries

Source: PISA 2000 surveys and authors' calculations.

Note: Because of normalization, the absolute values are meaningless.
a. The information on school location is not available for Peru.

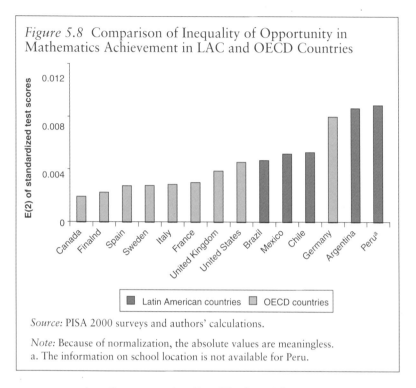

Figure 5.8 Comparison of Inequality of Opportunity in Mathematics Achievement in LAC and OECD Countries

Source: PISA 2000 surveys and authors' calculations.

Note: Because of normalization, the absolute values are meaningless.
a. The information on school location is not available for Peru.

An Opportunity Profile for Education

Much as was done for economic inequality in chapter 4, this section identifies the most-disadvantaged and most-advantaged groups for educational achievement opportunity by combinations of circumstances, and also quantifies the extent of the disadvantage faced by the most-disadvantaged groups. Again, the methodology starts by identifying the circumstance groups with the least opportunities, and continues adding groups until the most-disadvantaged 10 percent of the population is identified. The number of disadvantaged groups varies across countries, from only 4 in Peru to 26 in Brazil and Chile, with some representing thousands of individuals and others only a few hundred (table 5.2).[12] For instance, in Peru, the group of boys whose mothers and fathers are both uneducated, and whose fathers are in an agricultural or elementary occupation, is the circumstance group with the lowest mean achievement in reading, with a mean test score of 251 (to be compared with a national mean of 327), and that accounts for 6.6 percent of the population of 15-year-olds.

Males are typically large majorities in the disadvantaged groups for reading achievement. In Mexico, 96 percent of individuals in the lower-

Table 5.2 Characteristics of the Most Educationally
Disadvantaged Groups, Reading
(percentage of individuals in most-disadvantaged groups with characteristic)

Characteristic	Argentina	Brazil	Chile	Mexico	Peru
Female	15	10	32	4	33
Father without education	62	66	61	86	93
Father's education primary	21	24	31	6	4
Father's education secondary	17	10	7	8	3
Mother without education	75	80	76	87	96
Mother's education primary	11	14	20	9	3
Mother's education secondary	14	6	5	4	1
Father legislator, senior official, professional, technician, or service worker	7	5	4	23	1
Father worker, plant or machine operator, assembler, or with elementary occupation	16	21	35	6	4
Father skilled agricultural or fishery worker, or not reported occupation	77	74	60	71	95
School located in a village or small town (fewer than 15,000 inhabitants)	42	28	61	94	—
School located in a town (fewer than 100,000 inhabitants)	23	39	32	3	—
School located in a city (more than 100,000 inhabitants)	35	32	6	3	—
Group mean achievement	327.8	334.6	336.3	353.6	257.1
Country mean achievement	418.3	396.0	409.5	422.0	327.2
Share of group to country mean achievement (percent)	78	84	82	84	79

Source: Authors' compilation using data from the PISA 2000 and 2001 surveys.

Note: — = Not available.
   The unit of measure of achievement is arbitrarily defined such that the distribution of achievement of the overall population of the OECD countries has a mean of 500 and a standard deviation of 100.

achieving groups are males, followed by 90 percent in Brazil, 85 percent in Argentina, 68 percent in Chile, and 67 percent in Peru. This result is inverted with achievement in mathematics, where females form the majority of the disadvantaged groups in all countries.

Family background is also strongly associated with membership in a disadvantaged group. In the five countries, between 61 percent and 93 percent of 15-year-olds in low-achieving groups have a father who did not go to school, and between 75 percent and 96 percent have a mother who did not go to school. These shares are highest in Mexico and Peru. In four out of five countries (Argentina being the exception), fewer than 10 percent of individuals in the most-disadvantaged groups have parents with a secondary education or higher. Parental occupation is almost as strongly associated with educational opportunity, with 95 percent of 15-year-olds in low-performing groups in Peru being the children of agricultural workers, 77 percent in Argentina, 74 percent in Brazil, 71 percent in Mexico, and 60 percent in Chile. Mexico is the only country where the children of professionals, officials, technicians, and service workers have a substantial (23 percent) risk of facing a disadvantage.

Geographic patterns of disadvantage are more heterogeneous across countries. Spatial inequalities are strong in Mexico, where 94 percent of 15-year-olds studying in villages or small towns are in the most-disadvantaged groups, and 61 percent are in such groups in Chile. In Argentina and Brazil, however, students in villages and small towns account for 42 percent and 28 percent, respectively, of the profile. The information on school location is not available for Peru.

For the most-advantaged groups, females are the majority of 15-year-olds in high-achieving circumstance groups for reading, particularly in Argentina and Chile (table 5.3). In these two countries, females are also the majority of the high-achieving groups in mathematics, although to a lesser extent. There is, therefore, an asymmetry in the gender composition between the top and bottom types: while boys do worse in reading but better in mathematics among the disadvantaged types, girls dominate the advantaged types in both reading and mathematics.

Looking at family background, few people with uneducated fathers— only 11 percent in Brazil, 8 percent in Argentina, 2 percent in Chile, 1 percent in Mexico, and none in Peru—belong to the most-advantaged types. Similarly, there are few children of agricultural workers in the high-opportunity groups: 16 percent in Argentina, 4 percent in Brazil and Mexico, 2 percent in Chile, and none in Peru.

In Mexico and Chile, the most advantaged are as geographically concentrated as the most disadvantaged, with 84 percent and 80 percent of them, respectively, going to school in a metropolis. They are less concen-

Table 5.3 Characteristics of the Most Educationally
Advantaged Groups, Reading
(percentage of individuals in most-advantaged groups with characteristic)

Characteristic	Argentina	Brazil	Chile	Mexico	Peru
Female	95	51	84	53	61
Father without education	8	11	2	1	0
Father's education primary	22	21	28	14	7
Father's education secondary	70	69	70	86	92
Mother without education	11	4	1	1	0
Mother's education primary	42	35	38	43	17
Mother's education secondary	47	61	61	56	83
Father legislator, senior official, professional, technician, or service worker	77	86	85	94	99
Father worker, plant or machine operator, assembler, or with elementary occupation	7	9	12	2	0
Father skilled agricultural or fishery worker, or not reported occupation	16	4	2	4	0
School located in a village or small town (fewer than 15,000 inhabitants)	21	4	16	1	—
School located in a town (fewer than 100,000 inhabitants)	40	28	4	16	—
School located in a city (more than 100,000 inhabitants)	40	69	80	84	—
Group mean achievement	514.3	470.7	489.0	501.5	411.5
Group share of country mean achievement (percent)	123	119	119	119	126

Source: Authors' compilation using data from the PISA 2000 and 2001 surveys.

Note: — = Not available.

The unit of measure of achievement is arbitrarily defined such that the distribution of achievement of the overall population of the OECD countries has a mean of 500 and a standard deviation of 100.

trated in Brazil, where this share is 69 percent, and in Argentina where it is 40 percent. Argentina and Chile are the only two countries where significant shares (21 percent and 16 percent, respectively) of educationally advantaged 15-year-olds go to school in a village or small town.

The mean achievement in reading and math of the most-disadvantaged and most-advantaged group, compared with the country's overall mean achievement, gives an idea of how far ahead and behind these groups are from society as a whole. The mean achievement in reading of the 10 percent of individuals in the most-disadvantaged groups compared with the overall mean is 78 percent in Argentina, 79 percent in Peru, 82 percent in Chile, and 84 percent in Brazil and Mexico.[13] However, the mean achievement in reading of the 10 percent of individuals in the most-advantaged groups is 126 percent of the overall mean achievement in Peru, 123 percent in Argentina, and 119 percent in Chile, Mexico, and Brazil. As noted previously, however, the standardization of scores underlying these proportions means that they allow for rank comparisons across countries, but have no relevant absolute interpretation.

Summary

This chapter presented the results of a comparative assessment of inequality of opportunity in educational achievement in five Latin American countries, as well as in nine countries of North America and Europe. The analysis followed the same approach that chapter 4 applied to economic inequality: total inequality in educational achievement was decomposed into a component resulting from a set of predetermined circumstances and a second component encompassing individual effort and luck. The predetermined circumstances were almost exactly the same across countries: gender, mother's and father's education, father's occupation, and school location. Information on race or ethnicity was not available for any country.

Inequality of opportunity was estimated to account for between 14 percent and 28 percent of overall inequality in reading achievement in Latin America, and for between 15 percent and 29 percent in mathematics achievement, as a lower-bound estimate. The estimates varied somewhat across countries, but were not precise enough to provide a statistically significant ranking of countries by inequality of educational opportunity. The estimates also varied according to the method of decomposition used: parametric methods yielded lower estimates than did the nonparametric approach.

As in the case of economic outcomes, the circumstances that had the largest impact on opportunity shares were family background variables, notably mother's education and father's occupation. Nevertheless, school location was particularly important in Mexico, revealing large geographic inequalities in educational achievement in that country. The impact of gender on opportunity shares was found to be limited, but when looking at the composition of types at the extremes of the distribution (those with the lowest and highest mean scores), the gender profile was quite important. Girls dominate among the most advantaged in both subjects, as well as among the most-disadvantaged for mathematics. Boys are a majority of those in the most-disadvantaged groups for reading.

When compared with OECD countries, the median Latin American country seems to be more opportunity unequal with regard to educational achievement, with about 20 percent of total inequality accounted for by circumstances, while in the typical industrial country, 15 percent of inequality is associated with the same circumstances. Because total outcome inequality was also higher in Latin America, this pattern is even more pronounced in levels, with Argentina and Peru recording the highest gross amounts of inequality of educational opportunity.

Educational opportunity profiles of the circumstance types with the least and most advantage in educational opportunity reveal that for all countries, the most-disadvantaged groups tended to include a disproportionate share of children of agricultural workers and parents with little or no schooling. In Chile and Mexico, most disadvantaged individuals are studying in rural areas, whereas in Argentina and Brazil, a significant proportion are found in urban areas.

Notes

1. This chapter is based on Ferreira and Gignoux (2008). The reader is referred to that work for technical details.

2. See the *World Development Report 2006* (World Bank 2006) for a synthesis of the arguments.

3. This impossibility result was formally established by Zheng (1994).

4. $E(0)$ and $E(2)$ are two members of the generalized entropy class of inequality indexes. This class encompasses all inequality indexes satisfying a set of five properties. Among these properties are the Pigou-Dalton transfer principle, which requires that a transfer from a "poorer" to a "richer" person should not imply a decrease in inequality, while a transfer from a "richer" to a "poorer" person should not imply an increase in inequality. This class is preferred to other indexes, such as the Gini, because it also satisfies a decomposability property that requires that the measure should be additionally decomposable into between-group and within-group inequality. The different members of the class are obtained for different values of a parameter of sensitivity to income changes in different parts of the distribution. $E(2)$ is sensitive to changes in the upper tail, while $E(0)$ does not put more weight on changes in the upper or lower tails.

5. "Elementary occupations" is an ISCO88 category that encompasses occupations such as street vendors, domestic helpers, building caretakers, porters, garbage collectors, agricultural and fishery laborers, mining and construction laborers, manufacturing laborers, and transport laborers.

6. PISA also collected information on the mother's occupation. This variable was used in preliminary calculations, and results were unchanged, so they were omitted from this analysis.

7. See, for example, De Ferranti et al. (2004) and the references therein.

8. Exceptions include Mizala and Romaguera (2000) and Chay, McEwan, and Urquiola (2005) on Chile, and Albernaz, Ferreira, and Franco (2002) on Brazil.

9. Possible exceptions are comparative studies of intergenerational mobility in education; see, for example, Gaviria (2007).

10. Although Mexico is an OECD member, it is grouped here with the other Latin American countries, and the nine industrial countries are listed as "the OECD." There is some heterogeneity in sample sizes across the OECD: whereas the Canadian sample, with 29,687 participating children, is much larger than that in the other countries, the American one, with 3,846 participating children, is comparable to the Latin American ones, with about 4,000 participating children, but small in proportion to the population of the country. Results for the United States should thus be treated with caution. Rates of coverage by the surveys of the population of 15-year-olds attending school are higher than 80 percent in all OECD countries.

11. Because the scores are standardized with respect to a single mean and variance across all countries, these levels can be compared in relative terms. Nevertheless, the standardization does imply a simultaneous scale transformation and translation of the distribution, thereby making absolute values difficult to interpret.

12. The educational opportunity–deprivation profile is presented in full in Ferreira and Gignoux (2008). Peru is not fully comparable, because the definition of circumstance groups is more parsimonious in this country.

13. The overall mean for the country populations vary considerably—327 in Peru, 396 in Brazil, 409 in Chile, 418 in Argentina, and 422 in Mexico—in the PISA scale where achievement measured in all OECD countries has a mean of 500 and a standard deviation of 100.

References

Albernaz, Ângela, Francisco H. G. Ferreira, and Creso Franco. 2002. "Qualidade e Eqüidade n o Ensino Fundamental Brasileiro." *Pesquisa e Planejamento Econômico* 32 (3): 453–76.

Chay, Kenneth Y., Patrick J. McEwan, and Miguel Urquiola. 2005. "The Central Role of Noise in Evaluating Interventions That Use Test Scores to Rank Schools." *American Economic Review* 95 (4): 1237–58.

De Ferranti, D., G. Perry, F. Ferreira, and M. Walton. 2004. *Inequality in Latin America and the Caribbean: Breaking with History?* Washington, DC: World Bank.

Ferreira, F., and J. Gignoux. 2008. "Toward an Understanding of Socially Inherited Inequalities in Educational Achievement: Evidence from Latin America and the OECD." www.worldbank.org/lacopportunity. Washington, DC: World Bank.

Gaviria, Alejandro. 2007. "Social Mobility and Preferences for Redistribution in Latin America." *Economía* 8 (1): 55–96.

Mizala, Alejandra, and Pilar Romaguera. 2000. "School Performance and Choice: The Chilean Experience." *Journal of Human Resources* 35 (2): 392–417.

World Bank. 2006. *World Development Report 2006: Equity and Development.* Washington, DC: World Bank.

Zheng, B. 1994. "Can a Poverty Index Be Both Relative and Absolute?" *Econometrica* 62 (6): 1453–58.

Appendix

Table A.1 D-Index for Probability of School Attendance for Children Aged 10 to 14, by Circumstance, circa 2005 (*percent*)

Country	Urban or rural	Parents' education	Per capita income	Number of siblings	Gender	Presence of parents
Argentina	0.2	0.6	0.5	0.4	0.8	0.4
Bolivia	0.7	1.0	0.8	0.8	1.8	0.8
Brazil	0.3	0.5	0.4	0.4	0.8	0.4
Chile	0.2	0.3	0.2	0.2	0.4	0.2
Colombia	1.3	2.3	2.1	2.1	3.7	2.2
Costa Rica	1.0	1.3	1.3	1.2	1.8	1.3
Dominican Rep.	0.4	0.4	0.4	0.4	0.8	0.4
Ecuador	1.3	2.1	1.8	1.7	3.3	1.8
El Salvador	1.2	2.0	1.9	1.3	3.5	1.9
Guatemala	1.5	2.1	2.0	1.7	4.4	2.0
Honduras	1.0	3.5	3.1	2.8	4.2	3.2
Jamaica	0.3	0.9	0.8	0.7	1.0	0.7
Mexico	0.8	1.0	0.9	0.8	1.7	0.9
Nicaragua	1.3	1.9	1.7	1.5	3.8	1.7
Panama	1.2	1.9	1.5	1.3	2.9	1.5
Paraguay	1.2	2.1	1.8	1.6	3.2	1.8
Peru	0.6	1.0	0.9	0.8	1.5	0.9
Uruguay	0.7	0.9	0.7	0.7	1.1	0.7
Venezuela, R. B. de	0.6	0.8	0.7	0.6	1.3	0.7

Source: Authors' computation.

Table A.2 D-Index for Probability of Access to Water, by Circumstance, circa 2005 (*percent*)

Country	Urban or rural	Parents' education	Per capita income	Number of siblings	Gender	Presence of parents
Argentina	0.0	1.0	0.6	0.2	0.1	0.1
Bolivia	14.6	1.1	7.0	1.7	2.4	1.7
Brazil	1.1	0.7	0.6	0.0	0.0	0.0
Chile	1.5	0.2	0.1	0.0	0.0	0.0
Colombia	9.4	1.4	0.4	0.6	0.5	0.1
Costa Rica	0.2	0.2	0.1	0.1	0.1	0.1
Dominican Rep.	13.8	8.4	13.0	0.4	1.3	2.7
Ecuador	4.3	3.1	5.1	0.0	0.2	0.8
El Salvador	13.7	4.8	6.7	0.8	0.5	2.0
Guatemala	8.3	1.6	2.6	0.1	0.9	0.2
Honduras	5.2	2.8	3.0	0.7	0.1	0.2
Jamaica	18.7	1.2	1.6	2.9	2.6	2.0
Mexico	2.3	0.7	1.7	0.1	0.3	0.2
Nicaragua	22.8	6.0	6.0	0.1	1.4	1.8
Panama	2.5	1.7	1.1	1.1	0.5	0.6
Paraguay	16.2	7.0	4.8	1.4	1.0	1.9
Peru	15.4	3.0	8.9	1.1	0.1	0.4
Uruguay	13.8	8.4	13.0	0.4	1.3	2.7
Venezuela, R. B. de	2.0	1.4	0.7	0.0	0.1	0.6

Source: Authors' computation.

Table A.3 D-Index for Probability of Access to Electricity, by Circumstance, circa 2005 (*percent*)

Country	Urban or rural	Parents' education	Per capita income	Number of siblings	Gender	Presence of parents
Argentina	0.0	0.2	0.1	0.0	0.0	0.0
Bolivia	15.2	3.3	6.7	0.2	0.2	0.4
Brazil	1.3	0.3	0.2	0.0	0.0	0.0
Chile	0.1	0.0	0.0	0.0	0.0	0.0
Colombia	2.5	0.2	0.0	0.1	0.1	0.1
Costa Rica	0.1	0.0	0.0	0.0	0.0	0.0
Dominican Rep.	0.5	1.4	1.1	0.2	0.4	0.3
Ecuador	1.7	0.1	0.5	0.2	0.0	0.1
El Salvador	3.5	2.4	1.6	0.7	0.1	0.3
Guatemala	4.7	4.0	4.4	0.3	1.0	0.5
Honduras	13.3	4.7	6.8	0.1	1.7	0.7
Jamaica	2.2	0.6	0.6	1.2	1.3	0.1
Mexico	0.1	0.1	0.1	0.0	0.0	0.0
Nicaragua	17.2	5.5	4.9	0.8	2.4	0.3
Panama	8.3	3.0	7.0	3.0	0.9	0.4
Paraguay	0.7	0.6	1.1	0.0	0.0	0.1
Peru	15.0	3.8	3.3	1.0	0.7	0.7
Uruguay	—	1.9	2.4	0.2	0.1	0.1
Venezuela, R. B. de	0.3	0.1	0.1	0.0	0.0	0.0

Source: Authors' computation.

Note: — = Not available.

Table A.4 Profile of Inequality of Opportunity for School Attendance for Children Aged 10 to 14: Relative Importance of Six Circumstance Variables by Country

Country	Most important	2	3	4	5	Least important
Argentina	gender	parents' education	per capita income	presence of parents	siblings	location
Bolivia	gender	parents' education	per capita income	presence of parents	siblings	location
Brazil	gender	parents' education	per capita income	siblings	presence of parents	location
Chile	gender	parents' education	location	siblings	per capita income	presence of parents
Colombia	gender	parents' education	presence of parents	per capita income	siblings	location
Costa Rica	gender	parents' education	presence of parents	per capita income	siblings	location
Dominican Rep.	gender	per capita income	parents education	presence of parents	siblings	location
Ecuador	gender	parents' education	per capita income	presence of parents	siblings	location
El Salvador	gender	parents' education	presence of parents	per capita income	siblings	location
Guatemala	gender	parents' education	presence of parents	per capita income	siblings	location
Honduras	gender	parents' education	presence of parents	per capita income	siblings	location
Jamaica	gender	parents' education	per capita income	presence of parents	siblings	location
Mexico	gender	parents' education	per capita income	presence of parents	location	siblings
Nicaragua	gender	parents' education	per capita income	presence of parents	siblings	location
Panama	gender	parents' education	per capita income	presence of parents	siblings	location
Paraguay	gender	parents' education	per capita income	presence of parents	siblings	location
Peru	gender	parents' education	presence of parents	per capita income	siblings	location
Uruguay	gender	parents' education	per capita income	presence of parents	siblings	location
Venezuela, R. B. de	gender	parents' education	per capita income	presence of parents	siblings	location

Source: Authors' computation.

176

Country	Most important	2	3	4	5	Least important
Argentina	parents' education	per capita income	siblings	gender	presence of parents	location
Bolivia	location	per capita income	gender	presence of parents	siblings	parents' education
Brazil	location	parents' education	per capita income	siblings	gender	presence of parents
Chile	location	parents' education	per capita income	presence of parents	gender	siblings
Colombia	location	parents' education	siblings	gender	per capita income	presence of parents
Costa Rica	location	parents' education	per capita income	presence of parents	gender	siblings
Dominican Rep.	location	per capita income	parents' education	presence of parents	gender	siblings
Ecuador	per capita income	location	parents' education	presence of parents	gender	siblings
El Salvador	location	per capita income	parents' education	presence of parents	siblings	gender
Guatemala	location	per capita income	parents' education	gender	presence of parents	siblings
Honduras	location	per capita income	parents' education	siblings	presence of parents	gender
Jamaica	location	siblings	gender	presence of parents	per capita income	parents' education
Mexico	location	per capita income	parents' education	gender	presence of parents	siblings
Nicaragua	location	parents' education	per capita income	presence of parents	gender	siblings
Panama	location	parents' education	per capita income	siblings	presence of parents	gender
Paraguay	location	parents' education	per capita income	presence of parents	siblings	gender
Peru	location	per capita income	parents' education	siblings	presence of parents	gender
Uruguay	location	per capita income	parents' education	presence of parents	gender	siblings
Venezuela, R. B. de	location	parents' education	per capita income	presence of parents	gender	siblings

Source: Authors' computation.

Table A.6 Profile of Inequality of Opportunity for Access to Electricity: Relative Importance of Six Circumstance Variables by Country

Country	Most important	2	3	4	5	Least important
Argentina	parents' education	per capita income	siblings	location	gender	presence of parents
Bolivia	location	per capita income	parents' education	presence of parents	siblings	gender
Brazil	location	parents' education	per capita income	siblings	gender	presence of parents
Chile	location	per capita income	parents' education	gender	presence of parents	siblings
Colombia	location	parents' education	gender	presence of parents	siblings	per capita income
Costa Rica	location	parents' education	per capita income	gender	presence of parents	siblings
Dominican Rep.	parents' education	per capita income	location	gender	presence of parents	siblings
Ecuador	location	per capita income	siblings	parents' education	presence of parents	gender
El Salvador	location	parents' education	per capita income	siblings	presence of parents	gender
Guatemala	location	per capita income	parents' education	gender	presence of parents	siblings
Honduras	location	per capita income	parents' education	gender	presence of parents	siblings
Jamaica	location	gender	siblings	parents' education	per capita income	presence of parents
Mexico	parents' education	location	per capita income	siblings	gender	presence of parents
Nicaragua	location	parents' education	per capita income	gender	siblings	presence of parents
Panama	location	per capita income	siblings	parents' education	gender	presence of parents
Paraguay	per capita income	location	parents' education	presence of parents	gender	siblings
Peru	location	parents' education	per capita income	siblings	gender	presence of parents
Uruguay	per capita income	parents' education	siblings	presence of parents	gender	presence of parents
Ve…, R.B. de	location	per capita income	parents' education	siblings	gender	presence of parents

Table A.7 Decomposition of Changes in the Human Opportunity Indexes for Education (*average percentage point change per year*)

	Sixth grade on time			School attendance ages 10-14		
	Scale effect	*Distribution effect*	*Total change*	*Scale effect*	*Distribution effect*	*Total change*
Argentina	—	—	—	—	—	—
Bolivia	—	—	—	—	—	—
Brazil	1.48	0.74	2.21	0.69	0.24	0.93
Chile	0.51	0.24	0.74	0.07	0.04	0.12
Colombia	1.77	1.15	2.92	0.32	0.09	0.41
Costa Rica	0.67	0.22	0.89	0.49	0.26	0.74
Dominican Rep.	1.05	0.24	1.29	0.11	0.04	0.15
Ecuador	0.94	0.32	1.26	0.40	0.17	0.57
El Salvador	1.51	0.74	2.25	0.65	0.10	0.75
Guatemala	0.92	0.55	1.46	0.32	−0.04	0.28
Honduras	1.03	0.24	1.27	0.75	0.31	1.07
Jamaica	−0.21	0.13	−.08	−0.18	0.03	−0.15
Mexico	1.15	0.46	1.61	0.53	0.21	0.73
Nicaragua	1.13	0.34	1.47	0.87	0.35	1.22
Panama	0.25	0.32	0.56	0.24	0.09	0.33
Paraguay	1.97	0.44	2.41	−0.12	−0.11	−0.23
Peru	1.83	0.69	2.53	0.18	0.04	0.22
Uruguay	—	—	—	—	—	—
Venezuela, R. B. de	0.79	0.33	1.12	0.17	0.06	0.23

Source: Authors' computation.

Note: — = Not available.

Table A.8 Decomposition of Changes in the Human Opportunity Indexes for Housing Conditions (*average percentage point change per year*)

	Water			Sanitation			Electricity		
	Scale effect	*Distribution effect*	*Total change*	*Scale effect*	*Distribution effect*	*Total change*	*Scale effect*	*Distribution effect*	*Total change*
Argentina	—	—	—	—	—	—	—	—	—
Bolivia	—	—	—	—	—	—	—	—	—
Brazil	0.42	0.23	0.65	0.78	0.39	1.17	0.62	0.47	1.09
Chile	0.55	0.46	1.01	1.19	0.78	1.98	0.35	0.28	0.63
Colombia	0.24	0.33	0.57	0.17	0.13	0.31	0.30	0.22	0.52
Costa Rica	1.29	0.36	1.65	1.28	0.65	1.93	0.32	0.13	0.45
Dominican Republic	—	—	—	—	—	—	—	—	—
Ecuador	1.01	0.15	1.16	0.66	0.17	0.83	0.57	0.32	0.89
El Salvador	0.81	0.44	1.25	−0.11	0.12	0.01	1.01	0.61	1.62
Guatemala	1.18	0.17	1.35	0.97	0.58	1.55	1.20	0.43	1.63
Honduras	—	—	—	—	—	—	0.30	0.02	0.32
Jamaica	−0.76	−0.12	−0.88	−0.19	−0.03	−0.22	1.52	0.29	1.81
Mexico	0.81	0.52	1.33	0.88	0.64	1.52	0.50	0.33	0.83
Nicaragua	0.44	−0.16	0.28	0.43	0.02	0.45	0.55	0.02	0.57
Panama	0.29	0.37	0.65	0.11	0.26	0.37	0.45	0.47	0.92
Paraguay	1.79	−.02	2.81	0.65	0.44	1.09	0.90	0.46	1.35
Peru	0.32	0.21	0.54	1.47	1.06	2.53	0.55	0.40	0.95
Uruguay	—	—	—	—	—	—	—	—	—
Venezuela, R. B. de	−0.17	0.10	−0.06	0.33	0.15	0.48	0.10	−0.06	0.04

Source: Authors' computation.

Note: — = Not available.

Index

Boxes, figures, notes, and tables are indicated by b, f, n, and t following page numbers.

1804 90